A TEACHER'S TALE

A TEACHER'S TALE

BOB HAMMANN

ISBN: 978-0-9974659-1-4

Published and printed in the United States of America by the Write Place, Inc. For more information, please contact:

the Write Place, Inc.
809 W 8th St., Suite 2
Pella, Iowa 50219
www.thewriteplace.biz

Cover design by Rob Hammann and interior design by Michelle Stam, the Write Place.

Copies of this book may be ordered from the Write Place online at www.thewriteplace.biz/bookstore and at bobhammann.com.

Acknowledgments

A special thanks to my granddaughter, Kaitlin Maroney, who spent extensive time editing and helping with this book.

My gratitude also to my son, Rob Hammann, for his work designing the cover of this book.

A Teacher's Tale

Introduction

It's about 3 p.m. on Tuesday, June 30, 2004, and I find myself sitting at my desk for the last time as the high school principal and superintendent of the Ritzville School District in Ritzville, Washington. Retirement after more than thirty-two years of work as a public school teacher, principal, and superintendent has finally reached out and grabbed me. My feelings are mixed about this day. There is a sense of pride and accomplishment with regard to this moment, but there are also feelings of loss and grief. During all my years in education, my life has been full of challenges, purpose, and meaning, and now this career is going to end.

My career in education began in Mountain Home, Idaho, in 1971 as a substitute teacher in the Mountain Home School District, followed by a semester in the fall of 1971 at Boise State University completing my education certification requirements for the state of Idaho. Beginning in January of 1972, I spent seven-and-a-half years teaching math to seventh, eighth, and ninth grade students at Jenifer Junior High School in Lewiston, Idaho. Along with teaching a full six hours of mathematics classes, I coached basketball, baseball, and track. While I was teaching, I also attended the University of Idaho where I obtained a master's degree in secondary school administration in 1977. During my last three years at Jenifer, I was the acting athletic director for all the school's sports programs.

In August of 1979, I obtained my first administrative job and endured a two-year stint as a sixth through twelfth grade principal in Adrian, Oregon. This was followed by a three-year tenure as the junior high principal at South Junior High in Nampa, Idaho. In July of 1984, I began a seven-year term as the high school principal in Scappoose, Oregon. And, finally in June of 1991, I was selected to be the principal of the Ritzville High School in Ritzville, Washington, where my career has now come to an end.

However, before I even attended college from 1963 to 1967 at Bethany Nazarene College—now known as Southern Nazarene University—I grew up in a military home. My father was a World War II veteran who had a distinguished career in the United States Air Force beginning on October 1, 1940, as a crew chief servicing the AT-17 in the U.S. Army Air Corp and ending in 1974 as a lieutenant colonel piloting the KC-135 in the United States Air Force. He spent most of those thirty-three years in the Strategic Air Command, one of the toughest and most demanding military units in the Air Force.

I grew up moving all over the country. The whole family was never assigned overseas, but we sure got to see the United States of America. We lived in California, Texas, Florida, Arizona, New Hampshire, Kansas, Louisiana, and Michigan. I figured we moved over twelve times before I turned eighteen.

When I completed my college education at Bethany in 1967 with a degree in mathematics and a minor in physics, I married Martha (Marty) Nell Cook and met my military obligation by enlisting in the United States Air Force for four years. The Vietnam conflict was in full swing and at that time, it was either join the military or wait for the "Greetings" letter from the local draft board, so I decided to join a military branch with which I was familiar. During my tenure in the military, Marty and I had two children, Michelle and Robert III. After basic training and technical school, we spent most of those four years in Mountain Home, Idaho, where I worked at the Mountain Home Air Force Base servicing the inertial navigation equipment on the F-4 fighter and the inertial navigation and forward looking radar systems of the RF-4 reconnaissance jet. My tenure in Mountain Home was interrupted by a one-year tour of duty in Thailand from 1969 to 1970 supporting the war effort in Vietnam before I completed my military service and began my career in education.

One of the things I wanted to be sure to do during retirement was to tell my story. Most of the citizens of this great country sat in a public school classroom and learned from good, mediocre, and bad teachers. Many times we endured boring lectures from uninspiring teachers, but we also sat under the instruction of gifted and enthusiastic teachers. In my observations as a product of the public education system, and as a participant and leader in the system, I saw how these inspiring teachers loved their students and had a gift for teaching. These teachers stood out from all the others and they usually had a positive impact on every student they touch. During my time as a student in the public school system, I had a few such teachers who inspired me to discover my gifts and talents and to pursue them.

One of my high school teachers in particular had the ability to make learning fun and meaningful, and his enthusiasm for teaching and working with us inspired me to become a teacher as well. His name was Mr. Grant and I would like to dedicate this book to him and to all the other teachers whom I've had the privilege to know and who made a difference in the lives of their students: Mr. Crosby, Mr. Wimer, Mr. Green, Mr. Fox, Mr. Clements, Mr. Manley, Ms. Schultz, Ms. Rau, Ms. Wesche, Mr. Roehdell, Mr. Cole, Mrs. Peterson, Mr. Peterson, Mr. Covlin, Mr. Parker, Ms. Schwisow, Mr. Whitmore, Mr. Lynch, Mrs. Benzel, Mr. McGregor, and the list goes on. When you've attended several public schools across the country as a student and you've spent thirty-three years of your life working in five different school districts, you discover there are hundreds and even thousands of inspiring and caring teachers in the public school system. Each and every one of them deserves recognition, respect, and thanks.

My purpose in writing this book is to give readers my perspective on the public education system based on my many years of experience. I hope it will give readers a realistic perspective on the difficulty of teaching in the public school system. I also want the reader to realize that teachers become great when they look beyond their intellect, education, and motivation and realize they need to learn from every experience and circumstance, whether it results in success or defeat. I want you to truly see the inspiring and dedicated teachers who work tirelessly in the public education system to educate the children of this nation.

I intend to write other books to give my perspective on the public education system during my time as principal and superintendent. For now, this is not a treatise on how to teach or commentary on what is right or wrong with the public school system in our country. It is a book that will hopefully remind you of what effective teaching and learning was like in the 1970s. You will see the challenges, the humor, and the issues that were a part of that era and what I had to specifically deal with during my time as a teacher. Therefore, my approach will be to tell my story through a number of short stories. These stories are all true as I remember them, and they all happened on my watch. Most of the stories are humorous, but they all provide insights into education in the classroom during the '70s, which is not entirely different from what goes on today. I hope you will be entertained by these stories, but I also hope they bring back pleasant memories of your school experiences and give you a new respect for the men and women who stand before students day-in and day-out trying to prepare them for success in the world.

CHAPTER 1

First Lesson

"I expected to hear a lot of noise and find some off-task behavior when I re-entered the classroom, but I was pleasantly surprised to find a silent room where every student's head was down and focused on their work. In the back of my mind, I thought something just didn't seem right, but I couldn't put my finger on it. I got to the desk, still unable to shrug off my troubled feeling and kept looking at the students hoping to put my finger on what was troubling me. Not one of them looked up from their work as I pulled out my chair and sat down. Suddenly it became clear."

Upon my returned from Thailand in the summer of 1970 after a one-year tour of duty overseas, I found myself reassigned to a training squadron of RF-4 reconnaissance jets at Mountain Home Air Force Base in Mountain Home, Idaho. I had served three years in the Air Force including a year in Thailand and had one more year to serve in my four-year enlistment. I was promoted to sergeant while in Thailand and was now given the duties of supervising the midnight shift of enlisted technicians who maintained the inertial navigation and forward-looking radar systems on the RF-4 reconnaissance jets. I supervised maintenance of our assigned aircraft from midnight to 8 a.m. five days a week. The work was not too demanding since most of the missions occurred during the day, so this was much better than the hectic war theater hours we worked in Thailand.

Since I was eligible to be discharged in less than a year, and the workload during the night shift was usually light, I thought I could begin taking steps to pursue my dream of becoming a teacher. I began looking into the teacher certification requirements for the state of Idaho and found I needed at least one more semester of college to obtain the class credits needed for the formal beginning teacher certificate. However, I also learned that a person with a college degree could obtain a substitute teacher certificate in the state of Idaho and be eligible to substitute in any public school classroom in the state. Since I had a bachelor's degree, I decided to apply for the substitute certificate. I figured I could work the overnight shift at the base, substitute teach during the day, and get some rest from 4 p.m. until my shift started again at midnight.

My wife was expecting our second child, Rob, and we were in need of extra money, so I applied and was given the substitute certificate. Once I had the certificate, I submitted my name to be a substitute teacher in the Mountain Home School District in January of 1971. I was immediately inundated with requests to substitute in classes at all levels. I subbed in elementary, junior high, and high school classes. I taught physical education, math, algebra, physics and chemistry classes, self-contained elementary classes, and even an art class.

Now I need to stop here for a minute to describe the status a substitute teacher has in the public education system—basically, they have none at all. This is clearly evident in the compensation they receive, which is usually about one-third the daily wage of a teacher. In 1971, I received about $25 per day. As is evident just from this, substitutes were at the low end of the totem pole. I suppose that status is justified, since substitutes usually come into the classroom without having to prepare for the day's lessons. They don't know the students, and most regular teachers believe they will have to redo whatever material was to be covered when they come back.

On top of this, junior high and high school students usually view the substitute as fair game for all kinds of pranks. The junior high and some high school students will change seats for entertainment purposes when the substitute teacher tries to take role using the seating chart provided by the regular teacher. Usually, this is caught when the substitute notices a boy in a seat that has a girl's name assigned to it—but if they are really sharp, that won't happen. Students will change names—twins especially like to do this and have even been known to do it to the regular teachers. Secondary students tend to be noisier and less disciplined when they have a substitute teacher. They like to demand a "free day" where they can just visit. I learned quickly you never want to go there as a substitute.

A substitute teacher is the most difficult job in the whole public education system. Good ones are sharp and gain student respect quickly. The poor ones are either driven out or never called back to work. I learned first hand what it took to be one of the good substitute teachers: Be firm, but caring; follow the lesson plan script left by the teacher to the best of your ability; and most importantly, never fully trust the students. I also found it helps to build rapport with students by interacting with them in a positive manner outside of the classroom. For instance, when I subbed at the elementary schools, I always went out on the recess grounds and played basketball with the boys or four-square with the boys and girls.

I found myself quickly called upon to substitute teach when I got my certificate and made myself available to Mountain Home School District. As a man with a military background, they figured I should be able to handle almost anything. I too thought I could handle any situation.

Things went pretty well the first few times I taught as a substitute. In fact, they went so well there was a three-week period where I worked every day. I was putting in sixteen-hour days working at the base and at the schools. It was in the middle of this three-week work-a-thon that I let my guard down and they got me.

On this occasion, I had been called to substitute teach for a junior high math teacher at Mountain Home Junior High. The principal who called me indicated the teacher I was substituting for was seriously ill and would be out for at least three days. Most substitute teachers have no idea what the lesson plans are until they get there and even then may still not know what they are doing because the teacher has not left any written lesson plans. Fortunately, when I got there, this particular teacher had provided an adequate outline of her lessons for her seventh and eighth grade students. On top of her lesson plan, she had paper clipped a note which said, "Keep your thumb on the eighth grade class you have at the end of the day. They can be a handful!" I resolved to be on my toes with that group.

When I came into the building that first day, most of the students were in the hall milling noisily around their lockers, which is typical at most junior high schools. When the bell rang to start the day, students began to flow into the classrooms.

Seventh and eighth grade students are not dumb—they may act dumb, but that is only a ruse. They can spot a situation they can take advantage of in an instant. Each student came in the room and scanned their surroundings. Once they saw me, instead of going to their seats, taking out their books, and preparing for the lesson, they began to mill around and visit with each other. Some asked me the obvious, "Are you a substitute?"

When I responded in the affirmative, they would smile and return to visiting with a friend. It was clear I would need to communicate who was in charge and that we were going to be involved in academic activities during the class period.

When the tardy bell rang, I raised my voice.

"Students, you need to quiet down and go to your seats so I can take roll."

There was little movement or reduction in the noise level, so I raised my voice with a sharp, military tenor.

"LADIES AND GENTLEMEN, GIVE ME YOUR ATTENTION!"

Immediately, the talking stopped and they all turned to face me.

"Let's get something straight right from the beginning. I'm the substitute teacher and you are the students. I'm not someone you want to ignore, or someone you want to mess with. So, if you want this class to go well for you, you need to close your mouths and go to your assigned seats so I can take roll and review our activities for the class period."

Amazingly, they all went to their seats. I went to the seating chart and called out student names, and they answered.

"Bill."

"Here!"

"Kathy."

"Present!"

"Fred."

"Yo!"

This continued until I got to the next-to-last seat in row three. There, I looked up to see a boy sitting in the seat assigned to a girl on the seating chart. I called out her name.

"Sherry!"

"Here," he answered with a red-faced grin.

We all had a good chuckle over that before I told him to move to his correct seat, which he did. This seemed to break the ice, and for the rest of the class period we got along famously. For the most part, they were attentive when I presented the math lesson and were on task with helping me work problems. At the end of the period, students were given their assignment and I moved about the classroom providing individual assistance with most students on task and quietly working. When we got to within five minutes of the end of the class, some students got up to go stand at the door.

"Where do you think you guys are going?" I asked.

"We are going to stand here and wait for the bell to ring," one brave soul answered.

"No," I said. "That is not what you are going to do. You are going to go back to your seats and work until I release you."

With some grumbling, they all returned to their seats, with some returning to work and others just sitting there waiting for the bell to ring. When the bell rang, they all started to get up and I reminded them, none too gently, that they would be able to leave when I said it was time to leave.

"The bell is notification to me to release you," I said. "Not for you to get up and leave."

I was standing at the door and thankfully my presence there was enough to hold them in their seats. I waited about twenty seconds giving them my sternest look and then released them. For the most part, they all filed out meekly.

When I went out in the hall I could hear several of them talking about the new substitute teacher in the math room. I thought word would get out that I was not one of those substitute teachers you want to mess with and hopefully things would go well for the rest of the day.

Each of the next four classes went well. I had a few problems, but I dealt successfully with those the same way I had dealt with the first class. Then came the last eighth grade math class of the day. It became clear early on they were a group cut from a different cloth.

They came into class rather rowdy—some of the boys were physically pulling and pushing each other and talking in loud voices. When the bell rang to start class, they continued on without giving me even a glance. Most of the girls hung in the back, separating themselves from the boys.

"Please go to your assigned seats so I can take roll and we can begin class," I called out loudly.

The talking stopped and one young man looked at me with a cocky grin. "Who are you to be telling us anything?"

That was definitely the wrong thing to say to a military man who was ending a fourteen-hour day, six hours of which were spent trying to keep resistant junior high students on task. I took my 6-foot, 180-pound frame, walked over to him and put my face about two inches from his.

"The assigned substitute teacher for this class is telling you to go plant your butt in your assigned seat so he can take roll and we can begin class."

Now this young man stood 5-feet, 6-inches tall and maybe weighed 120 pounds. It was clearly evident from his body language that he was uncomfortable with my nose two inches from his. "Oh," he said simply. "I didn't realize you were the sub."

At this, they all went to their correct seats and I was able to begin class. This class was much different than the others. The girls were attentive and contributed to solving the problems associated with the math lesson presentation, but the boys were the opposite, and several times I had to tell them to stop talking. They would stop for a few minutes, but the talking would eventually pick up again. The young man I had confronted at the beginning of class was a particular problem and eventually used some profanity when addressing some comments to another student. I exploded, and sent him to the principal's office, which happened to be right next to the classroom. After I sent him to the office, things went much better.

The bell rang and the long day finally came to an end. I went by the office to get my coat from the faculty lounge before heading home for some much-needed rest, when the principal stopped me and asked if I could come back to sub in the same classroom the next day. The way he asked me seemed to indicate other substitutes in the past had rejected the invitation to return. I told him I would be glad to do it and he seemed rather pleased with my response.

The second day was much better. The tone had been set and it appeared the students knew I meant business. I didn't have to spend much time dealing with inappropriate or off-task behavior. The day was stressful, but rewarding. I saw students learning and I noted a grudging respect from most of them. Then came the end of the day with the eighth grade math class.

I had steeled myself for this class—I was prepared to deal with the disruptive student who had been sent to the office the day before. But surprisingly, they came into class with a different demeanor. The students came in and went immediately to their seats, visiting quietly until the bell rang to start class, and were attentive when I began to take roll.

The lesson presentation went fairly well and I only had to confront some talking during the presentation once or twice. Each time, they quit talking and paid attention. I thought, "Wow. These guys are quick learners—this class is going to be okay."

Now one of the things they never talk about in education preparation classes in college is how to find time to use the bathroom when you have three or four teaching periods in a row. I had been unable to use the bathroom facilities since lunch, which had been over two hours before. So during the last fifteen minutes of class, when the students paired off to work quietly on the assignment, I thought I could slip down to the bathroom, relieve myself, and get back before there could be any trouble. The students were working well, with a minimum of off-task discussion, so I slipped out of the room, went to the bathroom, and returned inside of five minutes.

I expected to hear a lot of noise and find some off-task behavior when I re-entered the classroom, but I was pleasantly surprised to find a silent room where every student's head was down and focused on their work. In the back of my mind, I thought something just didn't seem right, but I couldn't put my finger on it. As I moved to my desk, I stared at the students while they worked, trying to discover what had happened to cause the change of atmosphere. I got to the desk, still unable to shrug off my troubled feeling, and kept looking at the students hoping to put my finger on what was troubling me. Not one of them looked up from their work as I pulled out my chair and sat down. Suddenly it became clear. Piercing pain radiated from my backside, up my back, and into my brain. Instantly, I realized someone had put thumbtacks on my chair. I had heard about such things happening to rooky substitutes, but never dreamed it might happen to me. My mind quickly went into overdrive and I determined right then and there they were not going to get any satisfaction out of this. I somehow stayed seated and kept a serene countenance, even in the midst of incredible backside pain. As I sat there, I stared at the class, who still had their heads down, totally focused on their work.

I was sure the culprit who had placed these instruments of pain in that chair would want to look up to see the fruits of his handiwork. Sure enough, the young man I had sent to the office the previous day peeked up from his work. I stared dispassionately into his eyes and he quickly looked back down at his assignment. One or two others glanced up quickly with crooked grins on their faces, but the grins disappeared and they too returned to their work when we made eye contact. I learned a big lesson right then and there. If you have the look—the one that communicates you know what is going on in their little minds, even if you may not know for sure—you've got them.

I'm not sure how I did it, but I sat there and stared at the class for the next five minutes. They worked quietly during that time and then the bell rang. Some began to get up.

"Sit down," I ordered as I stood up. "I haven't excused you yet!" They all returned to their seats and I looked them over. "I really appreciate the way you all worked this period," I said. "I hope you will work just as hard tomorrow. It's been a good class for me. By the way, the next time someone puts thumbtacks on my chair, all of you will spend some time in detention. Do I make myself clear?"

They initially gave me a look of bewilderment like they really didn't know what I was saying. But I continued to stare at them and repeated myself. "Did I make myself clear?"

Finally, they all nodded their heads and filed noisily out into the hallway. As I followed behind them, I overheard the kid who I suspected of putting the tacks on my chair.

"I kind of like the guy," he said. "Old 'numb butt' is tough, but he's likeable."

From that day on at Mountain Home Junior High School, the students addressed me as Mr. Hammann to my face, but I'm sure I was frequently referred to as "Old Numb Butt" behind my back. I can say with certainty I enjoyed all my substitute-teaching days in that school from then on, and I developed a special rapport with many of them—including the young man I sent to the office the first day.

CHAPTER 2

First Job

> *Curious, I asked Mr. Walker, 'Who is the teacher I am replacing and why is that person leaving?' 'She has chosen to leave us and we need a teacher with your background to take her place,' he said stiffly. This was a little troubling, but I didn't ask any more questions.*

It was 9 a.m. Monday morning on January 24, 1972. I hesitated, as I thought about all that had occurred in the past few weeks to bring me to the entrance of Jenifer Junior High School in Lewiston, Idaho, to my first real teaching job. After receiving an "early out" from the military in August of the year prior, I took a semester of classes from Boise State University to qualify for an Idaho teaching certificate in mathematics and physics. After a student teaching experience at Mountain Home Junior High School, I had received my certificate the first part of January.

In December—while waiting for the state to issue my certificate—I researched college placement job openings at Boise State and the want ads in the Idaho Statesman newspaper. I found two teaching job openings in mathematics that would begin at the end of January. One job was for one semester only teaching high school math in Idaho Falls, Idaho. The other was a junior high teaching job in Lewiston, Idaho, that appeared to continue beyond just one semester. The job in Idaho Falls paid $5,800 per year and the one in Lewiston paid $6,500. I applied for both jobs at the beginning of December by sending completed application forms, transcripts, and resumes to each school.

My wife had a job teaching home economics in the Mountain Home School District, but I was out of work. Marty had just had our son Rob, and it was my responsibility to take care of him and my three-year-old daughter Michelle while my wife worked. I love my kids, but I was not called to be a child caregiver. It was driving me crazy not having a job while my wife acted as the breadwinner. During the week between Christmas and New Year's, I received a call from Mr. Harvie Walker.

When I answered the phone, he introduced himself as the principal of Jenifer Junior High School in Lewiston, Idaho. "Are you the Mr. Robert Hammann who applied for a teaching job in Lewiston, Idaho, and do you have a degree in mathematics and a valid Idaho teaching certificate?"

"Yes sir, that is me and I do have a degree in mathematics and a valid beginning teaching certificate," I replied.

"It shows on your resume that you have a military background. Is that true?"

"Yes, sir. I served four years in the Air Force and got out last August."

Mr. Walker went on to ask me about my teaching style and how I maintained discipline in the classroom. He asked me about my family and upbringing. His questions came fast and furious and his manner was brusque and forceful. It was evident this was a man who could lead, and he wasn't interested in small talk. Our exchange was short, only ten minutes, before he asked me, "Do you want to come here and teach mathematics this spring?"

"Yes sir," I replied quickly, surprising myself. "I would love to teach math at your school."

I thought he would have me come up for a formal interview in the next few days, but his response shocked me.

"Well, you're hired," he said. "The starting salary will be a pro-rated $6,500 per year and the district will pay for your personal health insurance. I'd like you and your wife to come up and see me this weekend so I can meet you both personally. If that meeting goes well, I'd like you to come a few days early before the new semester starts to observe the classes you will be teaching. The new semester begins Monday, January 24, but you can come up January 20, and observe. We can talk more about this when you get here this weekend. What time do you think you can get here Friday night?"

The entire time he was talking, I was thinking that I just got hired on a phone interview. "What is this all about?" I thought. "He doesn't know what I look like or what I can really do, and I don't know what he looks like much less what kind of administrator he is. I don't even know what the school looks like. This is insane, but it's a job and I've got to work or go crazy."

I gave him the approximate time we would arrive, and he gave me his home address. I assumed correctly I would have to find a motel at my own expense for Friday night, and then we would return Saturday. "Thank you for your time and I will see you in a couple of days," he said, ending the conversation.

My wife was standing next to me during the discussion and hugged me when I hung up, excited at the prospect of me getting a job. We spent the next few days planning the trip to Lewiston and began to make arrangements for the two of us to work in two school districts 320 miles apart. We would have to buy another car for her to use, find a cheap apartment in Lewiston for me, and get a motel for the one night we would be there. We developed a rough budget to cover the expenses of maintaining two households and found we should be able to make it with both our salaries.

That next Friday, Marty took a personal day of leave and after leaving both our children with friends, we made our way north from Mountain Home to Lewiston, Idaho. This was the middle of winter in Idaho, and wouldn't you know it, we had to go through a horrendous snow and ice storm to get to Lewiston.

We made it through the storm and got to Lewiston around 6 p.m. We immediately checked in to the motel and called Mr. Walker. He told us how to get to his house and encouraged us to come over. I was so excited about getting this job and wanted to be sure I did whatever was necessary to make a good impression, so we hurried right over. When we got there, we knocked on the door. A big, hulking man with a large mustache answered.

"You must be Mr. Hammann," he said. "My name is Mr. Walker and I'm going to be your new principal, and you are going to be one of my math teachers. Come on in!"

We were graciously ushered into his warm and comfortable home where he introduced us to his wife, who took our coats and encouraged us to sit in the living room. Mr. Walker told us his first name was Harvie, but most people called him "Slug" when students weren't around. Looking at the size of the man, I could see why he got that nickname. He looked and talked like a military man who had seen some action. He explained he was a retired military officer who had gone into public education to teach math and had eventually moved into administration. We talked at length about my military experience, and we talked some about my dad's military career and the fact that he was an Air Force pilot flying KC-135's out of Fairchild Air Force Base in Spokane, Washington, just ninety miles north of Lewiston. Harvie seemed to be more interested in my military background than in my knowledge of math and skill at teaching.

After about an hour, his wife brought us some pie and ice cream, and we talked about Lewiston and the surrounding countryside. There was hunting and fishing within minutes from downtown. You could catch salmon and steelhead out of the Clearwater River, which ran right through the middle of town. There was bird hunting and skiing as well. He was making it sound like a great place to live. When I told him I would need a small apartment for the semester, he said he had just the place and gave me a phone number and address of a boarding house near the school.

After about a two-hour visit, we were escorted to the door where he reminded me again that he wanted me to come up on January 20 to observe the classes I would be teaching. Curious, I asked him, "Who is the teacher I am replacing and why is that person leaving?" "She has chosen to leave us and we need a teacher with your background to take her place," he said stiffly. This was a little troubling, but I didn't ask any more questions.

Before we left Mr. Walker's house, he allowed me to call the owner of the boarding house to inquire about a possible vacant apartment. She answered and said she had a small studio apartment to rent and invited us to come by and look at the place. She said it cost $50 per month, which included utilities.

We said our goodbyes to the Walkers and hustled right over to take a look. It was a very small one-room studio apartment about fifteen feet by fifteen feet square with a small refrigerator, a small stove, two wooden chairs, a table, and a bed. The bathroom was down the hall with a toilet, sink, and bathtub with no shower. I would be sharing the bathroom with two or three other apartment renters. Considering our economic situation and the great price, I took it. I gave the owner the deposit, feeling that I was now ready for my first teaching job.

The next two weeks were full of activity as we prepared for me to move and Marty to stay in Mountain Home with our two children. I had to buy a cheap car for Marty to use, and we ended up buying an old brown early '60s Ford that seemed to run pretty well on the car lot. We bought it from "Oley" Olson who was a car salesman and member of the church we attended. He said the car might have some problems, but that it should start and run Marty safely to and from school. He said to let him know if Marty had trouble with it and he would take care of it.

The first morning after we bought it, we had trouble getting it started. It flooded once, but after keeping the accelerator pedal down while cranking the starter, the vehicle sputtered to life. Of course, the second or third time that happened after I left for Lewiston, Marty was forced to buy a new battery. After that purchase, it usually started after two or three tries.

On January 19, I had everything packed and was ready to go. We had decided I would come back twice each month during the semester, and then we would all move up to Lewiston in the summer. The next few months would be hard on both of us—Marty would be taking care of our three-year-old daughter and our infant son with the help of a great babysitter, but she would also be teaching five days a week.

So after moving up and getting settled in my new little apartment, I was ready to begin my formal teaching career—or so I believed. That night, I hardly slept in anticipation of my first day on the job in the morning. And little did I know the very first week would test my mettle and challenge my belief I had the skills and demeanor to be an effective math teacher.

CHAPTER 3

Observations

> *I thought the student behavior in the first class was bad, but this class reached a new level of misbehavior. ... I noticed two boys go to one of the outside windows near the back of the classroom, open it, and crawl out—giggling and laughing the whole way. Once outside, they made their way to the window at the front of the class and motioned at a student sitting in her chair, who opened that window to let them in.*

On the morning of January 20, 1972, I paused for a minute in front of Jenifer Junior High School to savor the moment. The L-shaped, two-story building was located about three blocks from the high school, just up the hill from downtown Lewiston. Across the street was the gymnasium with its curved metal roof along with the baseball and football fields. Both facilities looked less than twenty years old and appeared to be well maintained. This brick building would be my place of work for the foreseeable future, I thought as I stood in front of the junior high school.

Now, I had assumed I was volunteering my time to observe my future math classes those first couple of days, so I showed up around 9 a.m., knowing school started at 8:20 a.m. This assumption got me in trouble before I even saw the teacher I would be replacing or the classroom where I would be working. As I entered the building, I turned into the office area and a stern, frowning "Slug" Walker greeted me. "I'm here!" I said with a smile. "Where is my classroom?" "We need to talk in my office," he replied ominously.

He quickly led me into his office, shut the door, and proceeded to dress me down for not being on time. There was no, "Good morning, Mr. Hammann!" or "How are you this morning, Mr. Hammann?" or "We are really glad you're here, Mr. Hammann!" He just lit me up and he did it better than any drill sergeant I had in basic training. "Where have you been? Mr. Hammann, you need to understand in no uncertain terms that classes at Jenifer Junior High start at 8:20 a.m. sharp, and the teachers are to be here at 8:00 a.m. sharp. You are definitely starting off on the wrong foot by coming in late like this. My teachers are all here at 8 a.m. sharp getting ready for the school day, and I tolerate no tardiness or lollygagging around in the teachers' lounge during that time! Do you understand what I am saying?"

I started to tell him I thought I was volunteering my time to do these observations and could come in a little late, but he cut me off and told me that I was being paid for these extra days and he wanted me to observe each class from the beginning to the end starting with the first class of the day. He forcefully told me I needed to be on time, and that he would be watching me regarding that in the days to come.

I shamefacedly apologized and told him I was sorry and that it wouldn't happen again. All during this time I was thinking what a great way this was to start my first day in a new school with a new boss!

Mr. Walker also made it clear I was not to leave until 3:30 p.m. unless I had his permission to leave earlier. He said my classroom was on the first floor and was number 114. He indicated the teacher I was replacing was a Ms. Flowers—stressing the "Ms." with an undertone of contempt.

"You need to get going," Mr. Walker said as he finished up our talk. "The first period is about over, and they need to meet you before they go to their next class. Now git!"

I hustled out of his office, striding past the office secretary, whom I hadn't even met yet, and—once out of the office—I sprinted down the hall.

It took me a couple of minutes to identify the location of the classroom, and as I walked down the hall I looked into each room through a large window at the top of the door. Every door was closed, but you could see that some teachers were at the front of the room teaching their students, some were sitting at their desks, while others were moving about the classroom assisting students at their seats. Some rooms were quiet, while others were somewhat noisy. As I continued down the hallway, I heard a higher volume of noisy chatter coming from one particular class—room 114.

I stood outside the room trying to analyze the extremely noisy chatter I was hearing. I could hear a number of students talking loudly, and I could also hear an adult female voice trying to talk over the students. I peered through the window in the door, but it was difficult to see what was actually occurring in the room. As I listened, I could not hear anything that I could understand. I didn't even knock, since I doubted anyone would hear me anyway, so I turned the knob, opened the door, and walked in.

What I saw when I entered the room was astonishing. There were about thirty-five students in the classroom, and at the front of the class a small, pretty young lady sat in a student desk facing about six girls who were focused on trying to follow her instructions for solving a math problem. She had to raise her voice to give the instructions, because the other thirty students were involved in loud talking and horseplay around the room.

She was so focused on shouting her instructions that she did not notice I had entered the room. So, rather than disturb her concentration, I moved to the back of the room where I took a seat next to a boy who was talking to his neighbor. I assumed introductions would be made near the end of class.

The two young boys who were talking turned and smiled at me as I sat down.

"Who are you?" one of them asked. "Are you going to be our new teacher?"

I nodded, and they turned back toward each other and continued their discussion about a new movie they had seen.

For the next ten minutes I sat in that seat watching the chaos. As the teacher continued to try and talk over all the noise and help the young girls with their homework, the rest of the class continued on in disorder. Students were milling about, up and out of their seats without permission. Two students even left the classroom without asking—I supposed they were using the bathroom. Two other boys played rock, paper, scissors with the winner of each round hitting the other rather forcefully on the upper arm. Paper balls sailed across the room to either get someone's attention or to harass other students. At the same time, most of the inattentive students tried to talk over each other in order to be heard. The room was just chaos.

As the class period came to a close, the teacher stopped helping the five girls and pulled her chair to the front of the room next to the teacher's desk located at the front center of the classroom. She then walked back to me and smiled.

"Are you Mr. Hammann?" she asked. I stood up and extended my hand.

"Yes, I am! Are you Ms. Flowers?" With a nod, she shook my hand.

"Yes that is me," she replied. "I see you were a little late getting here. I'm sure Mr. Walker had something to say to you about that. Let me introduce you to the class."

She moved to the front of the room while I followed close behind. She raised her voice to a level I didn't know she was capable of reaching and shouted into the din. **"Class, give me your attention, please!"**

When the noise level of the class did not slack off, she put two fingers in her mouth and let out a shrill, piercing whistle that froze everyone mid-sentence. Then in a sweet, normal voice:

"I want to introduce you to your new teacher for the second semester," she said. "As you all know, I will be leaving after Friday's classes. This is Mr. Hammann and he will be taking over the class next Monday. Say hello to Mr. Hammann!"

"Hello, Mr. Hammann," the class sing-songed in unison before returning to their noisy chatter. As the noise level went back up, Ms. Flowers resumed her yelling.

"This assignment is due tomorrow. I'm available after class if you need help. Now I know some of you just hate math and that is why you didn't turn in today's assignment. Remember, I will take a one-page theme on any subject of your choice as extra credit to make up for your loss of points. Have a good day and I will see you tomorrow!"

She leaned over and whispered conspiratorially to me, "I have an English major with a minor in math, so I understand their feelings about math."

All the students then moved and stood at the door waiting for the bell to ring. They didn't even stand in a line. They milled around, talking loudly, some pushing and shoving each other like a herd of frisky calves waiting for someone to open a gate to let them out into a field of alfalfa.

As I observed them preparing to leave, I thought maybe this was just a bad group of students. Surely, the rest of the classes would be better behaved than this.

The bell rang and they all tried to move out of the room at the same time in a chaotic manner. I followed them out into the hall to observe as students moved to their double-stacked lockers and fingered combination locks.

I noticed one student really struggling with his locker, unable to open it after a few tries. So I walked over to him.

"Can I help you with that?" I inquired.

"Would you?" he replied with a look of relief. "I'm going to be late to class and I really need the book that is in there."

"What is your combination?" He gave me the three numbers and I quickly opened it on the first try. As he threw his books in the locker and grabbed another, I asked him a question. "What grade are you in and how long do you have to pass between classes?"

"I'm in the seventh grade and we have five minutes between classes," he replied. "Thanks for helping me, but I need to run." He moved off and assimilated into the densely packed flow of human bodies.

I turned back into the classroom and returned to the seat in the back to wait for the next group of students. A large group flowed in just before the bell rang, and several came in tardy after it rang. Ms. Flowers sat at her desk taking roll and organizing her materials in preparation for her lesson. A few students went to their desks, but most just stood around visiting loudly. The noise level was so high, I wondered if Ms. Flowers would ever be able to get their attention when the class started. It turned out she wouldn't.

Five minutes after the bell, she once again lifted her voice. "We are going to grade the assignment from yesterday! Those that have it done, please move to the front of the room so you can hear me!"

Out of approximately thirty-five students, six girls and two boys moved to seats at the front of the room and pushed the student desks into a semicircle facing the one Ms. Flowers was sitting in. The other students continued to talk and move around the room, oblivious to Ms. Flowers and the eight students gathering around her.

I sat in the back and watched her again try to lift her voice above the din to teach the students around her. She had them grade each other's papers as she called out the answers. It appeared they were doing long division.

I thought the student behavior in the first class was bad, but this class reached a new level of misbehavior. Talking and horseplay were of course happening, but incredibly, I also noticed two boys go to one of the outside windows near the back of the classroom, open it, and crawl out—giggling and laughing the whole way. Once outside, they made their way to the window at the front of the class and motioned at a student sitting in her chair who opened that window to let them in. They repeated this activity at least three more times, all while other students left and returned to the classroom without asking permission. Ms. Flowers continued to shout answers and instructions to the eight students sitting around her. I turned to the girl sitting next to me near the back of the classroom. "Do the students behave this way all the time?"

"Oh, this is a good day," she replied. "We've had a few fights break out and Ms. Flowers has to break them up."

"How does Ms. Flowers teach the rest of you?"

"If we don't want to listen to her, some of us just do the best we can to work the problems on our own, or we can turn in a one-page theme and she gives us homework points for that," was her reply.

"What about taking tests?" I asked, a bit confounded. "Does she give tests?"

"Yeah!" she said. "We have a test about every two weeks. If you do poorly on the test, you can write another theme and she will give you extra credit for that."

I asked a few more questions about where the students went when they left the room, the chapter they were on in the book, and how often those two students exited the room through the windows during a normal class period. After all I had seen, I was not shocked by the student's responses. The first period class, this class, and probably all of her classes were a discipline nightmare. I wondered what I'd gotten myself into.

Near the end of the class, I left and made my way down to the boys' restroom, which was located close to the library. As I approached the entrance to the library, a young woman stepped out and stopped short when she saw me. She motioned me over to where she was standing.

"Are you the new math teacher who is going to take Ms. Flowers's place?"

I smiled and stuck out my hand to shake hers.

"Yes, I am," I said. "My name is Mr. Hammann and I will start teaching next Monday. This is my first day in the school and I'm just observing her classes to help me be better prepared."

"Do you know what you are getting yourself into?" she asked with a frown. "Did Mr. Walker let you know what the situation is?"

I smiled back at her and replied, "I've observed only two classes so far, but I'm beginning to get an idea."

She quickly gave me a summary of the situation.

"Ms. Flowers is leaving. I guess it is one of those situations where both parties have agreed to part. She is a real honest-to-goodness 'hippie' who has lost control of her classes. The noise level from that end of the building is disturbing to all the teachers around her. Mr. Walker tried to help her, but she refuses to come down hard on the kids. She and Mr. Walker have gone round and round on a number of issues. Once, about a month ago, he confronted her at a staff meeting in response to several teacher complaints about the behavior of her students and the noise coming from her classes. She was coy and sugary with him to start with, but then argued with him about his tone of voice toward her in front of the teachers—then he really blew up. His military background came to the forefront and he lit into her. That meeting upset all the teachers. The next day, she sent him a flowery poem promoting peace and harmony. I guess that was the last straw. You are going to have your hands full getting those students back on track."

"Well, this is the first I've heard about the situation," I interjected. "I visited with Mr. Walker on the phone and met with him a couple of weeks ago and he never mentioned the reason for the vacancy. What you have shared with me explains a lot."

As she turned to go, she said, "I just can't believe Mr. Walker didn't fill you in on the situation. If I can be of any assistance to you, please come see me." She turned and went back into the library, and I went on to the bathroom. I observed two more classes until lunch and they were all the same. The students were out of control, and Ms. Flowers didn't seem to have the wherewithal to address the behavior.

When lunch came, Ms. Flowers took me to the cafeteria, which was located in the same building as the gymnasium across the road from the main building. As we moved through the lunch line, she talked about her students and the school. One statement she made was telling.

"Don't be too hard on the students," she said. "Most of them don't like math and it is important they enjoy their classes!" After we got our lunches, she led me back across the street to the main building and showed me where the teachers' lounge was and indicated she would eat in her room. Thankfully, she did not issue me an invitation to join her.

I took my lunch to the teachers' lounge, where I introduced myself to a number of teachers. In each case, they asked the same question: "Do you know what you got yourself into?" And in each case I said the same thing: "I'm getting a good picture of the situation."

After lunch, I returned to observing and the rest of the day was the same. Each class of seventh and eighth grade students was undisciplined and learning very little. The question became, "What am I going to do when I take charge?"

CHAPTER 4
Plan of Action

> *The one thing I knew was that it didn't matter so much what the rules said; it mattered that they were enforced justly. I knew from the military that when you were given orders, you obeyed them or there were serious consequences. I knew I had to come up with an effective classroom management and discipline plan and present that plan to the class the first day I stood in front of them to set the tone for the rest of the year.*

By the end of my first day of observations, I was seething. I had seen some undisciplined classes during my time substitute teaching, but never anything like what I saw at Jenifer Junior High that first day. As I made my way back to my studio apartment, I thought there was no way those junior high students were going to act like that with me. But what was I going to do about it?

I thought a lot about it that evening and even lost some sleep over it as I turned over in my mind what I had observed and what I might be able to do to bring discipline and order to each class. I needed more information—and some advice.

I observed again Thursday and Friday in preparation for taking over Monday. When I went back Friday, I determined to talk to the counselor, Mr. Al Kytonen, and Mr. Walker to seek their advice.

I got up early Friday morning and arrived at school at 7:40, twenty minutes before teachers had to be there. Fortunately, Mr. Walker was there so I asked the secretary if I could see him. He heard me ask her and came out of his office to invite me in. He closed the door and, as was his habit, waited for me to speak. I immediately gave a brief summary of what I had observed the previous day.

"Every class is out of control," I said. "Discipline is nonexistent and there is very little learning occurring."

"That's exactly what I have seen since the first day I hired her, and that is why she is leaving," Mr. Walker replied. "I hired you to fix the situation. I figured with your military background you could handle it."

I asked him, "Well, do you have any suggestions about how I can go about doing that?"

"Take charge!" he said tersely. "Let these kids know who is running the show and inspire them to learn. That is what I hired you to do. I will back any reasonable approach you take regarding that."

With that, he just gave me a look that said our meeting was over. Taking the cue, I said, "Thank you. I will give it my best shot," and left his office.

Well, that was a lot of help, I thought as I walked away. He didn't tell me anything I didn't already know.

My next stop was the counselor, Mr. Al Kytonen. Maybe he would give me some ideas. I went down to his office and made an appointment to see him during third period. I figured I could slip out and talk to him, fairly certain I wouldn't miss anything new in that class. Things would probably go as they had the day before.

First and second periods were just like the first day, with students totally out of control and little learning taking place. At the beginning of third period, I made my way down to the counselor and waited while he finished talking to a student, which gave me a chance to look him over. He was a short, somewhat balding, older gray-haired man. It was evident he was near the end of his career, and I thought he probably had enough experience and wisdom to advise me about what to do.

He stepped out of his office and introduced himself. He then invited me into his office and offered me the chair next to his desk. I seated myself while he closed his door. "I bet I know why you are here," he said. "You want some advice about what to do with Ms. Flowers's class, right?"

I responded hesitantly. "Yeah! I'm trying to get some advice from people who have more experience than I. I talked to Mr. Walker, but he wasn't much help, so I thought I would talk to you. Do you have any suggestions about how I might approach the situation? I know it will be really important that I get off on the right foot to overcome the discipline problems in all those classes."

He sat down at his desk and leaned conspiratorially toward me.

"Here is what I would do," he said. "I would put a trash can next to the door at the beginning of each class and stand out in the hall until each class has entered the room. Then, when the bell rings to start the class, come into the room and kick that trash can clear across the room and scare the piss out of them. That will get their attention and set the tone! Then tell them how you're going to run the class and what you expect of them. We are allowed to hack students here when they misbehave. So I would get a paddle, which the shop teacher will make for you, and I would show it to them and put the fear of God into them! They will get the message and the rest of the year will be a breeze."

He leaned back in his chair with a smile. "I know that will get their attention. You need to show them that you are going to be in charge, period." I was appalled at this extreme approach. It seemed like he was encouraging me to start a reign of terror rather than take control of the classes, teach them math skills, and instill respect for that academic discipline and me as a teacher. After listening to his ideas, I thanked him for his time and left his office to go back to class.

During the lunch period, I asked a few of the other teachers what they might do, and in almost every case they stressed that I needed to take control of the class. No one had a one-size-fits-all discipline plan they could articulate to me. It was clear I was on my own in this. I needed to come up with my own strategy for the year and an effective way to communicate that plan the first day I stood in front of the students. When classes ended Friday, I knew I would be busy planning my strategy during the weekend to come.

When I took my education preparation classes at Bethany Nazarene College and Boise State University, we learned very little on managing students and maintaining discipline. My education classes included Introduction to Education, Educational Tests and Measurements, Beginning Public Speaking, Math in Secondary Schools, Secondary School Methods, and a nine-week Secondary Student Teaching Experience. My supervising teachers during my student teaching experience provided me with the most help regarding discipline—although there was a general overview of classroom management and discipline in the Secondary School Methods class. One supervisor had a general rule that said, "Treat each other and the teacher as you would like to be treated." Another had a set of four rules:

- Don't talk while the teacher is talking.
- Stay on task with seatwork.
- Raise your hand if you want to say something.
- Stay in your seat.

When you student teach, the supervising teacher has already set the tone for managing the students and all you have to do is step in and follow through with their plan. When you start out with your first teaching job, you have to make and implement a plan that works for you and fits your belief system and teaching style. That is a whole different ball game.

The one thing I knew was that it didn't matter so much what the rules said; it mattered that they were enforced justly. I knew from the military that when you were given orders, you obeyed them or there were serious consequences. I knew I had to come up with an effective classroom management and discipline plan and effectively present that plan to the class the first day I stood in front of them to set the tone for the rest of the year.

I was busy the whole weekend. I had to review the seventh and eighth grade texts, come up with the lesson objectives for each day, and make sure I knew the lesson material and thought out how I would approach teaching it. This took some time, but the really big issue was reining in the out-of-control students in each class. I decided I had to be myself with these kids. I wasn't going to kick a trash can across the room to get their attention or threaten them with bodily harm if they crossed me. I was going to make a few rules, then communicate those rules and the consequences of breaking those rules as clearly as possible. Then I would strive to enforce those rules fairly and justly.

I decided I needed to assign student seating to help me break up student combinations that could lead to disruptions. I would then make a seating chart, which would make it easy to take roll at the beginning of class. I would adjust the chart to meet the needs of students who had social problems, problems seeing the board, or issues with hearing the teacher.

On Friday, Ms. Flowers had given me her grade book and I filled in student names for the new semester by ordering them alphabetically. I then took the semester calendar provided for lesson planning and wrote the first week's lesson assignments under the appropriate days. I also took time to look at the grades she had given students at the end of the semester.

Finally, I outlined my disciplinary plan and approach for the semester and came up with the following five rules for the classes:

- When students enter the room, they are to go to their assigned seats.
- Students are to come to class prepared with book, paper, and pencil.
- Students are to be attentive and not talk during lesson presentations.
- Students are to show respect to the teacher and others at all times.
- Students will stay in their seats unless they get permission to be out of their seats.

These rules were established to curtail all the negative behaviors I had seen during my observations. I suspected that, as I got further into the semester, there would have to be some adjustments. Indeed, about two weeks into the semester, when I observed some of the students had developed the habit of writing on and gouging their desks, I had to add a rule or two to address such issues.

I also outlined the consequences for students who chose to break the rules. The consequences I had in my arsenal included the following:

- Verbal warning, verbal reprimand, after-school detention, and removal from class into the hall.
- Administering hacks (the student bends over and you apply a paddle to the presented backside).
- Removal to the principal (used as a last resort because there was one principal for 840 students. And Mr. Walker made it clear he expected the teacher to resolve all but the most disruptive behaviors).

I wrote this all out in a three-ring binder to help me when I addressed the class on Monday, and I went to bed Sunday night feeling I was ready to take charge.

CHAPTER 5

The First Day as a Real Teacher

> *Today, many of the students visited quietly as they waited for the bell to indicate the start of the day. Finally, the bell rang and I stood at the front of the classroom wearing what I thought was a stern but friendly look as a few stragglers hurried to their seats. I tried to make eye contact with each student. I was nervous as any new teacher would be, but I didn't want them to see me sweat. I wanted to make every effort to communicate to the students that I was now in charge and things were going to be different. As I looked them over, the students stopped talking and the room became very quiet—it may have been the first time there had been silence in that class for many months.*

I awoke early Monday morning, January 24, 1972, before the alarm went off. I had slept fitfully during the night, feeling anxiety and some trepidation for the confrontation that was to occur. I got up, shaved, and put on slacks, a long-sleeve shirt, and a tie. Mr. Walker recommended his male teachers wear a tie most of the time when they came to work, although he said it was not a requirement. From the first time I met Mr. Walker—who always wore a tie—I knew it would be wise to implement all his recommendations.

After a bowl of cereal and a quick review of my written plan for the day, I got in my car and drove to the school. I made sure to arrive well before teachers were required to be in their rooms. I went to the classroom and made sure the chalkboard was clean and there was plenty of chalk. I laid out my textbooks, my lesson plans, and my outline for addressing each class. I had to make two preparations: one for my four seventh grade general math classes and one for my two eighth grade general math classes. I arranged the student seats in six rows of six seats each. I then printed my name, "Mr. Hammann," on the chalk board and wrote "7th Grade General Math" underneath my name since this was the first class of the day. After everything was ready, I poked my head into the classrooms of the teachers around me and greeted them. In almost every case, the teacher's response was, "I hope you can get those classes straightened out. They have really disrupted my classes this year." I assured each of them that I would do my best.

It wasn't long before students began to filter into the locker-lined hallways. After successfully working the combination locks, the students would clang their lockers open and pick up their materials for the first one or two classes of the day before wandering around the halls visiting with each other as they waited for the bell to ring. I stayed out in the hall and had several young seventh and eighth grade students tell me they were in Ms. Flowers's class and would be in my class sometime during the day. Most of the students were positive and friendly. I tried to positively greet those students who made eye contact with a smile and a friendly, "Hello!" I noticed there were a few students who wandered close, but were hesitant to say anything. I suspected they were trying to size me up through my appearance and interaction with the other students who approached me. I made a mental note to keep my eye out for those students in class.

Before I knew it, the bell rang and I stood at the entrance to the classroom while a large number of students filed into the room. I was amazed that almost all of them immediately sat down. This was not the behavior I had seen the week before. Were they more subdued because I was new and a man as compared to the meek, feminine Ms. Flowers? I discovered later that most junior high students entering a new class or dealing with a new teacher take a "wait-and-see" approach until they see how far they can push you.

Today, many of the students visited quietly as they waited for the bell to indicate the start of the day. Finally, the bell rang and I stood at the front of the classroom wearing what I thought was a stern but friendly look as a few stragglers hurried to their seats. I tried to make eye contact with each student. I was nervous as any new teacher would be, but I didn't want them to see me sweat. I wanted to make every effort to communicate to the students that I was now in charge and things were going to be different. As I looked them over, the students stopped talking and the room became very quiet—it may have been the first time there had been silence in that class for many months.

I cleared my throat and introduced myself.

"As you can see on the chalkboard, my name is Mr. Hammann and this is my first period seventh grade math class. I expect you to address me as Mr. Hammann and I will address you by your first name. The first order of business this morning is that I am going to give each of you an assigned seat."

There were moans and groans as I said that. Their response was not unexpected, but it did raise my ire a bit. My expression must have communicated that annoyance as I stood there and waited, because the groaning and moaning ceased almost immediately.

"Let me make something perfectly clear to each and every one of you right from the beginning of this class," I said firmly. "I am not Ms. Flowers."

There was a flippant comment from the back that I couldn't hear, but several students laughed. I chose to ignore it.

"Most of you can see that, but I want you to understand that I am not talking about looks. I'm referring to the expectations I am going to have for you. I am going to expect a lot more from you than Ms. Flowers ever did. I love teaching math and believe it is an important skill that every American student should master. I expect you to learn this skill to the best of your ability. I will not accept English themes as a substitute for math assignments. You will not be doing your own thing when I am going over assignments or making a lesson presentation. I will expect you to be attentive and taking notes. The quality of work on your homework assignments and what you get on tests will be reflected in the grade you get for this class. There will be no extra credit assignments unrelated to the math subject we are covering. I expect you to learn the math concepts that are going to be taught."

As I spoke with passion, keeping my voice firm and making eye contact with the students around the room, I saw that most were focused and attentive.

"We are going to focus our attention on learning math," I said. "But we are also going to have some fun. Now let's get this seating chart set up."

I went and stood by each student desk and called out the name of the student who was to sit in that seat. I immediately found myself in a dilemma. A few of the names were difficult to pronounce, and the students quickly made it clear they were displeased when I mispronounced their name. Some corrected me harshly in what I perceived to be a disrespectful manner. "I guess I messed that up and I'm sorry,"

I said after the third time it happened. "If I mispronounce your name, please tell me the proper way to pronounce it, and try to do it in a respectful manner. It is not my intention to embarrass you."

I continued working through the list, and the students moved to the seat as indicated when I called their names. I still butchered some names, but the students were good about correcting me. It took only about ten minutes to get everyone seated.

I went back to the front of the class.

"Now, let's talk about how things are going to run in this class! I want to make it clear again: I am in charge and we are going to run things my way. You are to come in at the beginning of class and go immediately to your assigned seat. You are to get out your materials for the day so you are ready to learn once I have taken roll. When the bell rings, I will take roll and then we will exchange assignments from the previous day and grade them in class. I will then work a few problems of your choosing to clarify any misconceptions you might have about a problem you missed. You will not wander around this classroom! There will be no one leaving this classroom without my permission. There will be no one climbing out the windows or throwing anything at another student in this classroom. You will be attentive to me when I am teaching and not talking to a neighbor during that time. I will let you assist each other when there is time given to work on assignments at the end of the class period, but you need to keep the noise at a level that is acceptable to me. You will remain in your seats unless you get my permission to get out of the seat. And you are to stay in your seats working until I dismiss you at the end of the class period. You are **not** to line up at the door as the end of the period approaches. You are to work until the bell rings! Do you all understand me?"

Several heads nodded and a few mumbled, "Yes!" In my mind, I'm thinking, "Hey, this is working. They are actually quiet, attentive, and with me on this. This is going to be a walk in the park." But in reality, it was going to take a lot more than a stern talk and setting some rules at the beginning of the semester.

After this declaration, I laid out the five rules regarding student behavior that I had prepared over the weekend. I then reviewed the consequences of violating these rules. To stress the seriousness of what I was saying, I brought out the "hacking" paddle I had found in the bottom drawer of the teacher's desk when I first got to school that morning. It was an inch thick and had several half-inch holes bored through it. It was a formidable weapon and for emphasis I swept it through the air. To my amazement, I found that the paddle was crafted so it whistled when you swung it. This was an unexpected and pleasant surprise, because there was a new depth of silence in the classroom as it whistled through the air and the eyes of each student widened to owl-like proportions. I was feeling more and more confident about turning this class around.

Before I gave the first lesson presentation, I reviewed the grading process and procedures. Students would be required to complete daily assignments on the math concept covered in class. I would give definitions, explain concepts, and work problems on the board to assist students with learning. They would then take a 100-point test at the end of each chapter. The assignments and the test grades would be averaged to determine their grades. An "A" would be assigned to students with an average of 90 to 100. A student could get a "B" with an average of 80 to 89, and a student could get a "C" with an average of 70 to 79. A "D" would be assigned for a 60 to 69 average, and anything below 60 would receive an "F." After this explanation, I began that day's lesson on the meaning of fractions. Amazingly, the students were very attentive during that presentation. I gave the assignment and moved around the classroom assisting students who had questions. I could tell about two-thirds of the students were doing the assignment correctly, demonstrating they had learned the concept properly, and most students were on task. When the class period was within five minutes of coming to a close, students began to close their books and put their papers away. I was helping a student when I heard the noise of books closing and chairs moving. I looked up and saw about five students moving from their chairs to line up at the door—I couldn't believe what I was seeing! My first thought was, "Do these children have a brain? Hadn't I said they were to stay in their seats until I dismissed them?"

I stood up to my full six-foot height and said in the sternest voice I possessed, "Hey! Didn't I say you were to stay in your seats until I dismissed you? Didn't I say you were to keep working until the bell rings? What do you think you are doing?"

There was an instant scramble by all the students at the door to get to their desks as quick as possible. Several other students quickly flipped open their books and feigned working on the assignment. I gave the whole class the "evil eye" until most were back on task. I then moved to the door to wait for the bell. This one breech of the rules on the first day was a clue that this discipline thing was going to take more diligence and persistence than I had originally thought.

When the bell rang, several students started to get up and leave. Once again, I put them in check.

"HEY! You sit there until I say you can leave!"

They all sat back down and after about fifteen seconds—enough time to remind them I was in charge—I released them and they noisily filed out.

I'd made it through the first class and it seemed to go pretty well. I now had five more classes to address before the end of the day. I did the same thing in each class and in almost every case, they responded the same way the first period class had. In every period, I had to confront students about lining up at the door just before the bell rang even though I had reviewed it at the beginning of each class.

After the first four classes, I got a thirty-five-minute lunch break. I went to the lunchroom, picked up my food, and returned to the teachers' room in the main building. As I entered the room, several teachers who I had not met during my observation time rose and introduced themselves and peppered me with questions.

"You survived the 'hellions' did you?"

"Did you kick a trash can across the room like I recommended?"

"What did you think?"

"Do you still want to teach?"

"What were the classes like?"

I assured everyone things had gone fine and that I was taking control of the classes. I then sat down at one of the tables and answered questions from staff members at the table about my personal background as I consumed the food. I quickly found the lunch period for staff was incredibly short—I was barely able to eat and answer a few question before the warning bell sounded. I was to discover that even your lunchtime had to be well organized in order to be back in the classroom to deal with the next class of students.

After lunch, I went back and addressed the students in the same manner I had addressed the class at the beginning of the day. Finally, the last bell of the day sounded and I moved out into the hall to watch the students noisily make their way to their lockers and then to their busses or homes. One small seventh grade boy came up to me.

"I like your class," he said. "I think we will actually learn some math this semester."

"Thank you," I replied. "I will do my best to make that happen." He smiled and ran down the hall to catch the bus.

I returned to my room and sat down, exhausted, at my desk and stared out the window. What a day—I had not worked this hard in a single day, even when I was in the military—and this was just Monday. I had been on my feet for six full hours and taught more than 160 students.

I got in my car and drove home to begin the process of preparing for the next day of school. As I drove home, I thought, "I will have to do this every day for the next four days. I wonder how tired I will be by the end of the week." I had no clue what the week was to hold.

CHAPTER 6

The First Week

> *I know this is hard to believe, but about five minutes before the end of the class, students began to close their books and visit, while a few were even bold enough to get up out of their desks and start toward the door. I was beside myself. I was now angry enough to actually kick a trash can across the room...*

On Tuesday morning I awoke and jumped out of bed before the alarm went off. I quickly cleaned up and ate a small bowl of cereal in preparation for the day. Today was Tuesday and Mr. Walker was holding his first staff meeting of the new semester. This was to be my first staff meeting as a real teacher—and needless to say, I was excited!

Mr. Walker told me during the two days of observation before I started teaching that he met with the staff every other Tuesday of the month to communicate on a number of issues. We were expected to come in early on those Tuesday mornings and meet in a classroom close to his office. We were to be there at 7:45 a.m. sharp—he emphasized the word "sharp" for my benefit.

So at 7:35 a.m., I sat alone in the classroom waiting for the other staff members and Mr. Walker to appear. About 7:40 a.m. teachers began wandering into the room sitting down at various seats. Sure enough, at exactly 7:45 a.m., Mr. Walker briskly walked into the room and wrote an acronym on the chalkboard: DWISLWBG. He then explained what it meant: "Do what I say and life will be good." He then had the whole staff repeat the phrase. The experienced teachers repeated it from memory in a tired monotone as if bored with this part of the meeting, while a few of us just read it off the board.

Mr. Walker said he ran the show and those who wanted life to be good in his school should follow his lead. He then went through some announcements: the high school and junior high staff would be involved in a donkey basketball game at the high school gym Thursday to support the high school's Future Farmers of America organization, he would be performing some evaluation visits during the month, weekly lesson plan objectives were to be turned in to him on Friday for the following week, etc. Some of the staff complained about class sizes and indicated a need for new student chairs. He said he was sorry about the large class sizes, but it couldn't be helped and assured those needing student chairs that he would get them. This continued until the warning bell went off and Mr. Walker dismissed us to go to our classes.

As I started out of the room, Mr. Walker waved me over.

"Would you be willing to be on the junior high staff team competing in the donkey basketball game this Thursday night? It would be a good way to get to know some of the other staff members in the district, and the students could see you in a different light."

I told him I'd be glad to, even though I had no idea what in the world donkey basketball was. But I was thinking that as a new teacher, I would do whatever was needed to help me keep this job.

After being dismissed, I walked quickly to my classroom, barely getting there as the bell rang to start class. When I got there, I found about half the students were in their seats and the other half were standing around visiting. I stopped just inside the door and just stared at them with the sternest countenance I could muster, and when those standing noticed me, they scrambled to their seats and fumbled around to get their books and assignments out. This method of staring quietly and sternly at the class worked well to get the students' attention and to remind them of what they should be doing. I had to really work on that look and knew I had it when the students reacted by giving me their attention or showing embarrassment for not performing as expected.

I moved to the front of the room.

"Now what did I say yesterday?" I said this with some angst in my voice. "Didn't I say that you were to come in and go to your seats and get your papers out to grade? Do I need to review that with you again?" Several students shook their heads and some said, "No!"

"Well, get your papers out and exchange them with the person behind you so they can be graded. I will get the roll taken while you do this."

I called out students' names on the seating chart and tried to match them with faces. I wasn't quite there yet, but I figured it wouldn't take long with the help of the seating chart. There were two students missing, so I marked them absent in my grade book, put their names on an absentee notice, and pinned it on a clip out in the hall. A student aide collected these about ten minutes after class started.

I returned my attention to the class and began giving answers as the students graded their neighbors' assignments. I was stopped on several occasions to clarify if an answer was correct even though it was different than the answer I had given. After grading the assignment, I called out names and the student who had graded that assignment responded by giving me their grade. I entered the grades in the grade book as they were given to me and then collected the assignments to review later. This first grading activity took longer than I expected, but we were done after about fifteen minutes.

I then moved into a lesson on reducing fractions. As I gave some definitions and worked some problems, I noticed two or three pairs of students talking as I spoke. At first it was in whispers, which I ignored—a bad mistake. When the volume of their voices went up, I stopped teaching and sternly stared at the class until they stopped talking. After I gave the assignment, there was about ten minutes left in the class, so I told the students they could work on the assignment until the bell rang. I sat down at my desk and when I looked up, there were about eight hands raised. I got up and went to the closest student.

"What do you need?" I asked.

"I don't understand this," he said, pointing to the first problem on the assignment, which was a simple fraction reduction.

"What part of reducing do you not understand?" I asked.

"All of it," he replied simply, in a way that made me feel like he thought it was my fault he didn't get how to do the problems. Needless to say, I was somewhat frustrated by his response and his failure to take some responsibility for learning the concept. I had just spent a significant amount of time outlining how to do the problems on the board and then working several examples just like the problems in the assignment. Most of the students appeared to be attentive. I thought maybe he really didn't get it, so I helped him solve the first problem by explaining step by step what to do. I then told him to work the second problem. His response was the same, saying he didn't get it. So I went through the material once again, this time asking questions at each step to help him work through the second problem more on his own. "You are on your own for the rest of these," I said after we'd worked the second problem.

I moved on to the girl behind him who had her hand up and asked her what her problem was. Her response was the same as the boy I had just helped. I used the same process, helping her through the problems step by step. In almost every case, the students with their hands up for help were giving the excuse that they didn't understand how to do the problems and were inferring by their body language it was my fault. I had to spend the rest of the class re-teaching the lesson to about a fourth of the class. About three-fourths of the class were understanding it, with a few of those only asking if their answers were right or not. I eventually came to realize this was typical for seventh graders—a high percentage of them need to be nursed through working math problems because typically, seventh graders have little initiative, but a lot of enthusiasm.

Of course, while I was working individually with students the noise level in the room went up.

"Hey!" I reminded the students. "You need to stop talking so students can focus on their work." In response, the students would quiet down for a few minutes before the noise level would creep up again. I had to remind them to stay quiet at least four times as they worked on the assignment.

I know this is hard to believe, but about five minutes before the end of the class, students began to close their books and visit, while a few were even bold enough to get up out of their desks and start toward the door. I was beside myself. I was now angry enough to actually kick a trash can across the room, but I refrained. Instead, I stalked toward the door and got in front of the students who had lined up there.

"SIT DOWN!" I commanded. "I'm beginning to believe that some of you are brain dead. I thought I made it clear yesterday—I expect you to stay in your seats until I release you after the bell rings. You will do this and if you can't, then some of you will face more serious consequences than a verbal reprimand. Now get back to your seats!" The bell rang just as I finished speaking and there was a surge from the students, trying to make their way through the door where I was standing. There were enough of them to bowl right past me, and for a moment I thought they might. But I stood in the doorway and just looked at them as sternly as I could. With a groan, they stopped and reluctantly turned around to return to their seats. Once they were all seated again, I dismissed them, stepping aside to let them out the door. As they passed, a few were mumbling and grumbling about how mean I was. This actually made me feel good—I wanted them to fear me, to some extent, hoping it would eventually lead to respecting me.

The rest of the morning classes went like the first period class. In the seventh grade classes, about the same number of students needed special help even when I tried to slow down and explain the concept of reducing fractions more clearly. I found that most of the eighth grade students were able to grasp the math concepts and needed less help. All six classes struggled with keeping quiet during lesson presentations and waiting for my dismissal at the end of class.

When lunchtime came, I hurried over to the lunchroom and returned to the faculty lounge with my lunch. And once more, I addressed questions and comments from other staff members regarding my progress in controlling Ms. Flowers's classes. "I can tell you this," said one of the teachers whose classroom neighbored mine. "His classes these past two days are much quieter, and I'm able to get some things done in my classroom."

I was encouraged by this comment, and it helped spur me on for the rest of the day. Finally, when the last student had exited my room, I sat at my desk exhausted. For two days now, I had worked harder at this job than any other job in my life and this was just Tuesday. I had three more days to go.

With a deep breath, I gathered up my things and took them to my car before walking over to the gym to watch the afternoon basketball practice.

I had met the coaches for the eighth and ninth grade basketball teams—Phil Crosby and Mic Wimer—during the lunch hour. During our conversation, I told them I'd played basketball in college, and they invited me to come over and watch them during practice.

Sure enough, I walked into the gym and the ninth grade team was going through a number of basketball drills as I stood on the sidelines. The bleachers were pushed back, making room for two shortened basketball courts that the team used to scrimmage after their drills were completed.

Now this was before the implementation of Title IX, so there was just one boys' basketball team for each grade. Each team had tryouts and each coach selected about twelve to fourteen players. As I watched the team practice, the old excitement of playing and being involved in the sport came back to me. There were some players who were pretty good, and it was fun to watch them and listen to the coaches encouraging and teaching them. One of my hopes was that eventually I would be able to coach basketball here. After about a half hour, I slipped out to my car and headed home to eat and get ready for the next day.

Wednesday and Thursday were much like Tuesday. I still had to be on my toes to keep students attentive, although the issue about staying in their seats until I dismissed the class seemed to be improving: I only had to guard the door and raise my voice at students in two classes over the course of those two days. Unsurprisingly, they were both seventh grade classes. At the end of the school day Thursday, the principal caught me as I was headed out to my car to remind me I had committed to participating in the donkey basketball game that evening.

"What time do I need to be there and what should I wear?" I asked.

"You need to be there by 6:30 p.m., and just wear blue jeans and a shirt," he replied. "I'll be there acting as the coach for the junior high team." I said goodbye and that I'd see him later that night, before I hustled home to grab a bite to eat, do a little planning for the next day, and change my clothes.

CHAPTER 7

Donkey Basketball and Bathtub Reflections

> *I got ready to shoot, and just as I started into my motion, the helper with a stick whacked my donkey and it bucked, sending me straight up into the air just as I released the ball in the general direction of the goal.*

After supper, I made my way to the high school basketball gymnasium where they were hosting the donkey basketball game between the junior high and high school staffs. I arrived about five minutes before the time set by Mr. Walker, who had made it clear my first day that punctuality was of the utmost importance to him. I was determined not to let him down in that area again. Ever since getting out of the military, I detested being dressed down by my superiors.

I was not sure what would be involved in this donkey basketball game, but I was anxious to participate with some of my fellow teachers and to show my prowess as a basketball player. I assumed my basketball skills would be needed to help the junior high staff triumph over the high school staff, although I was still unclear on how donkeys figured into the game. In the foyer of the gymnasium, there were was a table with three students wearing Future Farmers of America jackets taking money from parents, guests, and students. I got in line and informed them I was playing for the junior high faculty and, after looking me up and down, they let me in without paying, which was a relief since I didn't have much money and, since payday was the last workday of every month, it was going to be a long time before I would get my first full paycheck.

I entered the gym proper and saw three or four staff members from Jenifer Junior High sitting on the bleachers on one side of the gym with a few other people I had not seen before. It turned out some of the staff from Sacajawea Junior High School, which was located in what is known as the Lewiston Orchards, were participating as well. A few people were sitting in the stands and more were flowing in. On the other side of the gym, there were some other adults sitting on the first step of the bleachers, who I assumed were members of the high school staff team. I sat down next to Phil Crosby, an experienced teacher and the ninth grade basketball coach. "Did Slug talk you into doing this?" he asked me.

I nodded.

"Well, I'm not surprised. He's quick to go after the rookies for these extra kinds of things. Have you ever played donkey basketball?"

"No, never have," I replied. "Have you?"

"Yeah, I've done it a few times," he said with a smile. "It can be a lot of fun, but watch out which donkey is assigned to you. Most of them are mellow and easy to manipulate, but there are a few who will try to buck you off!"

"Really? Where are the donkeys?" I asked.

"They are just outside the gym over there," he replied. "They transport them to the event in a small stock truck and then corral them in a small pen near the truck. We'll be meeting them here in a minute. Don't get too anxious about this. You will have a good time and so will the spectators. By the way, are you in good shape?"

"Well, I think I am," I said. "I've played a lot of basketball during the months of November and December. I think I'm in pretty good shape."

"That will help," he said.

We continued visiting about school and how well his basketball team was doing. The gym was continuing to fill up with noisy spectators of all ages, getting louder and louder until we had to raise our voices in order to hear each other. At one point, the announcer walked over and had us put on jerseys with numbers on them. He wrote down our names and numbers, explaining that he wanted to know who was who as he announced the game. About twenty minutes before 7 p.m., a bearded man wearing jeans came through the door where the donkeys were supposed to be and called for the participants to follow him. The high school staff members and my team obediently filed through the door behind him.

Sure enough, there were about twelve donkeys standing quietly outside the door next to a small stock truck. The bearded man moved past the group of donkeys—who were being tended by a young man—and called us to stand around him. He introduced himself and gave us instructions about the rules of donkey basketball.

"Donkey basketball is played much like regular basketball," he said. "The object of the game is to score a basket when you are on offense and to defend your basket when you are on defense. Each team on the floor will have five players riding five donkeys. We will play four eight-minute quarters and make substitutions at the end of each quarter, so all of you will get a chance to play.

"Now here are some general rules: There is no out-of-bounds. You can go after the ball anywhere. There is no need to dribble, but you cannot advance the ball unless you are seated on your donkey. Once you are on your donkey, you can advance the ball by riding the donkey or passing it to a teammate while you are on your donkey. If the ball is loose, you can get off your donkey and get it, but you must maintain contact with your donkey in order to pick up the ball. Once you get the ball, you must remount your donkey to shoot or advance the ball. No basket will count unless it is shot while you are sitting on your donkey. A defender must be in contact with his or her donkey in order to steal the ball or block a shot. Are there any questions?"

All the staff members who had done this before said nothing, and the newcomers like me kept quiet. I didn't say anything because I didn't want to appear ignorant, and I suspect the others felt the same. "By the way," the bearded man continued. "When you go after a ball, you might want to avoid going directly behind any donkey. Some of these donkeys are a little skittish and you might get kicked! Also, they can be a little temperamental and may buck a little if things get too exciting. Now if you will just sign these waivers we will be able to get started."

We were being asked to sign waivers? We were going to play a game where you could get kicked in the head or maybe even a more sensitive area of the anatomy by a donkey. Or you might be bucked off a donkey onto a hardwood floor and break an arm or a leg. And now they were asking me to sign a waiver indicating I would take all the responsibility for any injury I might sustain in this activity? Somehow, this didn't seem right, but as a young and inexperienced teacher who wanted to please his students and employer, I signed it anyway. I was in this career to teach junior high students, yet here I was putting life and limb in jeopardy to help the high school FFA make a little money. At the time it didn't make much sense.

After signing the waiver, I walked around the corralled donkeys and looked the animals over. They definitely had an animal smell. They varied in sizes from three to four-and-a-half feet tall at the shoulders. Each donkey wore a rope halter and a small saddle with a horn for the rider to hold on to. I also noticed that the donkeys' hooves were wrapped in burlap to protect the basketball floor. As I walked around them, eyeing each one closely, the donkeys looked almost bored as they slowly chewed on straw. Well, I thought, maybe this won't be so bad.

Just then, the bearded man asked who was going to start the game. I quickly raised my hand, excited to be on the starting team. But as I looked around to see who else had volunteered, I found no one else on my team had raised a hand. A few seconds went by and reluctantly, four other staff members raised their hands—their hesitation should have been a clue.

After the starting teams were decided, each team member was given a colored helmet to wear—the junior high team got red and the high school team got blue. The helmets were light but durable and could be adjusted to fit any size head. The helmets being passed out raised my level of concern a little, but I was young and athletic and felt any threat of bodily harm was a remote one.

After the helmets were securely fastened to our heads, the bearded man told us to choose our donkeys, grab the ropes on their halters, and lead them into the gym. The door swung open and the junior high team started to lead their donkeys into the gym with the high school team close behind. We quickly found that "lead" was the wrong word—really, we had to tug and pull the donkeys into the gym with the bearded man and his young helper filing in behind us, each carrying a long, flexible stick.

As we entered the gym, cheers and jeers rose from the crowd. The stands were about two-thirds full of adults, teenagers, and children who had all come looking to have a good time at our expense. The starting team members were led to the center circle on the gym floor where we stood by our donkeys holding their halter ropes. The substitutes moved to their respective benches on each side of the gym. The announcer asked the crowd to stand and say the pledge of allegiance to the flag. Once that was done, the announcer introduced each starting player, and as our names were read, we mounted our donkey and raised our hands in turn. There were great boisterous cheers as each name came across the loud speaker.

After the teams were announced, the bearded man grabbed a basketball and, when the horn sounded, dropped it in the middle of the floor and walked away. Immediately, there was a mad scramble by those closest to the ball. Two of the high school teachers, both slightly overweight men, hopped off their donkeys and tried to reach the basketball while pulling their donkey by its halter rope. A couple of skinny junior high teachers did the same, each struggling to pull their donkeys toward the ball. The donkeys didn't want to be pulled anywhere by that lead rope, and the more desperately the player pulled, the more the donkeys resisted. The crowd roared, cheering and jeering as the struggle continued. One of the high school staff moved around to the back of his donkey to push him toward the ball, but he must have remembered what the bearded man had said about that and went back to pulling. The rest of the players sat helplessly on their donkeys, each of us awaiting the outcome of this wrestling match. Every donkey being pulled just dug in its heels and had to be physically manhandled to the ball. As this scene played out, I spotted the bearded man out of the corner of my eye, sidling up behind one of the waiting high school teacher's donkeys and tapping the animal's rear end. Immediately, the donkey began to buck and jump around the gym with the high school teacher hanging on for dear life. The crowd went wild.

After about three bucks, the teacher was tossed from the donkey and landed on his feet and hands without too much damage. He shot the bearded man a dirty look and tried to remount the small but surprisingly spry donkey. The animal continued to buck every time the teacher tried to mount her. Eventually, he gave up and stood in front of his donkey holding the halter rope and smiling, slightly embarrassed.

In the meantime, a high school teacher gained possession of the ball and had remounted his donkey. He tried to tell the donkey to "giddyup," but it refused to move until the young helper moved up behind it and tapped it on the rear end with his stick. This donkey was galvanized so quickly toward the offensive goal, that the rider almost dropped the ball and fell off the donkey. I kicked the side of my donkey to intercept him and prevent him from getting to the basket. My donkey moved slowly, but I had a good enough angle that I was able to get close enough to him to try and knock the ball out of his hand. He moved the ball to his other hand and passed it to another high school staff member close by. Slowly but surely, the high school staff moved the ball toward the basket we were defending. Finally, when one of the players was about ten feet from the basket, he shot the ball as his uncooperative donkey made a quick turn and, of course, missed. Again, there was a major scramble by players to get the ball. This time, I was close, so I got off my donkey and tried to pull it along to reach the ball. My donkey stubbornly dug in his heels, drastically decreasing my progress. Finally, with several great heaves, I was able to get to the basketball. I picked it up, pushing away a high school teacher, and tried to remount my donkey, but it kept sidling away. It really is difficult to hold on to a basketball and mount a stubborn, moving donkey while a crowd of wild adults and children scream and jeer.

After several attempts, I was finally able to get back on the donkey. Once I was seated, the young man with a stick came up behind me and tapped the donkey on the rear, and we began to move quickly toward our basket. He actually moved into a trot and I got pretty close to the goal. I got ready to shoot, and just as I started into my motion, the helper with a stick whacked my donkey and it bucked, sending me straight up into the air just as I released the ball in the general direction of the goal. Of course, I missed badly and there was another mad scramble for the ball as the crowd went wild.

The first quarter ended with each team having just three possessions and no baskets being scored. When the horn went off to end the quarter, we dismounted our donkeys and gave them to our teammates sitting on the bench. I went to the bench, grateful to get a rest. I was sweating and breathing hard and my muscles were screaming from exertion.

The second team did much better than we did. One of our players was able to maneuver his donkey just under the basket, close enough to shoot and score for our team. "Two points for the junior high team," the announcer said amidst wild screams from the crowd.

The high school team was able to match our basket and at halftime the game was tied two to two.

During halftime, the donkeys were removed from the floor and the FFA members conducted a number of drawings for home-baked pies with raffle tickets audience members had purchased as they entered the gym.

After the twenty-minute halftime break, the donkeys were once again brought into the gym, and I selected one at the suggestion of Phil Crosby as he grabbed one for himself. Again the horn sounded and the ball was tossed onto the floor. It was tossed close to Phil, who quickly got off his donkey and was able to get to the ball. He remounted his animal and, looking around, spotted me in the open at half court. He raised the ball with his right hand and tossed it to me. His pass was a little high and I had to reach up for it. Just as I stretched up to take the pass, the whiskered man, who was behind me, tapped my donkey on the rear. Wouldn't you know it—I had the donkey that had bucked the high school teacher off in the first quarter. And Phil Crosby, knowing this, had suggested him to me. Sure enough, the donkey reared and bucked at the touch of the whiskered man's stick. The momentum of my stretching for the ball and the bucking of the donkey coincided to send me into free flight high into the air. The crowd went wild.

It felt like I was watching this happen in slow motion. I found myself turning slowly in the air high above the floor, swinging my arms wildly, trying to get some control of my free fall. I gave up all thought of catching the ball and looked instead to see if there was any way I could land without getting hurt. But I was spinning so hard I couldn't gain any kind of control and eventually landed hard on the right cheek of my buttocks. The crowd groaned loudly in empathy with the loud thump of my landing.

I was stunned and my hip was hurting, but I managed to get slowly to my feet, although not without great pain. The crowd cheered as I came to my feet and looked around to find the ball. I quickly saw that the rest of the team was further down the court chasing the ball, as was my donkey. I limped after my donkey and once I reached him, tried to mount him, raising the leg that was unhurt over his back. Of course, he began to buck and rear. The whiskered man ran up and asked me if I was okay. When I shook my head, he said, "If I were you I would just try to pull the donkey around for now until the end of the quarter. I don't think he's going to let you mount him right now. He thinks he's in control." He then ran on down the court, touching a few donkeys on the rear end as he moved toward the action around the ball.

I stood near the top of the key at our offensive end and held on to my donkey, waiting to see if the ball would come my way again. Thankfully, it did not. We scored one more time before the horn sounded to end the third quarter. I was thankful to be able to limp to our bench and to sit down. Several of my teammates came to me asking if I was okay. "That's the hardest fall I've ever seen in a donkey basketball game," Phil Crosby said with a smile. "I think he bucked you about eight feet high. It's a wonder you didn't break a hip or a leg."

When I got to the bench, my hip was throbbing and I was evaluating my sanity for allowing myself to be roped into a game involving my beloved basketball with a bunch of dumb donkeys. The third quarter ended with the score tied, and the fourth quarter began with a set of fresh players.

I thankfully watched the rest of the game from the bench. I scanned the crowd and could see that almost everyone was having a good time and involved in rooting for their team or teacher. The kids especially were enjoying the game, shouting encouragement to some teachers and jeering others. What in the world could the benefit of this whole activity be except to raise some money for the FFA and give the paying attenders a good time?

As I was limping out of the gym after the game ended, several of my junior high students came up to me and patted me on the back or made comments. "Mr. Hammann, that was cool. I really liked how you played the game. When you got bucked off it was great!" said one.

"I didn't see how you were ever going to get up after being bucked eight feet into the air like that, but you did it! Wow!" said another.

"That was cool, Mr. Hammann! I never dreamed you would be out there doing something like that!"

Every one of these students had a friendly smile on his or her face. I realized this might be the greatest benefit of this ridiculous donkey basketball game: the students seemed to have more respect for me and I felt a better rapport with them because I took the time to play. It really was good for me to be involved in an activity like this—I made a mental note to make this a part of my role as a teacher and my efforts to build a positive relationship with my students.

The irony of Jenifer Junior High teachers playing in a donkey basketball game came to me as I thought about the mascot of Jenifer Junior High—the Jenifer Burros. I later found out that our cross-town rivals the Sacajawea Savages knew us more affectionately as the Jenifer Jackasses.

By the time I reached Friday night at the end of my first week as a teacher, I was totally exhausted. My hip was still sore from the donkey basketball game and rightly so, because I could see a large, dark, black-and-blue bruise on my hip after I undressed to take a bath before going to bed. I locked the door, filled the tub with the hottest water I could stand, and sank thankfully up to my neck in the tub. The hot water helped me relax and relieved some of the pain in my hip. As I soaked in the tub, I reflected on the day and week.

My thoughts went to that Friday morning, the first time I saw my classes after Thursday night's donkey basketball game. I stood at my door waiting for the first period class to enter after the warning bell sounded. Several students smiled at me as they entered and commented about the game and my participation. The demeanor of most of those who attended the game was much different than what I had seen earlier in the week—these students seeing me in a different, informal environment was a positive thing. Their comments and smiles communicated acceptance and respect, but it didn't noticeably change their behavior with regards to discipline. I still had students entering class and visiting instead of getting ready to grade papers; I still had students closing their books and preparing to leave class five to ten minutes before the bell rang; and I still had students talking during my lesson presentations. But I noticed the atmosphere in each class was more positive, and for that I was thankful. I still had to stay alert and keep my thumb on them.

I reflected on my new boss, Harvie "Slug" Walker. He appeared to be a rough-and-tumble kind of guy. He demanded certain things—

like being on time and following his orders. He seemed pretty gruff, but he didn't appear to treat students or staff unfairly. I liked him and respected him, I suppose because he ran the school like officers ran our shops in the military. I had spent four years learning to appreciate that kind of leadership.

As I soaked, I thought about the conversation I had with a teacher after school on Wednesday. I had asked him what it was like to work for Harvie. "I like working for Slug," he replied. "He's gruff but fair, and he doesn't put up with much nonsense. He expects his teachers to do their jobs and he stays out of their way as long as the job is done right. He had a hard time dealing with your predecessor, Ms. Flowers. He tried to get her to toughen up and take control of her class, but she was too much of a bleeding heart. She was always making statements that indicated she felt sorry for the students. She was always making excuses for them. She was a free spirit and he wasn't. He had an aggressive approach to dealing with students and she was passive-aggressive at best. They had a major clash and it became clear to everyone that one of them had to go and it sure wasn't going to be Slug. You replacing her is going to work out best in the long run for Slug, the staff, and the students. I've been here twelve years," he continued. "And I was here when they promoted Slug from a math teacher to an assistant principal at the high school. As the assistant principal at the high school, he dealt with discipline. The story goes that about two years into his tenure as the assistant principal, he went upstairs to the second floor at the high school to deal with an unruly male student who was giving one of the female teachers a bad time. When he got there, the student and the teacher were out in the hall and the student was cussing the teacher out using a lot of profanity.

"Harvie walked up to them and told the teacher to go back into the classroom. Without saying another word, he allegedly grabbed the student by the arm and aggressively guided him toward the stairwell to take him back to his office. There were no witnesses, but the student said Slug threw him down the stairs to the landing and then picked him up and threw him down the stairs to the first floor. This student was one of the football players and supposedly a tough kid, but I can believe he could pick this kid up and toss him down the stairs. Slug's a big man! The student wasn't injured, but his parents raised a ruckus with the school board about the allegation that Slug threw him down the stairs.

"The board held a hearing and at the hearing, Harvie testified that the student resisted him and slipped on the stairs. The board chose to believe Harvie over the word of the student since there were no other witnesses and the student had been in trouble with the staff and administration in the past. However, Slug was moved over to Jenifer to be the junior high principal the next school year.

"He has a no-nonsense reputation among the staff and the students. I've found it's best to do things Slug's way. The staff and most students have found life at Jenifer is much easier when you do that."

The story fit my informal observations from the past week. I had a lot of respect for Slug and I would do my best to follow his lead. He knew what he was doing.

I continued to reflect on my situation with the students since I took over on Monday. The things that were going on when Ms. Flowers ran the class did not occur this week. There were no students leaving class without permission, no students wandering around the classroom while I taught, and for the most part the students were attentive when I was teaching and grading papers. There were still problems with students staying on task after I gave the assignment, and I still had some instances of students trying to line up at the door before the class period ended. And about a third of the seventh graders still didn't seem to want to take responsibility for learning the concepts I was trying to teach. It seemed like I had to give the same students an incredible amount of time re-teaching the material after the lesson presentation was over. One thought jumped into my mind as I lay in the tub: I had taught for only a week and I was totally wiped out. Could I do this for the next thirty years?

I was wondering about that as I drifted off to sleep in that comfortably warm bathtub.

CHAPTER 8
The Hack

He looked up into my eyes like an injured puppy as he pleaded his case. I wanted to believe him, but things had gone too far now. If I let him off the hook, he and the other students wouldn't think I meant business, so I said, 'Jimmy let's get this over with. Bend over!'

The second week of teaching was fairly uneventful, although I noticed it was a constant struggle to keep students on task. It seemed like there were days when talking to the students just wasn't enough. In my discipline plan, I had consequences that included verbal reprimands, parental contacts, removal to the hall for the rest of the class period, detention after school, removal to the principal's office and the "hack."

About three weeks into my tenure, I sent a student to Slug for gouging his name on his desk. The student returned to the room about fifteen minutes after I sent him out with a note from Slug. The note said, "Please do everything in your power to discipline this student before you send him to me. I don't think gouging a desk meets the criteria of being serious enough to warrant my involvement. I expect you to send a student to me only as a last resort or when there is a serious violation of the rules."

After thinking about it, I could understand Slug's perspective on this. He and the lone counselor on staff had to deal with over 800 junior high students, and his request was reasonable. So, I kept the student after school and had him fill in the gouges and sand the desk. From then on, I determined to use my list of consequences first before sending a student to Slug unless it involved a student attacking another student or myself. And from those consequences, the hack would be the ultimate consequence before sending a student to Mr. Walker.

Now let me explain the policy for hacking a student during my first year as a teacher. If a teacher made the decision to hack a student, it could not be done in front of other students, so the teacher had to remove the student to the hallway. Once out of the view of the students, the offending student would be asked to bend over and grab his ankles. The teacher would then whack the offered backside with a paddle. At Jenifer Junior High, almost all hacks were administered to male students. I can't recall any female students receiving a hack while I worked there.

The severity of the hack depended on the instrument being used. A table tennis paddle would have a different effect than a one-inch by two-foot-long board full of holes. The number of hacks and the force of each hack to be administered would depend on the severity of the punishment. Most teachers gave a student one hack, but sometimes they would give two if they thought it was warranted. To my knowledge, no female teachers hacked students; instead, she would ask a male teacher near her room to come out and administer the hack if she felt one was needed.

The administration, the school board, and most parents in the district generally accepted the practice of hacking students, although I remember one member on the school board who opposed hacking. The school board member was a counselor working for the state children's home located in Lewiston, and she had a great distaste for the practice. This school board member and a minority of parents in the district were able to change some of the practices associated with giving a hack, but they were never able to banish the practice while I was there. In my second year at Jenifer, they instituted the rule that all hacks had to have a witness, which meant the teacher had to call a neighboring teacher out into the hall to observe the administration of the hack. This was mostly implemented to see that the hack was reasonably applied and not administered too zealously.

In my seven years at Jenifer, I hacked mostly seventh and eighth grade students. I felt that ninth-graders were just too old for that kind of punishment. I usually used after-school detention and calling the parent as last-resort consequences for those students. I can't recall ever hacking a freshman student.

I remember the first time I hacked a student—I was a three weeks into the semester and I was having real difficulty with a seventh-grade boy in my second period class. He just wouldn't stop talking while I was giving lesson presentations. Every day for more than a week, I tried to stop this behavior. I warned him the first couple of times, but he would return to talking to his neighbor within five minutes of the warning being issued. On the third occasion, I gave him a verbal dressing-down in front of the class. Within ten minutes of that reprimand, I observed him talking again. I gave him an after-school detention, which seemed to stop him for the rest of the period, but he came in the next day and started talking again. I changed his seat to get him away from the students he talked to the most, but that didn't change anything either. I was exasperated. I was spending valuable teaching time just trying to manage this one student. Finally, after confronting him again about his disruptive talking, I raised my voice.

"If you don't stop talking while I am talking, I'm going to give you a hack."

The class got very quiet. Some of the students looked at each other and smiled anxiously. Sure enough, it wasn't five minutes later that this student started talking and disrupting again. I stopped teaching and looked at him until he stopped what he was doing and made eye contact with me. I jerked my thumb toward the door and was amazed to see that he turned pale, got out of his seat, and plodded in the direction of the door as if he was going to the electric chair. I wrote the assignment on the board and told the students to work on it until I had returned. Dramatically, I slowly opened the bottom drawer of my desk and brought out the one-inch-thick hacking board. I strode purposefully to the door, went out into the hall, and pulled the door closed behind me. You could have heard a pin drop as I left, although I think they were being quiet so they could listen in on the interaction between me and the student and the inevitable hack.

This young seventh grader was a likable kid. He was short and a little pudgy—the other kids liked him and I really liked him—but he just couldn't seem to control his mouth. "Jimmy," I said to him once I was in the hall. "I've warned you and warned you to keep your mouth shut and not disrupt the class, but you won't listen, so I'm going to give you one hack."

"Mr. Hammann, I get it," Jimmy beseeched. "You really don't need to hack me. I won't cause you any more trouble. Just give me another chance."

He looked up into my eyes like an injured puppy as he pleaded his case. I wanted to believe him, but things had gone too far now. If I let him off the hook, he and the other students wouldn't think I meant business, so I said, "Jimmy, let's get this over with. Bend over!"

Jimmy must have been hacked before, because he assumed the proper position with no instructions from me. I pulled the board back and firmly brought it down on his ample backside. As had happened on the first day of class when I did a practice swing, the board whistled loudly until it struck pay dirt. I really didn't think I hit him that hard, but an amazing thing happened right after I made contact. He leaped up into the air and began hopping up and down crying in a high, squeaky voice, "Ow, ow, ow!"

"You've got to be kidding me," I thought. "I hardly popped him and he's jumping around like I killed him."

I thought he would get himself under control, but he just kept hopping and crying out. Finally, I just opened up the door for him to return to the classroom and he proceeded to hop through the door and all the way to his desk at the back of the room crying, "Ow...ow...ow!" The class was stunned at first, but then roared in laughter. I had to laugh myself watching this pudgy little guy with both hands holding his backside hopping back to his seat. By the time he got there, he had stopped hopping and crying and was soon beaming an embarrassed smile. What's really interesting is I never had much trouble with that student from that day until the end of the year. The hack really changed his behavior.

I was truly a rookie when it came to giving the hack, but the real expert on the hack was the physical education teacher, Mic Wimer. Mic had an office in the boys' locker room in the gym. Around my second week of teaching, I wandered over to the gym after school to watch the basketball teams practice. The teams weren't out on the floor, so I made my way to Mic's office where he was getting ready for practice. Mic's office was long and narrow, with his desk at the front of the room and a hallway leading to the back where other coaches had storage lockers. On the left side of the room near the entrance were glass windows so Mic and the other coaches could supervise the students as they showered and dressed. Hanging from the top frame of the window were a number of paddles. There had to be at least eight of them, from a relatively small ping-pong paddle, to a large boat oar.

When I entered Mic's office, I noticed the instruments over the window.

"What is this?" I asked.

"You mean the paddles?"

"Yeah," I replied. "Is there some significance to the arrangement and the size of the paddles?"

"Yeah, I have these all arranged to carry a message," Mic said. "They basically say 'Don't mess around in my class or you will quickly get a taste of these gems.' You see, if a student messes around with me, they get to choose the weapon that is going to bust their behind. The really dumb students pick the table tennis paddle thinking it is the smallest paddle and thus the one that will hurt the least. But most students only pick that once, because it stings like the dickens. I can really get my wrist into it. No one has ever picked the boat oar, but I suspect that one would cause the least harm. Could you see me laying a boat oar on some kid's rear end? It would be pretty cumbersome. I really don't think I could do much harm with that tool, but it is visually intimidating. I keep it there for that reason and that works for me. Most of the students will take that board in the middle with holes in it. It doesn't hurt as much as the table tennis paddle!"

Mr. Wimer was well liked by the students. He joked with them and teased them a lot, but they knew when he was serious. I asked a few students if they had ever been hacked by Mr. Wimer. One or two said yes and indicated they did not want to be subjected to that pain a second time. Most said no, but a couple of them said they had seen him hack a student in his office and they wanted nothing to do with Mr. Wimer laying one of his boards on their rear end.

Another teacher with a renowned reputation for administering hacks was Mr. Fox, the wood shop teacher. It makes sense that he would need this kind of reputation, because all of his classes were composed of male junior high students in a shop class full of tools and dangerous saws. He was a legend among the students—word had it that he designed and engineered his own wooden hacking board and made special boards for the other staff members. Three of the boards in Mr. Wimer's office were designed and cut by Mr. Fox.

Because of the all-male makeup of the wood shop classes, and the need for strict adherence to safety standards for operating the equipment, Mr. Fox was not tolerant of any misbehavior in his classes. He was not one for giving more than one verbal warning before moving directly to the hack. Students got the message within the first three weeks of school, during which time he administered a number of hacks, but once the students got the idea, the number of hacks decreased dramatically. But boys will be boys, and sporadically throughout the semester there would be some horsing around when they thought Mr. Fox was distracted, which led to a hack or two. This usually quieted the class down for a couple of weeks.

The students told me Mr. Fox gave the worst hacks with Mr. Wimer coming in second. Several other male teachers gave hacks as well. Amazingly, during my tenure at Jenifer Junior High, I never heard of Mr. Crosby the science teacher giving a student a hack. What I remember about Mr. Crosby and his classes was that a lot of laughter came from his room. I know this because he had a unique laugh and it was usually louder than the students' laughter. He was just down the hall from me after I moved up to the second floor, and when my door was open, I could hear laughter frequently coming from his room. He was a tall, athletic teacher and coach who had a jovial attitude and a great sense of humor. He seemed to always be laughing, whether in the staff lounge or in the classroom. Well liked by staff and students, he had a way with the kids that didn't require him to hack anyone, yet students were attentive to his presentations and on task with their work. I admired that and made an effort to emulate his approach to teaching. By the end of my seven years at Jenifer, I was able to teach my last year and maintain a positive learning environment without hacking one student—I took great pride in that.

During my first semester at Jenifer Junior High, I gave out hacks to nine of my own students and three to students of the female math teacher across the hall. When she found out I was willing to administer hacks, she asked me to help her deal with a couple of rowdy eighth graders, which I was happy to do.

In my opinion, the hack is a viable disciplinary tool to be used with students who are in the seventh or eighth grades, but it should be used with the support of the parents, the administration, and the school board. I found that it was the wrong thing to administer it when a student made you really angry. If I was really angry, I tended to administer it with more enthusiasm than was needed, and in some cases it caused me to be emotionally upset for the rest of the day. I just didn't feel particularly comfortable about hitting another parent's child, even with their support. So, I only used it as the last step before sending the student to the principal's office. This seemed to work best for me.

CHAPTER 9

A Slug Walker Confrontation and an Evaluation Visit

> *I can remember that moment to this very day. When he came into the room, I initially had feelings of panic and paused for a moment, which caused the students in the front of the room to look around to see what was causing the pause. When they saw it was Mr. Walker, they all turned quickly back to the front and gave me their full attention. They exhibited the best behavior I had seen since I took over the classroom.*

Mr. Walker had a reputation for being a rough-and-tumble, straightforward principal and from what I saw of him during my first month of teaching, this reputation was accurate. He was not a man to cross, nor was he one who would tolerate a casual conversation about your day. He was all business and he made sure you knew it. He would not hesitate to reprimand a teacher privately or publicly when it was needed, nor would he hesitate to verbally reprimand or administer hacks to students who had misbehaved. He was also not one who tolerated disrespect—whether from students, staff, or parents.

One way to get to the Jenifer Junior High teachers' lounge was through the general office area, which was surrounded on two corners by glass walls that faced the entry hall and the hall that led to the library. You could walk down the student hallway or come into the building and see the secretary or anyone else standing in the office area. After entering the office area and going by the secretary's desk, you could then turn to the left and go down a narrow hallway to the teachers' lounge at the end. Most of the time when I went to the lounge, I would go through the main office and past the principal's office, which was located just behind the secretary's desk.

Slug's office had a desk that faced a wall on one side of his door and he had a couch that was up against the wall on the other side of his door. When looking into his office, he could be seen working at his desk or—if he was talking to a student or a parent—he would be turned from his desk to talk to his guest sitting almost right next to him.

Slug was an administrator with an open door policy. If he was dealing with a student or a staff member, his door was usually open. Many times as I was making my way to the lounge, I would see him in his office talking to a student, a teacher, or sometimes a parent. Rarely was he in his office with the door closed unless he was disciplining a student or a staff member.

On one particular day in the month of February, I had come to school early and decided to go to the teachers' lounge to get a cup of coffee and maybe visit with any teachers who might be there. When I came down the hall from my room to the office area, I noticed a young man enter the building and march purposely into the office area. His posture and movements seemed to indicate he was upset about something. I was trailing just behind him and stopped at the secretary's desk to see what the situation might be. I could see that Mr. Walker was at his desk and the secretary had not arrived, so only Mr. Walker, this young man, and myself were present.

The young man marched brazenly into Mr. Walker's office without an invitation, sat down on his couch, raised his voice, and angrily said, "I'm here to talk about the way you treated my brother the other day!"

When I heard this, I paused by the secretary's desk, stunned that someone would talk to Mr. Walker like that. I saw Mr. Walker turn calmly in his swivel chair to face the man. "What did you say?" he asked.

Foolishly, the man raised his voice again. "You know damn well what I said, you old fool!"

What occurred next was surprising, but not necessarily unexpected if you knew Slug. Mr. Walker was out of his chair quicker than I thought was possible for a man of his age and size. He grabbed the front of young man's coat with one hand and shoved him to his back on the couch. As he pushed him down, he put his knee on his chest and delivered two quick punches to his head. He then stepped off the man and raised him with one hand to a sitting position. He then put his face down close to the man's face.

"Don't you ever talk to me like that in my office," Slug growled. "I won't tolerate this from you or any other person. How dare you come into my office and talk to me like that. Do you understand me?"

The man, evidently stunned, wobbled a little as he nodded his head in the affirmative and mumbled, "Yes."

"Now, what did you want to talk to me about?" Mr. Walker asked.

Just then, he glanced out the door and saw me. A jerk of his head indicated I needed to vacate the area, which I did quickly, making my way down to the teachers' lounge. I got my cup of coffee and went back through the office area where I saw the secretary at her desk. Behind her in his office Mr. Walker was again working at his desk as if nothing had occurred—the young man was nowhere to be seen.

At the end of the day, I went to the office and saw that Mr. Walker's office door was closed, so I asked the secretary who the young man was in Mr. Walker's office that morning. "Oh, that was Billy," she said. "He is the older brother of a student Mr. Walker suspended earlier in the week."

"Was everything okay when you got to work?" I asked.

"Yeah," she replied. "They were just talking about the reason for the suspension and Billy left just after I got here. I was a little surprised, because Mr. Walker had a lot of trouble with Billy when he went to school here two or three years ago. I hear he dropped out of the high school last year."

During the rest of my tenure at Jenifer, I never saw Billy again at the junior high. I respected Mr. Walker a great deal more after that day and was determined to never raise my voice to him. I also told myself never to refer to him as an old fool.

Later that week, I was in the teachers' lounge when one of the other math teachers came up to speak to me.

"Has Slug come in to evaluate you yet?"

"No," I said. "He hasn't been in, but he told me on my first day on the job he would be in to observe one of my classes sometime during the first month or two."

"Well, let me give you some advice," the teacher replied. "When he comes in to observe, it will be unannounced and he will come in and sit at the back of the room and observe you teaching for about fifteen minutes. Be sure you have your ducks in a row instructionally and that you have control of the class. When he comes in, don't make a big deal about it—just keep teaching. You need to know that he used to teach math, so I can guarantee you that sometime during the lesson he is going to interrupt and ask to continue the lesson for you. He will get up and do exactly that. Don't be offended, just stand aside and let him teach. He loves teaching and your cooperation in letting him do this will be positively reflected in your evaluation report."

I thanked the teacher for the advice and for the next two days, I fretted about Mr. Walker coming in to observe my teaching. I liked my job and I wanted to make a good impression on him during his first visit, so I made sure I was prepared and worked harder at maintaining discipline in each class.

Sure enough, the week after talking to the math teacher, I was five minutes into teaching my eighth grade math students a lesson on adding fractions with unlike denominators when my classroom door opened and in came Mr. Walker. Just like I was told, he moved quietly into a seat at the back of the room and just watched me as I taught. I can remember that moment to this very day. When he came into the room, I initially had feelings of panic and paused for a moment, which caused the students in the front of the room to look around to see what was causing the pause. When they saw it was Mr. Walker, they all turned quickly back to the front and gave me their full attention. They exhibited the best behavior I had seen since I took over the classroom. After fleetly faltering, my adrenaline surged from the fear that swept over me and I pressed on. I reviewed some definitions and how to find a common denominator before demonstrating how to change the fractions so they had the same denominator. I then showed the students how to add them once they had the common denominator and was about to work three or four sample problems when Mr. Walker got out of his seat and came to the front of the room. "Mr. Hammann, would it be okay if I picked up from here? Would it be okay for me work some sample problems for the class?"

Thankful for the advice I had received the week before, I said, "Sure, Mr. Walker. I think the students would be pleased to have you do that for them."

I stood off to the side as Mr. Walker worked three problems for the class. The class was abnormally attentive—there was no talking when Mr. Walker was teaching. They were polite, helping him work the problems when he asked for their assistance. As he worked the problems, he would occasionally look over to me and ask questions. "You taught them how to determine the least common denominator, right?"

"You showed them how to add the numerators and put the answer over the common denominator, right?"

I responded in the affirmative each time.

After working the three sample problems, Mr. Walker asked me if I had an assignment for the students. I put the assignment on the board and told the students to begin working on it. Mr. Walker then moved to the back of the room to watch as I moved about the room providing assistance where needed. Just before the bell rang, he left the room. As the door closed, it was like the air was being let out of a balloon. Several students let out their breath. "Mr. Hammann, you did fine!" one said boldly. "We tried to help you out and make you look good! How'd we do?"

The whole class, including myself, laughed. "You were great!" I said. "I wish you would act like this all the time, but I certainly appreciated your extra effort today."

The comments and the general response of the class indicated to me that maybe I was winning some of them over.

That evening I went to my mailbox in the teachers' lounge and found a note from Mr. Walker. It said, "Please see me tomorrow morning at 7:45 a.m. I would like to talk to you about my visit this morning." Needless to say, I went home feeling a lot of anxiety—at this point in my relationship with Mr. Walker, I perceived him to be a difficult man to please. What would be his evaluation of my performance? Was I doing okay? Would his evaluation help me know if I would be back next year?

I slept restlessly that night and got up early the next morning. I hurried to school, getting there at 7:40 a.m. When I entered the office area, the secretary had not arrived, but Mr. Walker was working at his desk with the door open. I thought back to Mr. Walker's confrontation with Billy just a week ago and with some trepidation, I walked behind the secretary's desk to his door and politely knocked on the door jamb. Mr. Walker looked up. "Mr. Hammann, come on in," he said gruffly. "Have a seat." He waved to the couch against the wall. Again, memories of what I had seen happening to the last person who sat on that couch flashed through my mind as I sat down somewhat uncomfortably.

He shuffled through some papers on his desk and pulled out a pink sheet and handed it to me. "This is a summary of what I saw yesterday in your classroom. Why don't you look that over and then we will talk about it."

I looked at this one-page summary. At the top was information such as the date of the observation, my name, the subject I was teaching, and the class period of the observation. In the middle of the page were some items with filled-in blank spaces on the side—things like discipline, lesson preparation, verbal articulation, organization, etc. In each blank space was an "S," which stood for satisfactory—there were no unsatisfactory marks. At the bottom of the form was a place for comments, and Mr. Walker had written three or four sentences, which were all positive. There was one comment in particular that stood out to me: "Things are much improved in this class due to the changes Mr. Hammann has made since coming on staff. I recommend he keep up the good work."

I finished reading the evaluation and looked up. "Well," Mr. Walker said. "What do you have to say?"

"Well, it looks good to me," I responded. "Thank you for the encouraging comments. It helps me a lot."

"Don't let it go to your head," Slug replied. "I can see that you could be a little better prepared and the lesson presentation could have been a little smoother. You're just a first-year teacher and you have a ways to go. I still expect my next observation to be as good as or better than this one. Do you have any questions for me?"

I didn't have any questions about the evaluation, but I did have a question about the possibility of coaching. "Is there any chance of coaching basketball next year? I played in college and I would love to have the opportunity to coach that sport."

"At this time I don't see us having an opening in that area," he said. "However, we are going to need a track coach this spring. I would really like you to consider coaching that sport. Our head coach left last summer. Mr. Bafus is the assistant coach and is not interested in moving up. He would like to remain as the assistant coach. What do you say?"

I was stunned—I didn't know anything about coaching track. I never participated in track and field in high school, although I tried out as a long jumper in junior high. "Mr. Walker, I don't know anything about coaching track," I told him. "I have the knowledge to coach basketball or even baseball, but I don't know anything about track."

"Mr. Hammann, you really don't need to know anything about coaching track," he said. "Mr. Bafus has been coaching track as an assistant for the past five years, and he can be an invaluable help to you. We just need someone to be the head coach even if it is in name only. Based on what I've seen of you over the past month, I think you could do a good job. The kids like you and are already beginning to respect you, and being a coach would add even more to your ability to relate to kids. What do you say? Will you be willing to give it a try? You can pick up an extra stipend of about $450 for the effort."

If I wasn't such a rookie and in need of a little more money, I would have said no. But I was feeling good about the evaluation and wanted to do whatever it took to be a better teacher and make a difference in the lives of kids. I also wanted to please Mr. Walker and stay in his good graces. "Sure," I conceded. "I'll be glad to do that."

He then had me sign the evaluation form and gave me a copy before he stood up to indicate our meeting was concluded. He slapped me on the back good-naturedly.

"I think you will do a great job as our new junior high track coach," he said. "I'll get the contract to you. Keep up the good work in the classroom. Now you better get on to class before the bell rings. I don't want you tardy for your first period class."

With that, he ushered me out of his office.

I left feeling a little dazed. First, I was glad my interaction with Mr. Walker was vastly different from the confrontation with Billy I had seen the week before. I came away from that first evaluation meeting with even a deeper respect for Mr. Walker. I viewed him as a demanding leader, but now realized he would be encouraging when someone was doing the job to the best of his ability. Second, did I really say I would coach track? I didn't know anything about coaching track—I felt certain I could coach baseball or basketball, but I knew next to nothing about track. Mr. Walker said Jerry Bafus could help me with the knowledge part of the sport, so I would need to get together with him soon to help prepare for the first track practice, which was a little more than a month away. I went to class with a bounce in my step and a determination to be the best math teacher and track coach Jenifer Junior High had ever seen. I was going back to Mountain Home for the weekend and would have a lot of news for my wife—it was already stacking up to be a busier spring than I had originally anticipated.

CHAPTER 10
Track Coach

> *This was my first attempt at formally coaching a sport. I found that my approach to coaching track had to be different than how I might approach coaching basketball or baseball. In track the coach has to do a lot of encouraging and be a sympathetic counselor. I had to know when to challenge the athletes to extend themselves beyond what they thought they could do, and when to back off and just listen to them.*

During the months of my first semester of teaching, I made every effort to make the trip to Mountain Home to see my wife and two children every other weekend. My wife Marty was teaching science and home economics to the high school students of Mountain Home High School, and her life was busy and full between working and caring for our two children. We had some babysitter issues at first, but by the end of February we had found a great caregiver for our children and that helped significantly.

It was those weekends together that helped us make it through this semester of working in different school districts over 300 miles apart. On those weekends, I had a chance to spend quality time with my children and cultivate my relationship with my wife. We were both under a great amount of stress, and those weekends together helped us lower our stress levels, spend time as a family, and survive.

I would leave Lewiston right after school ended around 3:30 p.m. on Fridays and travel the 313 miles to Mountain Home. The drive was slow because it was on two-lane roads that wound through mountains and along the Salmon and Payette Rivers. The trip would take about five-and-a-half hours, and I would arrive in Mountain Home exhausted from the long drive and a full week of teaching. On Sunday, I would leave Mountain Home around noon and get back to Lewiston at 5:30, which would give me just enough time to get ready for the week's classes. The short two days we had together were precious—my wife was and is my lifeline for living and working.

When I got home, she would always patiently listen to my tales, frustrations, challenges, and dreams with regard to teaching those Jenifer Junior High students. She would always give me her perspective, which thankfully was different from mine. She always encouraged me and helped me see the whole picture. So going home every other weekend was critical to my success that first semester at Jenifer.

The Friday after Mr. Walker's evaluation, which was near the end of February, I made my way to Lewiston for my twice-monthly rendezvous with Marty. When I got there, the kids were in bed, but because of everything that had happened in the past two weeks, we stayed up late talking about our teaching experiences. I told her about everything that had happened in the past few weeks, including Mr. Walker's first observation of my teaching and the offer to coach track. She encouraged me to pursue the coaching position because we were going to need the extra money to make the move from Mountain Home to Lewiston. She shared with me her frustration with the used car we had purchased to get her to and from work—there had been several cold mornings when it wouldn't start and she had to call on "Oley" Olson to come and help. Amazingly, he was always willing to come and help her get it started. She told me about her classes, issues with the kids, and the babysitter situation. Soon, we were talking about our plans for the future.

We had already made the decision to move to Lewiston if it looked like I would have a continuing job there. My first evaluation seemed to indicate I would be there next year. Once in Lewiston, Marty wanted to spend the majority of her time staying home with the kids while I worked, so we decided she would be a stay-at-home mom and I would be the breadwinner for the next year. Unfortunately, it would be difficult to live on $6,500 per year, which was my current salary. This was one of the reasons I was so eager to take on the track coaching position.

We also decided I would have to pursue some summer work as well to help supplement our income. One of the options included applying for graduate school under the GI Bill. The University of Idaho in Moscow, Idaho, was just thirty-five miles away from Lewiston. The GI Bill paid for tuition and books while providing a monthly stipend—it was possible I could attend graduate classes in the summer during the morning and work as an umpire for baseball games in the evening. I had played baseball at the junior high level and had done some informal umpiring while stationed at the Mountain Home Air Force Base. Lewiston was known as a baseball town with numerous Babe Ruth teams and an outstanding American Legion team. I could look for any other temporary summer work to supplement my salary and also see if there were any coaching positions open for the next school year. After brainstorming options, we went to bed that night excited about how things were going and the prospects for the future.

I returned to Lewiston the next week and continued my routine of teaching during the day and preparing for lessons in the evenings. I occasionally attended junior high and high school basketball games. The junior high teams played on Tuesday and Thursday nights, and the high school team played on Fridays and Saturdays. Attending the games provided an escape and helped relieve some of the stress associated with teaching. I also played some pick-up basketball games with Mic Wimer and a few of his friends in the junior high gym after the boys' teams were done practicing. We would play full-court and half-court games for a couple of hours depending on how many players showed up. This not only gave me the exercise I needed to stay fit and reduce my stress level, it also was an opportunity to get to know Mic and some of his athletic friends.

During the first week of March, I sat down with the assistant track coach, Jerry Bafus, and quizzed him about running a track program, which was of great help. He said there were usually a large number of seventh and eighth graders out for track and field and a much smaller number of ninth graders. The low ninth grade turnout was because many of the athletes played baseball, which was really the primary sport in Lewiston. Baseball was played as part of the public school athletic program in the ninth grade, but not in the lower grades because of the outstanding Babe Ruth Baseball program in the community. Jerry said he would set up the initial practices and help organize the two track meets we would host during the season. After I became more knowledgeable, I would take a more active role in these areas. He also said he would take care of getting volunteers to run the various events at the meets since he was familiar with what was needed to put on the various events like the discus throw, the long jump, the pole vault, and the shot put. He would recruit timers, a starter, an announcer, and people to post scores. He said most of the volunteers were usually staff members quite capable of running an event, since most had done it for years. My discussion with him greatly reduced my stress level until he informed me we usually hosted the league championship meet at the end of the season. Not only was I going to coach a sport I barely understood, but we were also going to host the league track meet. Jerry assured me it would not be a big deal, he would help out, and he reminded me he had done this for more than five years. It was obvious he had talked to Mr. Walker and had been told I would need a lot of emotional support and encouragement to be the head coach. After talking through a number of issues, we decided our first priority would be to have a meeting with all the students interested in turning out for track.

We placed our announcement in the daily bulletin, which was read by each teacher at the beginning of the first period of the school day. The announcement indicated there would be a meeting for all seventh, eighth, and ninth grade boys interested in participating in track and field in Mr. Bafus's classroom immediately after school on Tuesday, the second week of March. The day rolled around and we had about twenty-five seventh graders, twelve eighth graders, and fifteen ninth graders show up. We did not have enough seats for all of them, so some stood in the back of the classroom. The students were joking and clowning around, and there was an air of excitement in the room. Some went over to Mr. Bafus and greeted him—it was obvious he was very popular with the eighth and ninth graders. I had a few seventh graders come over and say hello, with many expressing surprise to see me coaching track.

Since this was my first time to stand before a team as their head coach, I wanted to get off on the right foot. I was a little nervous, but I jumped in with both feet and called for their attention by welcoming them to the team meeting. I introduced myself since none of the ninth graders knew me, although I'm sure a few recognized me. I started off by saying we were going to have a great season and we had a real shot at winning the league title, although I was clueless about our chances. Jerry had indicated the ninth grade team had some good athletes, the eighth graders had some great athletes, but he was unsure about the prospects of the seventh graders. We passed out parent permission slips and an information sheet asking them to print their names and state which track and field events were of interest to them. They were only allowed to participate in four events, with some stricter limitations regarding those running in the distance events. I found out in a hurry that most of the athletes were not interested in the long-distance events.

Jerry Bafus then informed the team that our first practice would be the following Monday right after school. We would be doing some conditioning activities at the football field, and after about three days of that, would eventually get over to the track, which we shared with the high school team. They were told to show up for practice with the proper clothing and shoes. The meeting lasted about ten minutes and ended with us asking them to encourage their classmates to come out for the team—Jerry told them that we could always use more participants.

Between that meeting and the first practice, I spent a lot of time reviewing a few books on track and field, which I had checked out from the public library. I tried to familiarize myself with the specific techniques for running the sprints and distance events and long jumping and high jumping. Jerry said he would work with the athletes on the hurdles, the shot put, the discus, the middle-distance running, and the relay teams.

I quickly found out that coaching track is vastly different from coaching basketball and baseball at the junior high level. During the first three conditioning practices, only about half the eighth and ninth graders showed up, although most of the seventh graders were there. Jerry and I caught many of those absent students in the hallway during the school days to ask where they'd been. All of them had one excuse or another—some said they forgot their clothes and shoes, while others said they had something they had to do at home. Those students who were at the practices regularly said the real reason was they didn't want to participate in the conditioning practices at the beginning of the season. Once we moved to the track and began to have track meets, the attendance was much better.

When we practiced at the high school track, we had to wait until the high school team had finished, which often didn't happen until 4:30 p.m. The first three practices went fairly well—we started every practice by taking attendance while they did some stretching exercises to warm up. We did a number of evaluative events during those first five days of conditioning and practice to see who could sprint, who could run distance, and who was good at the field events.

The remaining practices leading up to our first meet were focused on improving conditioning and working on a variety of techniques associated with the various running and field events. Students were always coming up to me and asking for advice on their technique in their track event. I could help them with sprints and distance running because that's what I had read up on, and I was very knowledgeable with regard to the long jump and high jump, but I was pretty vague in my assistance when it came to the shot put and discus. We were a month into the season before I had time to read up on the techniques for throwing the discus and discovered our discus throwers were throwing the discus off their little fingers instead of their forefingers. After helping them with this change of technique, they began throwing ten to twenty feet farther. I was learning on the fly and without Jerry's knowledge and experience, I would have been very discouraged.

Because of our low turnout, we had to require that our athletes participate in the maximum number of events. When we announced the lineups for the first track meet, there was a lot of moaning and groaning. I heard comments like, "I don't want to run the mile."

Or, "I don't want to run the hurdles. I'm really better at the 100 and 220 yard dashes."

Jerry and I would try to explain that this was the best for the team. Some understood, but others were only interested in their own comfort and agenda. There were some meets when it was difficult to field enough athletes in the various events to give us a chance to place well. What was most frustrating was that some athletes were always coming up near the end of the meet, when they were going to participate in their fourth event, and telling us they were going to scratch that event. They used excuses that they were tired or had a minor injury. Sometimes, we could convince them to gut it out for the benefit of the team, but many times we had to just scratch participating in that event if we were unable to find a replacement. Track and field can tell you a lot about the character of the students who participate in the sport.

The seventh and ninth grade teams did okay during the season, but the eighth graders were outstanding. We had eight boys who were excellent athletes, and when we distributed them appropriately to the right events, they would regularly beat the other teams. They were also strong enough to handle participating in four events and to do each one well. Some of them were somewhat arrogant about their abilities as evidenced by their irregular attendance at practices, but when the meets came, they were there and they did an outstanding job.

The season came to an end with the league track meet, which Jenifer Junior High hosted. As Jerry had said, the staff members had the meet covered. We had timers, a starter, an announcer, and one staff member with a student for each field event. The meet was carried off without a hitch. I found it was difficult to oversee the meet and coach three teams as well, but with Jerry's help we were able to do it all. The seventh and ninth graders finished in the middle of the pack, but the eighth graders won the meet with only eight participants. The team finished first in many of the events, giving them the maximum number of points. Our one weakness was in the distance events, but we had one outstanding runner and he finished well in the 800 and won the mile. Many of the league coaches were astounded we could win the meet with only eight participants. I tried to stay humble about it, but it was difficult to restrain my pride in the team and our accomplishments.

This was my first attempt at formally coaching a sport. I found that my approach to coaching track had to be different than how I might approach coaching basketball or baseball. In track the coach has to provide a lot of encouraging and be a sympathetic counselor. I had to know when to challenge the athletes to extend themselves beyond what they thought they could do, and when to back off and just listen to them. I couldn't be too demanding or they would just shut down or quit, which I discovered early on when one or two quit because they thought I was too demanding. In basketball, you can sit an athlete out when they miss practice or lack effort in practice or a game, and they will usually respond by improving their attendance or making a better effort. In track, that person is needed to participate in order for the team to have a shot at winning, so you have to take a different approach.

I learned a lot from Jerry Bafus about organizing meets and coaching individual skills, and I looked forward to the next season, although I would rather be coaching basketball or baseball. I was certainly happy for the opportunity to coach, as I could see definite benefits in the classroom. The students I had in class who were out for track were well behaved and respectful in class during the track season. Once again, I was finding that interacting with students outside the classroom made for more positive relationships inside the classroom.

CHAPTER 11

The School Year Ends

> *Right then, a water balloon soared through the air and made contact with the middle of my back, totally soaking the back of my shirt and pants. There was a loud 'Ohhhhhh!' from the students standing behind me.*

March, April, and May were busy with me working hard in the classroom and coaching track after school. I continued to prepare lessons, grade papers, and grade tests after school, and during the school day I gave class presentations, assisted students as they worked on assignments, gave tests, and maintained order and discipline in the classroom, which included hacking a few unruly boys. I figure I handed out a total of nine hacks to students during the course of that semester, and by the end of the year, I found that hacking was not a pleasant thing for me. But felt it was a necessary tool for maintaining order and helping students to have a healthy respect for my position as their teacher. Because of my distaste for that form of maintaining discipline, I made a commitment to keep that level of punishment to a minimum and rely more on after-school detentions and contacting parents.

One of the interesting experiences I had was related to spring break, which happened during the first week of April. As we approached the Friday before spring break, there was real pressure from students to have "free days." Now a "free day" is when a teacher allows the students to work on whatever subject appeals to them or to just sit around and visit or play games. Somehow, during the week before spring break, they caught me in a weak moment. The students whined and begged for me to give them that "free day" the Friday before break. Wanting to please them to some degree, I caved in. I promised to give them that Friday if they worked hard for me on the days leading up to it.

Some of the students did a great job of working hard the week before spring break, but there was a substantial minority whose effort was minimal. It was only when I kept reminding them the free day would only happen if they worked hard in class that they picked up their effort.

Finally the free day came, and they filtered into class wanting to get right down to doing their own thing. But we had to grade Thursday's assignment and look at some of the problems they struggled with. When I told them this, the class moaned and groaned, but made a reasonable effort to focus on grading the papers and giving me their attention as I worked a few problems on the board.

It took about ten minutes and after we finished, I laid out the ground rules.

"Okay, this is your free day, but there are a couple of rules," I said to the class. "You need to keep the noise down and stay in a seat. You can group up to play a game or to visit, but don't be wandering about the class. Do you all understand?"

They nodded their heads and then moved to begin their activities. What a disaster. Some students had brought card games, and they grouped up to play Hearts, while others just began visiting. It wasn't long before the noise level was beyond tolerable. Several times I had to yell at the students to keep the noise down. It would quiet for about two or three minutes and then steadily increase until, again, I had to raise my voice and tell them to quiet down. I also had to tell students to sit down on several occasions—there was some horsing around by some of the boys, which I sternly addressed. By the end of each class I was exhausted from trying to maintain a semblance of order. At the end of the period before lunch, I promised myself I would never have another free day—a promise I have kept. In fact, I've found the best way to handle the day before a vacation is to schedule a test. Discipline problems disappear when the students are taking a test. So from that point forward, on the day before three-day weekends or Christmas and spring breaks, I always had a test scheduled. It was much more rewarding on those days to see the students frustrated and exhausted at the end of the class period rather than me.

Another thing I observed was that students perceived spring break as the dividing line between focused work and getting ready for summer break. After spring break, at least for many students, their effort plummeted while their penchant to goof off and have a good time increased. Discipline was always more difficult to maintain after spring break than before. And the closer you got to the last day of school, the worse it became. When that last day came, and all the students were gone, I was totally physically and mentally exhausted, as were most of the other junior high teachers.

Near the end of the year, Mr. Walker came to my room to tell me I would be retained to teach another year and asked if I would be willing to move to a new classroom and teach ninth grade algebra and general math next year. The new room would be next to the other algebra teacher, Mr. Chavez. He told me I was the only teacher on staff with a math degree and that made me a strong candidate for this position, so he strongly recommended I take the offer. Of course, when Mr. Walker makes a strong recommendation, I had already learned you better take him up on it, which I did. He said I would be receiving a new contract and my salary would be increased to $6,800 plus the $480 stipend for coaching track. This meant I would be receiving a whopping $300 raise—but even with this extra money, Marty and I would be hard pressed to make ends meet during the coming school year. I was still going to have to find some supplementary work in the summer.

When the last day came, I was in for an eye-opening experience. The Tuesday before the last week of school, Mr. Walker had a teachers' meeting to communicate staff responsibilities for closing school. We had to have our grades in by the end of the day after the students were released, and our rooms had to be organized so the custodial staff could begin the summer cleaning and repair projects. A list of all recommended repairs for the room and an inventory of equipment had to be submitted to the school secretary on a sheet of paper with the grades. We also had to inventory everything in our classroom and present our list to Mr. Walker's office before we could check out. He announced that the Lewiston District provided teachers with their last three paychecks of the contract year on the last day of June. This meant you had to make all three checks last until the end of September when you got the first check of the new contract year. This would prove to be a significant challenge for teachers like myself who were being paid below the poverty level. Mr. Walker also said students were to turn in their textbooks to their respective teachers, who would then sign each student's checkout sheet indicating, when appropriate, whether there were fines for defacing or losing the books. About fifteen minutes before the students were to be released on the last day, he instructed all teachers to be out in the hall inspecting lockers and signing off checkout sheets. He gave us a list of the students and their locker numbers and told us to be sure each locker was cleaned out and there was no serious vandalism. Mr. Walker then passed out a sheet of paper indicating assigned areas for each teacher for the purpose of supervising students as they left the building and grounds. Some were assigned spots in the building, while others had spots assigned outside the building. I noticed several longtime teachers roll their eyes when he made that announcement. I wondered at their response.

The last day came, which was a half-day of school, and the students came into the classes with an extraordinary amount of energy and enthusiasm. Each class period was shortened to about twenty minutes to allow teachers to collect books and sign checkout sheets. My day was busy and chaotic trying to keep some semblance of order while signing sheets, issuing fines for lost or damaged books, and collecting late assignments. The bell to end the day finally rang at 1:30 p.m., just as I completed checking the lockers and was signing off on the last few students. I quickly tried to move to my assigned supervision area, which was outside near the entrance to the building. As I walked down the hallway, several students stopped to say goodbye and wish me a good summer vacation. However, most of the students were totally focused on getting outside. After talking to a few students and making my way through the crowd, I moved out to the front of the building where students would be loading in the busses. When I stepped outside and onto the sidewalk, what met my eyes was beyond belief.

Almost all the students were armed with squirt guns, squirt bottles, or water balloons and it looked like a war zone. As a naïve first-year teacher, my initial response was to diligently carry out my assigned responsibility to supervise students as they loaded the busses, but it quickly became evident this would be extremely hard to do. Mr. Walker had said about half the staff were to be in their assigned area outside the building to maintain order and I was there. But as I looked around to find some other teachers to help restore some kind of order, none could be found. In fact, not even Mr. Walker was there. I and two other teachers were the only ones out there to supervise and try and bring order to approximately

800 wildly excited and armed students. I moved out away from the building and shouted at the students as they battled it out.

"Hey! Stop that!"

Right then, a water balloon soared through the air and made contact with the middle of my back, totally soaking the back of my shirt and pants. There was a loud "Ohhhhhh!" from the students standing behind me. I swung around to find the culprit, but there was just a mass of running and laughing students. Seventh, eighth, and ninth graders were running around trying to get each other as wet as possible, and no one seemed to be focused on me. As I scanned the area, another water balloon from a different direction splattered near me getting the lower half of my pants wet. Realizing I was not going to bring order to this mess, I quickly retreated back into the building dodging one or two balloons that I saw arcing toward me. Once inside, I stood at the door and watched the pandemonium until the last bus pulled away from the curb. I made my way to the teachers' lounge where I found four or five other teachers silently drinking coffee or smoking a cigarette. As I sat on a couch feeling emotionally numb, I looked at the faces of my fellow teachers and saw haggard, worn-out expressions. I suspect I looked much like they did. "Did you go outside?" one of the teachers asked.

"Yeah, I went out there like Mr. Walker told us to, but there were hardly any other teachers there," I replied. "It was like a war zone. As you can see, I had a number of students throw water balloons at me—one of them hit me dead center in the back and that is why my shirt is soaked. What is this water fight chaos all about?"

Another teacher spoke up and said, "A water fight on the last day of school has been a tradition here for some time. Most of us know what is going to happen, and we just don't go out there. Mr. Walker has not ever mentioned the lack of supervision, because I think he is relieved the year is over just like the staff and students.

He's as tired and worn out as we are, and so he just lets it go as long as no one gets hurt."

"Well, I guess I'll know what to do next year," I said. Suddenly, it made sense why some of the teachers rolled their eyes when Mr. Walker said to supervise students outside the building on the last day. They knew what was going to happen and they knew this would be one directive they would not be following. I guess that is part of gaining experience as a teacher at Jenifer Junior High.

After visiting a few more minutes with the other staff, I went back to my classroom and sat at my desk to evaluate the semester. This exercise was one I would do every year and proved to be a valuable process for me. I graded a few of the late papers and compiled my grades for the semester. I reviewed them all, looking to see what improvements I could make to enhance learning and improve student effort.

I noticed that most of the students earned Bs, Cs, and Ds. I had a small percentage of As and a slightly larger number of Fs. Most of the Fs were earned by students who did not do their homework and did poorly on tests. I noted that many of those same students also had attendance problems.

Based on this, I elected to keep my grading system the same for the coming year, but to do some things to improve learning. I decided to have each student keep a notebook of the lesson presentations and turn that in for a grade at the end of each quarter. The notebook would be worth a total of 100 points depending on the completeness and quality of the book. I figured most students could get 80 points or more just by copying down what I put on the board during presentations, which would raise the overall grades of each class. And I thought writing notes on the lecture and copying problems as I worked them during the presentation would improve their learning and retention as well.

I evaluated my disciplinary system and decided to put my rules on a poster next year along with the possible consequences for breaking them. I had only stated my rules verbally this first year.

I took out a pad of paper and wrote down the changes I was going to make and put it with the materials I was going to move into my new room. After completing my checkout sheet, my grades, and the inventory, I took these to the office secretary to get Mr. Walker's signature. I then took everything to the new classroom and put them in the teacher's desk or in the storage closet. The teacher I would be replacing had already removed her materials, and I wanted to put my things in place so I would be ready to implement my plans for the new school year. I picked up the algebra and ninth grade general math textbooks to look over during the summer and made my way out of the classroom.

It was about 4 p.m. on the Thursday following Memorial Day weekend when I walked out of Jenifer Junior High to enjoy my first summer break. I was tired and worn out, but I felt good about what I had accomplished during my first semester of teaching. I was now ready to move my family to Lewiston and settle into the community.

CHAPTER 12

Summer Break and Graduate School

> *"We were all seated around a table and there was thankfully another student sitting between her and me. She was so angry, I think she would have taken a swing at me had I been close enough. She ranted at me for some time and initially, I was able to appear calm."*

About mid-April, when I was assured I would be extended another contract for the coming year, I had investigated the possibility of pursuing a master's degree at the University of Idaho. Initially, I wanted to get a degree in mathematics, but quickly found that no graduate program existed that included only summer and evening classes. Students in that program had to be able to take day classes during the regular year, which was impossible for me. I looked into the possibility of a degree in a scientific discipline, but again ran into the same problem. I was assigned a college counselor who assisted me in this process. When I shared with him my frustration about the lack of graduate programs during the summer, he suggested I look into a master's degree in school administration. He said it would be compatible with my teaching degree and would allow me to qualify as a building administrator in the public school system. He indicated that all of those classes could be taken at night during the school year or during the summer term. He suggested I initially enroll in the secondary school administrator program and take a couple of classes that summer to get a feel for the program. If I didn't like it, I could change my major. This seemed like a good idea, so he helped me enroll in that particular program, a process that took more than a month. I had to submit an application along with transcripts and recommendations from a few of the professors I had at Boise State University and Bethany Nazarene College. I also had to take a test indicating I had attained appropriate skills in reading, writing, and mathematics from my undergraduate work.

I also went to a representative at the veterans' liaison office on campus, who helped me fill out the paperwork needed to qualify for the funding. The GI Bill paid my tuition and book fees and provided a small monthly stipend to cover living expenses. I had used the GI Bill for my classes at Boise State University the fall of 1971, which made this application easier. By the middle of May, I was enrolled in the master's program and scheduled to take two morning classes—Secondary School Curriculum and Supervision of Instruction—that met four days per week for six weeks. Around that same time, Marty came to Lewiston to help look for housing. We were able to find a rental house in the Lewiston Orchards that charged us about $145 per month. It was a little more than we could afford, but it met our needs. We were set to move the weekend after I finished the school year, and since Marty's school district was finishing at the same time, we were able to move as scheduled.

So, school ended and we rented a U-Haul trailer, loaded up our things in Mountain Home with the help of some of our church friends, and made our way to our new home in Lewiston. Since we didn't own a whole lot of furniture, we were able to unload the trailer and return it to a Lewiston U-Haul dealer by Sunday afternoon. Since I would be starting summer school Monday, Marty was left with the responsibility of unpacking boxes. I always hated moving, especially the packing and unpacking of boxes. Two weeks before moving and two weeks after moving there would be boxes everywhere—the house would look cluttered for weeks and it drove me crazy. It was a good thing Marty could deal with it, so I always left most of the packing and unpacking in her very capable hands.

The first Monday of June came and I was off to my first day of graduate classes at the University of Idaho. I had a little trouble finding the Secondary School Curriculum class, but when I finally got there, I found myself in a class of about twelve students. Most of the students were men, with only three women in the class. Almost all of us were classroom teachers from school districts in northern Idaho. The professor seemed to be friendly and likable. On the first day the professors handed out their syllabi and I found that the requirements of both classes involved reading a number of books and presenting reports. There would also be discussions on the issues of the day associated with supervising instruction and selection of curricula for the secondary level of education. There would be little instruction in the form of lecturing, but there would be a lot of group discussions and debates. A few written themes summarizing some of our discussions were required. This troubled me because I was not a great writer—my major was math and we had to do little writing for that discipline. Many of my undergraduate general education courses had some writing projects, which also caused me to struggle. But usually I could get them done well enough to pass the class.

Overall, the classes were very enjoyable. During the '60s and '70s, great changes were occurring in the American culture and in public education in particular. We discussed the "new math," special education, developing instructional objectives, separation of church and state, and employment equality between the sexes. Many of these issues were directly discussed, but others were addressed indirectly.

One indirect discussion activity in particular stood out to me early in the class and had an impact on me for the rest of my educational career. It came when the professor provided a scenario regarding the hiring of a secondary teacher and making a selection based on the qualifications of the candidates. The scenario involved two equally qualified individuals who were under consideration for employment as English teachers. Both substantially met the requirements equally with regards to education and experience. One was a single female and the other was a male who was married with three children. After providing this information, he opened the discussion with this seemingly innocent question: “Which one would you hire and why?”

I was raised in a military family where my dad was the breadwinner and mom stayed at home to manage the house and care for the kids. I also attended a conservative Christian college where the traditional family, consisting of a husband breadwinner and a stay-at-home wife, was promoted as the ideal. In the military, I saw only one woman in a leadership position. I had just spent the past school year trying to correct a mess made by an inept female teacher. Understanding this was my experience with women in the work force, you can imagine what happened when I naively blurted out, “I would hire the man with the family. He has four mouths to feed.” Up to this point, all of our class discussions had been cordial and respectful even when we disagreed, so I was surprised when what I thought was a quiet female student turned beet red and stood up out of her chair.

“WHAT? Are you kidding me?” she sputtered with loud vehemence. “That is the most asinine statement I have ever heard come out of a male mouth. You call yourself a teacher? You are talking like a male chauvinist pig! I’ve got a thing or two to say to you…”

And for the next minute or two she railed on me about my mental stability, my upbringing, my narrow mindedness, and my lack of intellect with a vocabulary that might have been learned from the drill instructor I had in the Air Force.

My first thought was that I was now under verbal attack from a hardcore, militant feminist. I'd read about such women in newspapers and magazines and seen a few protesting on the television, but I had never met one in person. The articles I'd read and what I saw on TV seemed to say they were all about burning their bras and protesting loudly in public venues about how unfair life was for them. I immediately checked to see if there were any visible bra straps, but it was difficult to tell because she was moving around her chair and waving her arms wildly. I decided that not wearing a bra was not a prerequisite to being a hardcore feminist, but what I was hearing from her snarling mouth made it clear she fit the mold. I was amazed and then angered at her rage.

We were all seated around a table and there was thankfully another student sitting between her and me. She was so angry, I think she would have taken a swing at me had I been close enough. She ranted at me for some time and initially, I was able to appear calm. I had just come out of the military a year earlier and was accustomed to such behavior from my superiors and had learned how to take a verbal beating and stay cool, but I had never been addressed like that by a woman, especially one I barely knew.

While she ranted, I saw that some of the other students around the table were hanging their heads, while others sat smiling, enjoying the show. "What in the world is your problem?" I thought to myself. "I'm just giving my opinion here. What tripped your button? I'd be glad to hear your opinion without all the demeaning and unladylike rhetoric."

I was also surprised the professor did not intervene immediately, but allowed her to continue for some time. A quick glance at him indicated he was smiling as well, but he was smiling at me. Finally, he intervened and asked her to stop and to sit down. She reluctantly sat down, but glared at me with a look that could kill. I was not to be intimidated, so I stared back at her in as calm a manner as I could muster. "I think we have a misunderstanding here," the professor said. "I certainly understand where Mr. Hammann might be coming from with his response to my question, but it is possible that he has not kept up with current developments in our laws and culture."

He then began a lengthy lecture about the Civil Rights Act of 1964, which stipulated there could be no discrimination in employment based on race, religion, national origin, color, or sex. He indicated the prohibition of discrimination based on sex was added later in the 1960s. He then talked about another bill making its way through Congress called Title IX, which would expand the rights of women into other areas such as sports. I was to fully realize the impact of that bill on sports during the 1974-75 school year.

At the end of the lecture, he paused and looked at me clearly communicating he was giving me an opportunity to correct my reasoning for hiring the man with a family over the single woman applicant. I had listened closely, and based on the legal information he provided, it was clear my response was inappropriate and did not fit the current changes that were occurring in our culture. But inside, I was disturbed and still somewhat angry myself. It was obvious I did not know the new laws, but that did not mean I should be subjected to the angry and degrading rant of the young lady who felt she had been offended. So I cleared my throat and looked the young lady straight in the eye

"You know, the professor is correct," I said. "I did not know anything about the Civil Rights Act with regards to women. I knew about the non-discriminatory portion of the law with respect to race, culture, national origin, and color, but I did not know that women had been added. Based on that new information, I might change my choice and my reasoning. That might take some time considering my family and background, but I'm willing to re-evaluate that. If my original choice and reasoning offended you, I'm sorry. But I have a real problem with the emotion and the language you directed at me because of my lack of knowledge of the law. No one should have to be subjected to what I have just experienced no matter what is under consideration. I thought we were educators who could discuss all perspectives and positions like civilized human beings, and through that discussion, our perspectives and positions may be changed. Am I wrong in thinking that?"

I had just apologized for offending her while trying to maintain my own dignity and I thought it was fair to allow her an opportunity to apologize for her emotional overreaction, which was embarrassing to me and to many of the other students in class. But she refused to accept the invitation. She just continued to glare at me until the professor intervened. "I'm sure the young lady realizes she could have communicated her position differently, and I know she will strive to do that in the future. Let's continue our discussion of this scenario. Who else wants to provide a choice and the reasoning for that choice?"

One of the other women in class said she would hire the female teacher if there were an unbalanced ratio of female to male teachers in the school. One or two of the male students supported that position as well. I noticed the professor smile broadly and then go on to verbally reinforce that response.

For the rest of the term, the angry student and I kept our distance. When we had some team debates over our reading, the professor was careful to put us on separate teams, and that set well with me. The conflict I experienced with this young lady taught me that education was changing. Public school was quickly becoming quite different from the public school I had attended as a child and teenager in the '50s and early '60s. The change was occurring fast and I needed to keep up with the changes if I was to be successful at working in the public school system. I learned to listen more and not speak until I knew the lay of the land. I also learned that facts, knowledge, and a clear ability to articulate those in an argument carries more weight than an emotional outburst based on a perceived offense. Emotional outbursts tend to alienate those in opposition as well as some who might be supportive. I believed that understanding those concepts would help me if I chose to pursue an administrative career.

Except for this one incident, I truly enjoyed the class. I learned a lot and made some great friends. I finished the class with a B grade, and after talking to my advisor I made up my mind to pursue a master's degree in secondary school administration. This meant I would have to take thirty semester credit hours in a variety of classes during the summer and at night during the next few years in order to reach this goal.

CHAPTER 13

Summertime and Baseball

"The legend, Dwight Church, had come all the way up in the bleachers to ask me, a rookie math teacher, a question that might help his team in obtaining a regional championship. I didn't have a mathematical answer right at the forefront of my mind, but I didn't want to let him down. He stood there and looked at me expectantly. He was hoping I could give him an answer that might give him and his team an edge."

My summer days were busy commuting to Moscow, taking my graduate classes, and doing the homework. I earned a small stipend through the GI Bill, but I needed to make more money during the summer in order to pay my bills and care for my family, since the salary I was making as a teacher fell far short of meeting those needs. Fortunately, near the middle of April, Mr. Wimer, the Jenifer Junior High PE teacher, gave me the number of the Lewiston Babe Ruth League manager, who was hiring umpires for the summer. Mr. Wimer had already talked to him, so I called and we had a short visit, after which he quickly hired me to umpire games for the older Babe Ruth teams. I thought it was a little unusual to be hired so quickly, but I would find out why as the summer progressed.

Lewiston was and still is a baseball town as was Clarkston, Washington, just across the Snake River from Lewiston. I learned Lewiston had a small, first-class college baseball team at Lewis-Clark State College. They also had an outstanding AAA high school baseball team that had won an inordinate number of state championships over the past ten years. They also had a first-class American Legion team composed of Lewiston and Clarkston high school athletes. One of the reasons the high school and legion teams were so good was because of the Babe Ruth Baseball program in the city. The parents and community were accustomed to champion baseball programs, and winning was very important to them—something I learned very quickly.

I was scheduled to umpire my first set of baseball games on the first Monday after school let out. I showed up at the community baseball complex about an hour before the first game dressed in black slacks and a black T-shirt to meet with the Babe Ruth League manager. The complex was composed of two fenced fields with the backstops back to back. On the first baseball field, the bleachers were along the first base line, while the other field had bleachers along the third base line.

When I arrived at the fields, I noticed a middle-aged man with a notebook sitting next to a box in one of the bleachers. Since I didn't see anyone else around, I asked him if he was the Babe Ruth League manager and he said he was. We shook hands and introduced ourselves, and then he quickly explained my duties as the head umpire. He handed me a copy of the summer schedule and said I would be umpiring two games per night at this same baseball field—as the only umpire! I would call balls and strikes from behind the plate and also make calls on the bases. Normally, there would be a minimum of two umpires, but he said they could not afford to hire a neutral base umpire, and there had been serious problems in the past when they asked parents to volunteer to umpire the bases. Some of those parents had trouble remaining neutral in their calls, so he had gone with one umpire for each game.

I would be paid $10 per game and there would be two games per night Monday through Thursday. Games cancelled because of rain would be made up on Friday or Saturday. That meant I would make $80 per week for ten weeks. This, along with the stipend I was making while going to graduate school, would just about help my family make ends meet.

The manager said the league would provide the umpiring equipment needed for behind the plate. From the box next to him, he took out a set of shin guards, a vest, a counter, and a mask and handed them over. He indicated I could keep these with me and return them at the end of the season. He then quickly reviewed the mechanics for calling balls and strikes and making calls on the bases. As the only umpire, I really had to move quickly from behind the plate to the middle of the infield when the ball was hit in order to be in a position to make any reasonable call at the bases. I could see that if I were to do a somewhat credible job, I would need to be focused and on the move. The manager then gave me a rulebook and wished me luck. While I was visiting with the manager, the teams and some parents had appeared. By the time we were through talking, the teams were already warming up on the field and the parents were beginning to fill the small set of bleachers. I put on the equipment and waited to begin the first game. Just before the start time, the coaches came over to me at home plate to introduce themselves and give me the lineups. They returned to their respective dugouts and I called out to signal the beginning of the game. "Play ball!" I yelled, and the fun began.

I can safely say that the Lewiston Babe Ruth parent fans, coaches, and players are baseball fanatics, and they know the game. That first game really went pretty well. It took an inning or two to settle in, but soon I was able to do a credible job of calling balls and strikes while also calling the bases, at least in my own eyes. It became evident early on that the players, coaches, and fans had a different opinion. I was booed on some calls at the bases and on a few ball and strike calls from behind the plate. Most of the derision was made in good fun and was not too demeaning—I was a new face and they were trying to test me and see if they could influence my calls. I understood that and did my best to be consistent.

Both pitchers were fairly good and could throw strikes most of the time. I found that games go well and are relatively enjoyable when you have good pitching. The second game, however, was a different story. Both pitchers had trouble throwing strikes, and I found out that poor pitching makes the game an umpire's nightmare. Ball after ball comes in outside the strike zone, and a lot of walks are issued. Players, fans, and coaches become frustrated. Players stand out in the field for lengthy periods of time watching runners cross the plate as these walks are issued. Or if there is a hit, the play is usually poor because the fielders are caught off guard. If a pitch gets close to the strike zone, but is not a strike, and you call a ball, all of the onlookers begin booing and criticizing the umpire as if it were his fault and not the pitcher's. Those types of games lasted more than two hours, and there was always great relief to all in attendance when the last out was called. I learned to expand the strike zone some to try and help keep the game moving along if I noticed the pitching was particularly poor.

The first night of umpiring went well for me, as did the second night. In fact, the whole week went well. It appeared this was going to be a breeze until the second week rolled around. It was Thursday night and I had umpired all the teams in the league at least once and was becoming familiar with the faces of the coaches and some of the parents. By that point, I knew pretty well who was fair-minded and supportive, and I definitely knew who was not.

Two middle-aged coaches coached one of the teams in the first game that night. When I had umpired them the first time, they were on me after every close call. "Come on, blue, that was an awful call!" they'd say.

Or, "Get your lazy butt out from behind the plate so you can make the call!"

Or, "You're blind! There is no way that was a strike!"

This particular game was close and both pitchers were fair, but at least two walks were being issued each inning on both teams from the first inning on. Those two coaches were on me from the beginning, verbally abusing me for any call at the plate that did not go their way. After the third inning, one of them came out from the dugout and moved behind the backstop to see if I was making the right calls. And some of the parents were following their lead, berating my efforts with one or two dads also moving behind the backstop. I didn't like the fact there was a small crowd gathering behind the backstop, but I let it go for the moment. At one point when the opposing team was at bat, I called out a strike for a close pitch. The coach who was behind me began yelling.

"No way! Are you blind? Get your head out of your ..."

The last word was barely out of his mouth before I reacted. "Time!" I called out harshly and whirled around to face the group behind me. "I've had enough from you guys," I said in a subdued tone, aiming to make my message clear without embarrassing anyone. "I'm directing you to go back to your appropriate seats. I will not tolerate any more of your trash talk. The next time I hear any more talk like that, if you are the coach, I'm kicking you out of the game. And if you are a parent you will be asked to leave. Do you understand me?"

The look on their faces was priceless. They were stunned—I hadn't really responded to their goading up to this point, but now I was hot and they must have seen it in my face. The parents grumbled as they trudged back to their bleacher seats somewhat subdued. The coach did not move at first, but looked me up and down. After a second or two, he reluctantly returned to the dugout.

Things went better for an inning or two. It was a close game. Both teams had changed pitchers, and now the pitching was improving and there were a lot of good plays in the field. The fans and coaches were more focused on the game and not so much on the umpiring. The sixth inning rolled around and the bases were loaded with one out. The team at bat was that of the coaches who had been critical of my calls. The batter at the plate hit a hard grounder to the third baseman, who pounced on it and went for a double play. The second baseman took a perfect throw from him, pivoted, and made a good throw to the first baseman. The play at first base was close, but I determined that the batter was out, which ended the inning. I was in the best position possible to make the call, which was about ten feet in front of home plate.

The coaches of the team at bat went wild. "You missed it again!" they said loudly. "You're totally out of position. You are so blind. Get a new pair of glasses! You still haven't pulled your head out!"

When I heard the last comment, I went over to the dugout, glared at the two coaches, and demonstratively jerked my thumb over my shoulder and yelled out in a loud, clear voice for all to hear: **"YOU'RE OUT OF HERE!"**

I'd seen umpires at professional baseball games make the same motion when kicking a coach off the field, and I wanted to make this declaration in a manner that emulated theirs. It was a little dramatic, but I didn't think I overdid it. The response was again a stunned one. One of the coaches looked at me dumbstruck, and the other stammered in disbelief, "What? Are you really kicking us out of the game? I've never been kicked out of a Babe Ruth game in my life."

"Well, I guess this will be a first for you and for me," I said. "I've never had to eject a coach in my short life as an umpire either. You have five minutes to vacate the field. I don't want to see you or hear from you until this game is over. Otherwise your team will forfeit this game. Do you understand what I just said?"

One started to say something but stopped. The other just looked at me dumbly for a second and then turned to call one of the parents to take over coaching the team. Meanwhile, I moved back to my position behind the plate. As they moved out from the dugout, I resumed the game.

"Play ball!"

The teams had exchanged places and began to warm up. Just before the batter was to come to the plate, I heard someone behind me call out.

"Mr. Hammann, could you just give us a minute?"

I turned around and there stood the two coaches I had just kicked out of the game. They were looking sheepish and a lot more subdued than they had been five minutes earlier.

"Okay," I told them. "But say what you have to say and then leave."

The head coach cleared his throat and looked me in the eye as he spoke.

"Look, we messed up," he said. "We didn't intend for things to go this far. We both apologize for our conduct, and I can assure you we won't do anything like this in the future. Is there any way you could let us back into the game?"

The other coach stood beside him nodding his head in agreement. I was tempted to give in to their request—their apology was sincere, they appeared to be contrite, and I didn't think I would have any more trouble from them, but I couldn't just back down on a decision like that as someone in charge. "I'm sorry, guys," I told them. "I'd like to let you back in, but it just isn't possible. You went too far and I made my decision in front of everyone at this game. I just can't let you back into the game. You are welcome to coach at any games I umpire in the future, but now you have to vacate the area for this game."

They both respectfully thanked me for considering their request and said they would honor my decision. They then moved to a position behind the bleachers, and I didn't hear from them for the rest of the game.

We went ahead and played the next half of the inning. As the teams exchanged positions for the next half inning I heard another voice behind.

"Hey, Bob!" I took off my mask and turned around, and there was the Babe Ruth League manager standing there with a wide grin on his face.

"I was back here when you dealt with those two coaches," he said. "Just for your information, I think you handled it right. I might have sent them packing sooner, but you did just fine. You're new and you need to let the coaches, parents, and athletes know you are in charge, but I want to make sure you know those two men are Mr. Stellman and Mr. Mosman. Mr. Stellman is the chairman of the Lewiston School Board and Mr. Mosman is a local attorney, soon to be a judge. I know you just finished your first year as a teacher here in Lewiston, so you should know you just ejected the chairman of your school board. I'm quite sure he's going to remember you for a long time!"

I must have turned pale, because he laughed and reassured me. "Don't worry about it. They're good guys and they'll get over it. At least I think they will!"

With that he laughed loudly, turned around, and walked away.

I was stunned! What had I done? I had just kicked my boss out of a Babe Ruth baseball game and embarrassed him in front of kids and parents. I had kicked out an attorney who could probably sue me. What in the world had I done? I stood there trying to come to grips with the revelation and wondered what the consequences might be. But just then, the catcher called out to me. "Hey. blue! We're warmed up. Let's play ball."

So I pushed those thoughts out of my mind and went back to finish umpiring that game and the next.

What impressed me was that Mr. Stellman and Mr. Mosman never brought the issue up again. For the most part, they acted like perfect gentleman for the rest of the summer. They still disagreed with some of my calls, but they did it in a manner I could tolerate. There were even times between games when we had some good discussions about the game of baseball and the talent exhibited by some of the young players.

The baseball umpiring went pretty well for the months of June and July, as did graduate school, but I was still looking for another opportunity to make some money. Word came to me from the Babe Ruth manager that the Lewiston/Clarkston Twins legion baseball team was looking for bus drivers who would transport the various teams from the Lewis-Clark Hotel in downtown Lewiston to the baseball facility during the regional tournament scheduled for the end of August. He gave me a contact number, and after meeting with Dwight Church, the coach of the Twins, and the regional game manager, I had a job driving one of the busses. There would be two of us driving the seven teams in the tournament. I would be paid by the hour during the week of the tournament, which should give my family that last bit needed to make it through the summer and still have a short vacation just before school started.

I was excited about this job because I would drive the players to their game, wait until the game was over, and then drive them back to the hotel. I would get paid for driving them to and from their games, and they also paid me during the time I waited to drive them back. I would make some money and get to watch some great baseball. How could you beat a deal like that?

The tournament week came and there was an air of excitement running through the towns of Lewiston and Clarkston. Hosting the legion regional tournament was a big deal and had not happened in Lewiston for years. Because Lewiston hosted the tournament, their legion team, the Lewis-Clark Twins, received an automatic invitation although they had also qualified by winning the state championship game. Therefore, the Boise Gems would get an entry because they finished second in the state tournament. The word was also out that Lewiston had been selected to host the 1973 Legion World Series, which would take place next summer, and this added to the excitement.

That year's regional games would be played at Bengal Field, which was the high school baseball field that was maintained at a professional level by Dwight Church and the school district grounds crew. The Lewis-Clark State College baseball team used it as well as the local legion team. It was located behind Jenifer Junior High's football field and was fully fenced with a large grandstand capable of holding more than 1,000 fans that stretched down both the right field and left field lines. It was more than adequate for the high-profile regional tournament that was to take place.

The tournament would last about a week, and I would be driving several of the seven teams every day of the tournament. The teams competing included teams from Sheridan, Wyoming; Yakima, Washington; Elmendorf Air Force Base, Alaska; Portland, Oregon; Great Falls, Montana; Boise, Idaho; and of course, the Lewis-Clark team from Lewiston. Coming into the tournament, the legion team from Portland, Watco Electric, was selected by the media to win the tournament and move on to the Legion World Series. This was a double elimination tournament, so two losses put a team out of the running.

I greatly enjoyed the tournament. Because there were so many games, there were times when a team played twice in a day. I would pick up a team at the hotel and bring them to Bengal Stadium about an hour and a half before their game. I would watch the last part of a game and then watch the game of the team I was transporting. I got to see some great baseball, but I also got to visit with some of the fans in the stands. When the team I was transporting played the Lewis-Clark Twins, I had the opportunity to talk with some of the other fans about the coach, Dwight Church, and some of the players.

I learned a lot about Dwight Church. He played on the Lewiston legion team in 1939 at the age of fourteen when they won their first Idaho State Legion Championship. He continued playing on the high school and legion teams until he graduated from Lewiston High School in 1943 and joined the navy. He served on the battleship USS *California* in the Pacific until he was discharged in 1946. After leaving the navy, he played one year of professional baseball with a minor league team called the Globe Miami Browns. He attended college and worked in the private sector until 1955 when he returned to Lewiston to coach baseball and some football, but it was in baseball that his coaching career excelled. He was already a legend. By 1972, he had led the Lewiston Bengals to numerous state championships and the Lewis-Clark Twins to an impressive ten consecutive state championships and three Legion World Series appearances.

I watched him as he coached the Twins against the Sheridan team I was bussing. He knew his baseball, and he had the respect of each and every one of his players. Lewiston was in the tournament because they won the state tournament, but no one expected Lewiston to do well against teams like Portland and Yakima.

But by the end of the tournament, there was a three-way tie between the Lewiston, Yakima, and Portland teams. Portland had gone through the tournament undefeated until they faced the Yakima team, who had one loss. Amazingly, Yakima went off offensively and beat the Portland team 14 to 1 resulting in the three-way tie.

I was assigned to drive the Portland team to the final tournament games. All three teams were at the field after Yakima beat Portland, and there was some uncertainty about how to play off the tie. But soon after the game ended, I saw Dwight Church and one of his assistants making their way up to my seat in the bleachers. I was surprised when I realized he was coming up to speak with me. "Bob—that is your name, right?"

I nodded my head.

"We have decided to set the play-off format by drawing numbers out of a hat," Dwight said. "There will be three numbers in the hat. If a coach draws a one or a two, they will play each other while the team that draws a three sits out. The team that sits out will then play the winner of the play-off and the winner of that game will be the representative to the Legion World Series. You're a math major, right?"

I again nodded my head.

"Mathematically," he continued, "would it be better to choose first, second, or third?"

I was stunned by the question. I had taken statistics and was familiar with the theory of probability, but the problems I had dealt with were textbook problems. I had never been faced with an application problem like this. The legend, Dwight Church, had come all the way up in the bleachers to ask me, a rookie math teacher, a question that might help his team in obtaining a regional championship. I didn't have a mathematical answer right at the forefront of my mind, but I didn't want to let him down. He stood there and looked at me expectantly. He was hoping I could give him an answer that might give him and his team an edge. I didn't have a pat answer, so I verbalized my thoughts. "If you choose first, you have a two out of three chance of drawing a one or a two, which means you would probably play in the first play-off game," I said. "If you let one of the other two teams pick first and they draw a one or a two, which probability says is likely to happen, then there will be two numbers left with one of them being a three. That means whoever draws second has a 50/50 chance of drawing the three and receiving the bye. I would recommend you choose second. I wouldn't choose last, because you would not really have a choice. You would just get what is left over. I would choose second."

"Are you sure?" he asked. "This might make all the difference."

"I'm sure!" I responded.

He and his assistant coach turned and went back to the field. The tournament manager and the umpire then called all three coaches to home plate, where the umpire held a baseball cap in his hand, and sure enough Dwight Church made the second draw—and he drew the number three.

After he saw the number, he lifted it up and turned to his team and the crowd. "It's a three!" he shouted.

Everyone went wild, hopping up and down and cheering. This play-off game between Yakima and Portland was scheduled for the next day at 1 p.m., which was a Sunday. The championship game between Lewis-Clark and the winner would be Monday. After determining the play-off format, the Portland and Yakima teams loaded into their busses and returned to the hotel.

That Sunday, I drove the Portland team to the baseball field and got to watch a classic defensive gem and a duel between two great pitchers. The Portland Watco Electric team, the team picked to win it all, finally won by a three to one margin. I noticed the Lewis-Clark coaches and team were there to watch the event, and I'm sure they left the game proud that they would be playing the team everyone said would win it all. I'm sure they had it in their minds to write a different ending to Monday's game, even though they would be facing Portland's undefeated pitcher Gail Maier, who touted an 18-0 record.

The championship game was scheduled for 7 p.m., and I was the driver for the Portland team. We arrived at the field two hours before game time, about the same time as the Lewis-Clark Twins. Both teams and coaches had their game faces on. Portland and Lewiston went through the warm-up process in a crisp manner. Lewiston had a strong pitching staff, but I was not sure they could match up with Gail Maier. He had won all three games he had pitched in the tournament—it certainly looked like Portland had the edge.

The game began and as predicted, it was an excellent contest with good pitching and some solid defense. Both teams scored, but never in bunches. There were a lot of strikeouts on both sides, and by the time they got to the ninth inning, the score was tied five to five. Portland was up in the top of the ninth. They were able to get a runner to third base, but couldn't bring him home. The final out of the inning was a strikeout. Lewiston came into the dugout fired up, realizing they had a chance to win it all.

The first batter up got an infield single. An attempted sacrifice bunt by the second batter was hit too hard, but since the infielders were in it flew over the second baseman's outstretched glove. That put men on first and second. With no outs, the next batter tried to sacrifice both runners to second and third, but he popped the ball up to the third baseman. The next batter hit a fly ball to left field, which was dropped, filling the bases. The next batter struck out on four pitches. The bases were now full with two outs, and Lewiston's pitcher was up to bat. Dwight Church put in a pinch hitter to face Gail Maier, who had pitched the whole game. The first pitch was taken for a strike, but the second pitch was laced into the gap between the left and right fielders. As the ball fell untouched in the outfield, the crowd of 1,500 people went wild. Lewis-Clark had beaten the number one team in the region. I watched as the fans continued cheering loudly and the Lewiston dugout emptied onto the field. The players jumped up and down and pounded the player who hit the single on the back. Lewiston had won and was going to the Legion World Series. This would be Dwight Church's fourth appearance at that special event.

What an end to my first summer in Lewiston, Idaho. I finished the summer with "B" grades in my first graduate classes and had enough money—thanks to the GI Bill, umpiring, and driving bus at the American Legion Regional Tournament—to make it to the first school payday, which would come at the end of September. And now, I had been part of watching and making a tiny contribution to the Lewis-Clark Twins making it to the Legion World Series. After an eventful summer, I felt like I was now ready to begin my second year as a math teacher and coach at Jenifer Junior High School.

CHAPTER 14

Teaching Algebra and Ninth Grade Math

> *I thought this was ironic. Here they had been using crude and profane language in my class far beyond the word 'slut,' and now they were going to complain about me using the word 'slut?' Besides, I hadn't called them sluts. In reality, I had said, 'You are acting and talking like a bunch of sluts!' They had surely missed what I really said.*

The start of the 1972-73 school year began the Wednesday before Labor Day weekend. Teachers were given one day before the students returned on Wednesday to have meetings and to get organized for the new school year. We all met with Mr. Walker in the morning, and he reviewed a number of things, including submitting lesson plans, when teachers were to be in the building, the use of the intercom system, and making announcements. He also introduced some new teachers and had returning teachers introduce themselves to help orient the new teachers. Toward the end of the meeting, Mr. Walker made an exciting announcement: the school district was going to expand the basketball program by forming two teams for each grade level in the junior high school. He said he would be looking to fill two positions to meet the coaching needs for those teams. I caught him as we were leaving the meeting and said I would like to be considered for one of those positions. He indicated he would get back to me.

As Mr. Walker had informed me at the end of last year, I was going to be teaching four sections of ninth grade algebra and two sections of ninth grade general math. I was excited about teaching a higher-level math and especially looked forward to the challenge of teaching algebra. I considered this a golden assignment at the junior high level. I had taken the algebra and general math textbooks home to review, but was unable to spend much time with them, considering all of my summer activities. Still, I wasn't too concerned. A brief review of the first four chapters of each book indicated I understood the material and should not have a problem teaching those two courses.

I was moved from the first floor classroom to a room on the second floor. Across the hall was an English teacher who was near the end of her career. On one side of me was another math teacher, Mr. Chavez, who also taught algebra along with some general math classes. On the other side of me was another math teacher who taught seventh and eighth grade math.

I spent that Tuesday afternoon preparing my lesson plans for the rest of the week and the next week. Mr. Walker required us to write our daily learning objectives and the measurement we would use to ensure those objectives were met. So I listed the math objectives for each day in a spiral calendar notebook and then wrote the assignment that would be given for that day, which should meet the measurement requirement of planning. I also had a list of the students who would be in each class, which allowed me to enter the names in my grade book. I learned later to delay putting the names in my grade book, because there were a number of students who would transfer out of algebra and into general math within the first week, and there would be new students entering my class within a week of the start of school. This year, it looked like I would average around 30 students in the algebra classes and 22 in the general math classes. I would be teaching about 160 students over six periods with no preparation period for planning. At the time, this was not a concern—I thought it was just a normal thing. Preparation and grading papers would be done on my time after school.

Since I was in a new classroom, I put up some posters on my bulletin boards that highlighted the field of math and science and wrote the disciplinary rules and consequences on one corner of the chalkboard at the front of the room. I loved this classroom because it had two walls covered with chalkboards, which gave me a lot of space to work problems. I rearranged the classroom, putting the seats in rows and placing my desk at the front of the room. I went to the school supply closet near the main office and retrieved the chalk and erasers I needed to start the year. By the time I had done all this and spent some time visiting with the teachers around me, it was 4 p.m. and well past the time to go home. I went home excited about the new school year.

The first day of school went well. The first day of classes was devoted to introductions, assigning seats, making a seating chart, reviewing disciplinary rules and consequences, and a general orientation to the course. I approached assigning seats to my ninth grade classes a little differently than the previous year, since the students were older and I thought they would be able to handle selecting their own seats. Once they had selected a seat of their choice, I filled out my seating chart, which would help me take roll in a quick and efficient manner. This proved to work well for my algebra classes.

I was ecstatic with my algebra students—they were respectful and most of them were eager to take the class. Those classes organized themselves quickly, and we were able to get through the agenda with little difficulty. We even had time at the end of each class to visit about the coming sporting season and what they had done during the summer.

The general math classes were a different story. During my time student teaching, I had not experienced teaching ninth grade general math. So I was unprepared for the mindset of these students. Some of these students were bright enough to take algebra, but were not interested in that kind of challenge. Instead, they were looking for an easy grade in math, which every student had to take at the ninth grade level. There were other students who had very poor math skills. Many of them hated math and resented the fact they had to be there. I quickly saw that most of these students were poorly motivated and many were potential discipline problems.

Lewiston was the home of the Northwest Children's Home, a facility for troubled youth who had been abused and separated from dysfunctional families in Idaho. In almost every case, these children were deeply troubled and had some behavior problems. Most of these students were enrolled in the Lewiston Public Schools and most of these students were assigned to a general math class rather than an algebra class. I found I had several of these students sprinkled through my two general math classes.

After my delight with my algebra classes, I quickly saw that the general math students had entirely different attitudes. It took far more time to get them seated to set up the seating charts, and there was evidence of disrespect when some carried on conversations while I was trying to get them arranged and oriented to the class. Once I realized some were being less than cooperative, I moved quickly to my rules and consequences for behavior and had to firmly state I was not going to tolerate an attitude of disrespect in any class. After I covered this, most of the students quieted down and settled in to let me finish reviewing the course. We had little time to talk informally at the end of class like I was able to do with the algebra classes. The rest of the week went well in both classes, although there was a building atmosphere of disruption in my general math classes.

Jenifer Junior High provided sporting programs for the boys, which included seventh, eighth, and ninth grade football; seventh, eighth, and ninth grade basketball; ninth grade baseball; and seventh, eighth, and ninth grade track. They also provided volleyball for the ninth grade girls. The seventh, eighth, and ninth grade football teams and the ninth grade volleyball team began their practices after school on the second day of school. A significant number of male students were out for football with Mr. Wimer assigned as the ninth grade football coach. After the first week, school was in full swing with the majority of students focused on learning and preparing for the football season. During the third week of school Mr. Crosby, the ninth grade basketball coach, came to me and asked if I was willing to coach the second ninth grade basketball team. If I took him up on that offer, we would hold a week of tryouts where he would pick twelve players for the varsity squad, and then I would take the rest and play a junior varsity schedule. The junior varsity would play teams from some of the smaller districts around as well as playing junior varsity teams from Pullman, Moscow, and Sacajawea, who were members of the league. Mr. Crosby assured me he would see that I got at least one or two good players to help make us competitive. Of course, I was eager to take the job, which meant I would have another slight increase in my salary while coaching a sport I loved.

I quickly settled into a routine with teaching algebra. The first part of the class was devoted to taking roll, making announcements, and then grading papers and working problems on the board that were of concern to the students. Then I would provide a fifteen- or twenty-minute lesson, which would include defining algebraic terms, working through algorithms for solving algebraic expressions or equations, and working several sample problems similar to those they would find in their assignment. During the last part of the period, I would move about the class providing individual assistance as they started the assignment for the next day. There were very few problems with discipline. Occasionally, I would have to ask students to quiet down, but for the most part they stayed on task. Approximately three-fourths of the students learned the concepts and were able to work the assignments effectively.

The general math classes were totally different. I had a great discrepancy of abilities in these classes. There were those students taking the class to get their math requirement out of the way and were quite capable of taking algebra. They pressured me to get through the lesson presentations quickly so they could do the homework and move on something else. These students usually did not have homework—instead, they finished the assignment five minutes before the bell rang, and then spent the remaining time talking to friends or working on assignments from other classes. Some of these students were disruptive and had to be confronted.

Most of the other students had incredibly low math skills and could not learn the material very quickly. They did not have a good grasp of math basics and were often unable to finish the assignment by the end of the period, so they had homework. Most of these students didn't know their addition or multiplication tables, and it appeared many of them had not been required to learn them in the lower grades. The elementary schools were adopting the educational progressive concepts of the "new math," which emphasized the use of manipulatives to show how adding, subtracting, multiplying, and dividing numbers worked. Based on what the students told me, it appeared elementary teachers were abandoning the discipline of memorizing basic math facts for the numbers one through twelve. Without these skills, most of my math students struggled to understand and work simple math problems that took a number of steps. I had to provide a lot of assistance to these students, and I knew they would struggle when and if they ever took an algebra class.

The students who lacked those fundamental skills were easily frustrated because they felt we were moving too fast. Out of that frustration, they would misbehave and were sometimes very disrespectful towards myself and the other students. There was a real tension between these students and those who should have been in an algebra class.

Because I had significantly more behavioral problems in the general math classes, I tried to be more structured and found that if I relaxed with those students and tried to develop a friendly relationship with them, some of them would take advantage of that. I quickly learned that, in most cases, you couldn't be a friend to those students. By the end of that school year, it was apparent that for my general math students, I had to convey that I was in charge and would execute discipline fairly and justly on all those who tried to be disruptive. The lessons that taught me this were painful at times.

In particular, one situation in my last period general math class burned a lesson in my mind that solidified my approach to discipline and addressing inappropriate behavior. At the beginning of the year, I approached discipline with these ninth grade general math classes from the same perspective I used with the algebra classes. After all, I reasoned, the students were the same age. As with the algebra classes, I let the students pick their own seats at the beginning of the year, a choice that proved to be a disaster with the general math students. And in the case of my last period general math class in particular, there was a group of four girls who were quite close who chose to sit together near the back of the room. As the year progressed, their behavior became more and more disruptive—they would talk while I was teaching the lesson, forcing me to stop and ask them to quiet down. They would stop talking for a short time, but eventually start again. Also, their conversations were laced with profanity and some crude sexual language. They would try to talk low enough to mask their words, but I could hear what they were saying and I knew that most of the other students could as well. This situation came to a head about a month into the school year. I was trying to teach the lesson and they were talking again. This time, they were pretty loud and I had to stop the lesson twice to tell them to stop talking. After the second time, I moved them to different seats in the class that put significant distance between the four of them. In defiance of what I had done, they continued to talk even louder as I finished the lesson. I gave the assignment to the rest of the students and told the girls they would need to stay after class so I could talk with them. They grumbled and griped under their breaths, again using profanity and crude language. The class ended and two of them tried to leave by falling in behind the last student filing out of class.

I moved between the two girls and the door and directed them back to their seats. After a short stare-down, they both complied. They sat down and astonishingly began to talk to each other and the other two students who had stayed in their seats using offensive language. By this point, I was pretty frustrated.

"Enough!" I said. "I want you to hear me." They all grudgingly gave me their attention, but had looks that said they really didn't care what I was going to say. This infuriated me even more.

"I've had enough of your talking while I'm trying to instruct students," I snapped. "I've had enough of your profanity and crude talk. You are all acting and speaking like a bunch of sluts!"

Bingo! I knew I had hit them right between the eyes with that statement, because the same two who had tried to leave when the bell rang turned beet red and stood up angrily. "You can't talk to me like that!" one of them declared. "You can't call me a slut!"

I thought this was ironic. Here they had been using crude and profane language in my class far beyond the word "slut," and now they were going to complain about me using the word "slut?" Besides, I hadn't called them sluts. In reality I said, "You are acting and talking like a bunch of sluts!" They had surely missed what I really said. "I don't have to put up with that," one of the other girls said. "We're out of here!"

She and the other standing student started for the door. The other two stood hesitantly, as if they were thinking about leaving as well. I realized I needed to get the situation back under control, so I moved to block the door. "You aren't leaving this classroom until I say you can leave this classroom," I told them. "I did not call you sluts. I said your attitude and crude talk make you behave like sluts. I'm trying to encourage you to act and talk in a respectful manner instead of what you have been doing this whole semester! You can change your behavior so you appear more ladylike, and I'm trying to help you do that by reflecting to you what your behavior looks like!"

While I was talking, the most defiant girl continued to make her way to the door, which I assertively blocked with my full six-foot, 180-pound frame. She got within three feet of me and looked me up and down.

"I'm leaving this room!" she said. I stood up as tall as possible and looked back down at her, putting as much authority in my voice as I could.

"Then you're going to have to go through me, because you are going to stay here until I dismiss you! Are you ready to take me on?"

We stared at each other, both of us trying to portray a demeanor of strength and unbendable purpose. After what seemed to be minutes, she reluctantly turned and sat down at the desk near the door. Inside I was relieved—I really hadn't been sure what I was going to do. If she tried to physically move me aside, I don't think I would have tried to physically restrain her, although I was prepared to block her with my body and make her try to fight her way past me. In reality, I had bluffed and won—at least I thought I had won.

Once she was seated, I stood quietly for about a minute more then stepped aside to let them leave. "I hope you will come to class with a better attitude tomorrow," I said as they left. "And conduct yourselves like young ladies so we don't have to go through this again."

They left sullenly without saying a word.

On this particular week, I had been assigned the duty of supervising students as they left the school at the end of the day. My post was near the main entrance next to the office, so as soon as the girls were out of my room, I closed my classroom door and hurriedly made my way down to my post. I stood there with another teacher, and we watched the students as they filed out after getting their books from their lockers. Just as the last few stragglers were leaving, the four girls I had just chastised came down the stairs from their lockers and turned to leave the building. All of them glared at me as they turned and headed out the building. I chose to ignore their looks as they left.

After they passed me, I watched their backs as they started through the doors. To my surprise, the student who challenged me the most lifted both arms above her head, made fists, and extended her middle fingers. She was giving me a double dose of the "bird!" Here she was defiantly giving me the double whammy and the mother of all insults. At first I was stunned, and then angry. I was ready to chase her down and bring her back to face Mr. Walker, but then decided against it. I was not ready at that moment to deal with her again, so I let her go. But, I thought, that display reinforced what I had surmised—she was determined to continue acting like a slut!

After they were gone and I had completed my duty, I went back to my desk and worked on grading an algebra test I had given to my algebra classes. I was just preparing to gather my things and head home, when Mr. Walker's voice came over my classroom intercom.

"Mr. Hammann, are you there?"

I went over and pushed the transmit button. "Yes, I'm here. I'm just getting ready to go home."

"Well," he replied, "we have a situation down here and you need to come to my office right now."

"Okay," I said. "I'll be right there."

It was almost 4:30 p.m. and well past the time we were required to stay. I was concerned about what situation might cause Mr. Walker to call me to the office. As I came down the stairs and rounded the corner toward the office, the reason for the situation became evident. There in the office was the girl who gave me the "double whammy," and with her were two adults, which I guessed to be her parents. It looked like I was going to find out who really won in the standoff in my room.

As I entered the office area, Mr. Walker spoke.

"Here he is. This is Mr. Hammann and these are the parents of this young lady, whom I think you know. Please come into my office." If only Mr. Walker knew how wrong he was to call her a young lady, I thought to myself. The parents introduced themselves to me with glares as we were ushered into Mr. Walker's office. The girl looked at me and flashed a cocky, confident grin.

After we had all been seated, Mr. Walker closed the door and moved his desk chair so he could address us. The girl and her parents were sitting on one couch, and I was sitting by myself in a chair along the other wall. As we took our seats, I was trying to figure out how this would turn out. Would Mr. Walker support me or was I going to find myself in deep trouble? "Mr. Hammann, this student and her parents just came into my office about ten minutes ago," Mr. Walker began. "She and her parents were pretty upset, as I think you can see. She had told her parents that you called her and her friends a bunch of sluts in your class today. Is that true?"

As her parents looked at me accusingly and she sat there with that cocky grin, I said, "Mr. Walker, that is not exactly accurate. She and three of her friends have been disrupting my math class for several weeks by talking while I am trying to teach. They were also using language that was totally inappropriate. They were using profanity and some crude words with sexual connotations. I warned them several times over the past two weeks to stop, but it has continued off and on until today. Today, I reseated them and told them to stay after class so I could address their behavior. After the other students had left, I tried to communicate my displeasure at their behavior and language. I tried to make them see how disruptive and inappropriate it was. I told them they were acting and talking like a bunch of sluts—I did not call them sluts. I was trying to help them see how their behavior might be categorized in the eyes of others. It's obvious it didn't work, because they left class pretty upset. Her anger was further evidenced when she flipped me off as she went out the door at the end of the day!"

To my amazement, the father turned to Mr. Walker. "He can't talk to my daughter like that. It just isn't right. Mr. Walker, you need to deal with this teacher. What Mr. Hammann said is totally wrong—I want my daughter out of this man's class!" Had he heard what I'd just said? Had he heard me say his daughter was using profanity and disrupting my class? Had he heard me say she had flipped me off in front of a bunch of students as she left the building? He was upset with me, but he hadn't even said anything about his daughter's inappropriate behavior. What kind of parents were these?

Mr. Walker sat quietly for a minute, looking from the father to the daughter and then to me. He finally locked eyes sternly on the daughter.

"Young lady, you were totally out of line for talking while Mr. Hammann was trying to teach. You were even more out of line for using profanity and crude language on the school grounds, and Mr. Hammann did the right thing trying to reason with you and your friends about your behavior. His intentions were good, but he may have gone too far with the language he used. Is it true you flipped him off as you went out the building?"

She looked at her dad and didn't say anything. "If that is true," Mr. Walker continued, "I will not tolerate any student in my school treating one of my teachers in that manner, and you can count on me taking swift action if I hear of it again. The next time you exhibit this kind of behavior, whether it be using foul language or flipping him the 'bird,' I am directing Mr. Hammann to send you to me and I will deal with you accordingly. Do you understand?"

The girl had now lost her cocky grin and looked somewhat abashed. "Yes, I understand," she replied, then looked at her dad with a glare.

"What about him?" her dad asked.

"Sir, that is between Mr. Hammann and myself," Mr. Walker replied to his credit. "You, as her parents, need to help your daughter understand what is respectful and what is not. Is there anything else you would like to say?"

The father looked at his daughter and then at Mr. Walker. "I still want her out of his class," he said.

"I can arrange that since we have another teacher teaching general math," Mr. Walker replied.

Turning to me with a knowing, stern look, Mr. Walker asked if I had anything I wanted to add.

"It was never my intention to insult your daughter or to insult you, her parents," I said, taking what I thought was his cue. "If she and you feel insulted because I used the term 'slut,' I apologize for using that term. I could have used other terms to confront the behavior of your daughter and her friends that may not have been interpreted as insulting."

The father grudgingly nodded his head and stood with his wife and daughter, who were clearly unhappy with the results of the meeting. I'm sure the daughter wanted to see me crucified for what I had said. Her father shook Mr. Walker's hand and mine and thanked us for sitting down with them. I wasn't sure the dad and his daughter were going to discuss her behavior anytime soon.

As they left, Mr. Walker motioned for me to stay. Once they were out, he closed the door and turned to me with a small grin and little bit of a twinkle in his eye. "What you said was probably right on. I've had her in my office before for this kind of behavior and she can be a pill. But, don't use the word 'slut' or any other word that carries that kind of connotation. It just makes the situation worse for you and for me. Criticize their specific behavior, but don't use terms like that. Do you get what I'm saying?"

"Yes sir!" I replied. "I will do my best to not use terms like that in the future."

With that, he dismissed me and I went to my room, gathered my things, and went home.

I learned a valuable lesson that day. As the teacher and the one in charge of a classroom of students, I needed to avoid inflammatory words like "slut" to address inappropriate behavior. Using such language is judgmental and demeaning, and needs to be avoided. I could have just told the girls what specific behaviors I was not going to tolerate and given them the consequences if they refused to correct those behaviors. I also needed to address those inappropriate behaviors quickly, rather than letting them continue until I'd reached a point where my emotions took over.

It was interesting that two of the four girls transferred out of my class and into another math class, which turned out to be a real blessing. This one change made my last period ninth grade general math class more manageable and the atmosphere more positive. I was, however, concerned for the teacher who got her. She would be a handful for anyone if she didn't change her attitude and behavior.

The front of the Jenifer Junior High School gymnasium, where Bob coached many basketball games while teaching at the school.

The front of the Hammanns' home. Bob lived here for the majority of his time teaching at Jenifer. The house was just a few blocks from the school.

The front entrance to Jenifer Junior High in 2015. The building has seen little change over the last forty-five years.

Lewiston, from the top of what is affectionately known as "Lewiston Hill." Bob spent many evenings fishing on the Clearwater River, seen in this photo.

Bob's first ninth grade varsity team from the 1974 season.

CHAPTER 15

The Golden Assignment—Coaching Basketball

> *Jerry was getting beat on defense and was really slow getting through our offensive plays to the spot where he could get a good shot. He also was not getting out on the fast break for the easy layup as he had been in our previous games. I asked him several times during the first half if he was okay, and every time he said he was fine. However, he looked pale and had little energy throughout the half. By halftime, he had two points and we were down by eighteen. I went to him at halftime and asked him again if he was feeling okay.*

November was fast approaching, and I was looking forward to coaching basketball for the first time. About two weeks before tryouts, Mr. Crosby met with me and we worked on formulating our plan for tryouts, putting together parental permission slips, and making announcements. We decided to put an announcement in the daily bulletin instructing ninth grade boys interested in trying out to sign up with either of us. We scheduled a meeting after school with interested athletes to give them the parental information slips, outline our expectations, and give them a list of what they would need to bring for the first day of tryouts. We had approximately twenty-four boys sign up to try out, and during our meeting a week before tryouts we had approximately thirty-four boys in attendance. There were ten athletes who had not signed up, so we passed out parental permission slips and told them they needed to be returned before they would be allowed to get on the basketball floor to practice. We instructed all of them to bring tennis shoes, shorts, and shirts to all practices. Mr. Crosby then told them no one would be cut from the team, as had been the practice in the past. The tryouts were to determine a varsity team and a junior varsity team. The varsity team would be composed of twelve athletes, and the rest would be on the junior varsity team with myself as the coach. There was a general atmosphere of excitement as the boys left the room.

The first day of practice came on a Monday, and Mr. Crosby and I waited in the gym as about thirty-five boys swarmed in from the locker room, all excited about the start of the season. Mr. Crosby immediately took charge and started practice by having the athletes jog two laps around the gym. Next up, he asked the boys to do five suicides, which are stop-and-go wind sprints. Six to eight athletes at a time lined up on the end line of the basketball floor where they awaited the coach's signal. When the whistle blew, they sprinted to the first free throw line extended, touched it, and sprinted back to the end line to touch it. This process was repeated with the half-court line, free throw line extended at three-quarter court, and finally the end line at the opposite end of the court, where they would stop with most of the students panting and holding their sides. Then the next group would step to the end line and perform the same drill while the first group recovered. He had each group do five of these! Generally those who were not in shape were walking around with their hands on their hips gasping for air.

After the suicides, the students did layup and jump shot drills, dribbling and rebound block-out drills, and half-court and full-court defensive slide drills. Practice culminated with full-court scrimmages on two courts where we could see twenty students at a time performing in game situations. After the scrimmages, the practice ended with five more suicides. On the first day or two, these suicides usually had a few athletes puking in the drinking fountain or on the floor. The rule was if you puked on the floor, you cleaned it up. The athletes learned quickly to not snack before practices if they didn't want to embarrass themselves by throwing up.

During the five days of tryouts, it was easy to see who the talented basketball players were. After practice on Friday, Mr. Crosby and I sat down and he chose the twelve players he wanted to keep for the varsity. These lists would be posted in the gym on Monday. The talent pool dropped dramatically after he chose his twelve. I pointed out he promised to give me one or two players to help me be competitive, but after some debating, I only got one. He was a great shooter and knew the game, but he was incredibly slow of foot. I like to win, but it would be near impossible to win too many games with the athletes he left me. I knew we would mostly be working on the fundamentals and running simple plays. I thought we might still be competitive if my team learned to play defense, but it still would be hard to win many games without a few good shooters.

Since we were starting a new program, we needed to purchase new uniforms to clothe the team. The varsity was able to purchase fourteen brand new, classy red-and-white uniforms, while the JV team got the hand-me-down uniforms from the varsity—the uniforms left over from the last two purchases. There were fourteen that were used, but in pretty good shape and another fourteen that were old, ragged, and faded from an older set that had been used years earlier. This gave our team a motley look, but we didn't really care. What did give me some concern was the name across the front of the jerseys, which was JACKS. What was that all about?

After the tryouts, we practiced an hour and a half per day for two more weeks on half the court while the varsity practiced on the other half. Fortunately, I was able to schedule the whole gym for extended practices on the two Saturdays before the start of competition. We worked hard on fundamentals and on learning some simple plays. They worked hard, but except for the one student who could shoot, we just didn't have much natural talent.

The season began the first week of December. Mr. Crosby was acting as the athletic director of our school and had scheduled fourteen games. We played four games with the Pullman JV team and four games with the Moscow JV team, where we were soundly thumped. We played two games with the Clarkston JV team, where we were also defeated soundly, and four games against our cross-town rivals the Sacajawea Savages, where we proved to be very competitive, winning half the games. In my first season as a coach, we finished with two wins and twelve losses. But the skills of my team improved significantly. They worked hard and did what I asked of them.

One of the problems with coaching the ninth grade JV team was that I had twenty-two members on the team, and I was expected to play all the players if possible. This was just one of the factors that contributed to our losing. We began to play a fifth quarter at the end of many of the regular games to allow athletes to play for a longer period of time, which helped some.

I remember one game where we were to play the Pullman ninth grade JV team on Pullman's home court. We had played well against them when they came to Lewiston the week before this game, so I thought we might be able to win this time around. At Lewiston, we had kept it close with our defense and the shooting of my one good player, Jerry. I had designed our plays to give him as many shots as possible. He was really good at hitting long shots, but this was well before the installment of the three-point line, so he would only get two points. Even without the three-point line, he was averaging double figures.

We travelled on a school bus to all away games. As the coach, I usually sat at the front of the bus with the athletes sitting behind me. We always took all of our athletes to away games, so there would be about twenty-six players on the bus plus two team managers. There was always some competition about who would sit in the back of the bus. In traveling to and from this particular game in Pullman, my best player and four of his friends sat in the back of the bus. Discipline and behavior on the bus had not been a problem up to this point, so I was pretty lax about moving to the back of the bus periodically to monitor their activities. The bus was usually noisy, but there were few incidences of disruption. And when the trip was over, all the players were expected to help clean up the bus. Many brought sack lunches to snack on as we travelled, so there was usually a mess by the time we got home. One thing I did stress to the students was that they should eat lightly until after the game, since it would impede their play if they ate too much. On this particular trip, which took about an hour, everything seemed to be normal.

Once we got there and the game began, it didn't take me long to see that my best player was playing badly. Jerry was getting beat on defense and was really slow getting through our offensive plays to the spot where he could get a good shot. He also was not getting out on the fast break for the easy layup as he had been in our previous games. I asked him several times during the first half if he was okay, and every time he said he was fine. However, he looked pale and had little energy throughout the half. By halftime, he had two points and we were down by eighteen. I went to him at halftime and asked him again if he was feeling okay.

"What's going on out there? You are moving like you are wading in molasses. Are you sick?" I asked.

"I'm okay," he replied. "I'm not sick. I'll get it together this next half."

He went out the second half and looked even worse than the first. He was playing so badly that I finally took him out. He ended up with six points, and we needed him to score fifteen or more to keep us competitive. We ended up getting beat by thirty-two points. Since this was Pullman, we played a fifth quarter and that proved to be competitive, but we still lost by two points. As the players were loading the bus to head home, I pulled one of them aside and asked him what was wrong with Jerry, our best shooter.

"Oh, Jerry brought a big bag of hard candy on the bus. He shared it with everybody in the back of the bus. The bag was empty when we got to the game."

"How many did he eat?"

"Let's see," he responded, taking a minute to think. "I think he had most of the bag. I do remember him saying he was sick to his stomach when we got off the bus."

Needless to say, Jerry and I had a long talk on the way back to Lewiston about eating appropriately and the negative affect eating all that candy had on him and the team. The team also got a firm talk from me at the next practice about proper eating habits before any basketball game. I don't think Jerry snacked before a basketball game for the rest of the year, although I can attest he ate well on the way home. I was also much more diligent about supervision on the bus from that point forward, making several trips to the back of the bus as we went to and from games.

I developed a special love for these boys who dedicated a couple of hours each day to becoming a team and playing the sport I loved so much. I was truly proud of these athletes and their accomplishments, even though we did not have a very successful season as far as wins and losses were concerned.

The year before, when I coached track, and during this first season as the ninth grade JV basketball coach, I was concerned about our team mascot. The burro didn't seem to be a mascot I might choose for a team. When I first found out our mascot was a burro and our name was the Jenifer Jacks, I wondered what school in its right mind would choose a burro for a mascot. Well, some investigation showed there was quite a discussion in the community about the mascot for the Jenifer Junior High School sporting teams when Jenifer was built. At the center of the discussion was Mr. Walker. He believed it would be valuable to have a live mascot that could be trotted out at games and pep rallies. The community rejected any canine mascot as too common. Lions, tigers, cougars, and the like were impractical, so Mr. Walker suggested the burro. He felt it would be easy to get one to parade around at games and pep rallies. Most of the parents seemed to think that was a good idea, so the burro was adopted as the official mascot. I don't think they really thought that through too well, because someone then came up with the bright idea of giving us the nickname of the Jenifer Jacks, and from that time on, "Jacks" was printed across all the jerseys and on the center court of the gym. I remember having team pictures taken around the center court in the gymnasium. Those pictures showed the players, managers, and coaches all standing with smiles on their faces in a semicircle around the center court, which featured a smiling burro surrounded in a half-circle by the logo "Jenifer Jacks." Of course, all the team members had Jacks stenciled across the front of their jerseys.

I know first hand that our crosstown rivals, the Sacajawea Savages, had a great time with that mascot. I can't count the number of times we trotted out on their floor to hear several fans shout out,

"You bunch of JACKASSES!" This all could have been avoided had they chosen a more macho mascot. We worked around it, though. We always thought if we won we could let those fans know they had just been beaten by a "bunch of jackasses!"

Another great tradition at Jenifer with respect to sports was the end-of-the-season sports assembly. When each sporting season concluded, we would have an awards assembly at the end of a regular school day, which was usually a Friday. At these assemblies, the full student body and staff would be in attendance along with a number of parents. Each participant and manager would receive a certificate, and the team would give the coach a small gift of appreciation, which was usually a cake baked by one of the parents. This year was my first awards assembly, since for some reason we didn't have an assembly for spring sports like track and field. At this first assembly, I tried to say something positive about each player and to thank the parents for lending him to me for the season. I pointed out to all in attendance that I was not so much interested in developing a winning basketball team as I was in developing positive character attributes in each player who turned out. I wanted them to see the positive results of teamwork, hard work, discipline, and integrity. I saw most of the athletes embracing that idea and becoming better young men, which therefore made us a better basketball team. What better place to teach these concepts than in the arena of sports, especially basketball?

CHAPTER 16

Teaching Algebra and Track Season Conflicts

> *"Our strategy was to confront the four athletes with their absences when they came to school. If they were open and honest with us about playing hooky and going for a swim, we would suspend them from the afternoon track meet. But if they lied to us about the reason for their absences, we would remove them from the team for the rest of the season, which would cost the team a possible league championship."*

As the school year progressed, I found myself settling on a regular routine regarding the instruction of algebra. I found the algebra classes had a wide spectrum of skill levels, just as those evident in the general math classes. At one end of the spectrum of student abilities, I had students who were bright enough and motivated enough to pick up the algebraic concepts by focusing on the class presentations and the sample problems worked on the board. Students at the other end of the learning spectrum had a more difficult time. They needed to see a lot of problems worked and needed the concepts reinforced by a lot of review and instruction from a different perspective. Again, the difficulty to me as a teacher was to find a balance to meet the needs of the students at both ends of the spectrum.

After some experimentation during the first semester, I developed an instructional routine skewed more toward those who were struggling and needed as much reinforcement as possible. By doing that, I sacrificed providing more challenges to the students who picked up the concepts quickly. I figured these motivated students would continue in a math track at the high school that would include challenging classes like algebra 2, geometry, pre-calculus, and calculus. So the instructional routine I settled on for the rest of the year looked like this: I would start class by working three or four problems from the assignment that students found difficult. Then, I would have students exchange their homework assignments from the previous class day and give the correct answers as they graded them. After giving the answers, the students would write the number of correct problems at the top of the paper and read them out loud to me as I entered them in my grade book. I then collected the papers to look through later that night and see where any glaring gaps in understanding might exist.

After the review and grading exercise, I would teach concepts again, if necessary, based on the problems they had me work at the beginning of the class and from reviewing assignments the night before. I would then move into a lesson presentation to meet the learning objectives for the day. This would usually include defining terms, stating theorems, and reviewing problem-solving algorithms. I would finish the lesson by working three to five problems similar to those the students might have in their assignment for the day. Usually by the time I finished this, there would be ten to fifteen minutes left in the class period during which time I let the students work on that day's assignment in groups of two or three until the bell rang. I would be available to provide assistance if needed as they worked.

There were times when it was evident that many of the students were struggling with a particular section or group of sections. When this happened, I would deviate from this routine to have a day where we worked on problems from these difficult sections. I would try to make the review as competitive and intense as possible. This process seemed to work best for those students who needed more help.

At the end of a chapter, I would provide a worksheet with problems similar to those on the chapter test. Included with the worksheet would be a copy of the answers. This review sheet would be given the day before we were to review for the test. When the review day came, we would work the problems using a variety of methods. Sometimes I would have a few students come up to the board to work problems from the worksheet and would review or correct their work before the whole class. Sometimes we would make a game out of it, and I would divide the class into two teams and four students from each team would come up to the board to work a problem. Each team would be given a point for every problem completed correctly. The team with the highest score at the end of the period received a small reward. Sometimes it was candy or the team that won was excused from class first while the losing team waited. The students usually enjoyed the review days.

Mr. Chavez, the other algebra teacher who taught in the room next to me, had a different process that seemed to work well for his students. He simply gave a short presentation lasting about ten minutes at the beginning of class and then gave the assignment, working as many odd-numbered problems from the assignment problems as he could. He would then assign the even-numbered problems for homework. The students would copy down the odd problems as he did them, because they were needed as part of the graded assignment. They then could use the odd problems as a guide to help them work the even problems at home. The textbooks we had provided the answers to the odd problems in the back of the book, but did not give the answers for the even problems. Mr. Chavez graded the assignments at home and returned them to the students the next day.

Both Mr. Chavez and I found that our students resisted reading a textbook to learn the math concepts—something I found to be true at every grade level. At best, they struggled, and at worst, refused to learn the math information on their own from the textbook. Most of the students responded best when a teacher provided the material as a lesson presentation. Because of this, students who missed a lot of class rarely did well in algebra or other advanced math classes. We also noticed some students responded well to his instructional process, but not well to mine and vice versa. We found that to be true when one student was transferred from his class to mine because he was struggling in Mr. Chavez's class. After working in my class for two weeks, the student told me the concepts were easier to understand after receiving my instruction and his grades reflected that. Another student who was struggling in my class was transferred to Mr. Chavez's class, and that student found she could grasp the concepts better through his method of instruction. It took a year or two for us to figure this out. Once this was understood, we would look to transfer students before we considered letting them drop algebra to take the general math class. Of course, some students were not ready either intellectually or motivationally to take algebra at the ninth grade level, so in those cases we allowed them to transfer to a general math class.

Before I would approve a transfer from the algebra class to the general math class, I would try to counsel the student to stay and work harder. Many of these students were smart enough to do the work, but they were not motivated. They wanted to take the easiest track to a diploma and in many cases had an aversion to math. I tried to reason with these students and make the case that education was the key to well-paying jobs, and a strong background in math and science was especially valuable. But in almost every discussion the students would resist.

"When I graduate from high school," they'd say, "I will go down to PFI and my father will get me a better paying job than you have right now with all your education! I'll probably start out making twice what you are making!"

A little research on my part showed that what these students told me was absolutely true. PFI, Potlatch Forest Industries, provided a number of entry-level jobs at their tissue plant in Lewiston starting at about $8 per hour, which means that person could make more than $12,000 annually compared to my paltry $7,200 per year.

I tried to make the argument that the forest industry has its ups and downs and that sometimes there are large layoffs, but that logic fell on mostly deaf ears. The forest industry and most manufacturing companies were in high gear at that time, and well-paying jobs were there for the taking. Those students set their mind on making good money right now instead of investing in education, which would have a long-term positive effect financially and provide more opportunities in the future. Of course, history has proven me correct. I wonder if any of those students remembered our conversation ten to fifteen years later when things like the movement to save the spotted owl habitat dramatically changed that industry?

Mr. Chavez and I found that some students would transfer from algebra to general math within the first month of school or at the end of the first month of the second semester. The transfers during the first month of the second semester usually occurred because the course material became more difficult as we began to work with factoring and solving quadratic equations.

We would usually lose ten to twenty percent of our students out of our algebra classes by the first month of the second semester. Of course that meant my general math classes would become extremely large, with some class sizes topping forty students. Having numbers this high in a general math class made the maintenance of discipline extremely challenging.

Algebra is, for many students, the first class taken that deals with abstract concepts and it can be very difficult. I came to believe there are some students who are just not ready to take algebra at the ninth grade level. Their brains are not ready yet to deal with abstract thinking, but I believe they might be ready to deal with it successfully at the tenth or eleventh grade levels.

As spring approached, Jerry Bafus and I prepared for another great track season. This would be my second year as the head coach, and the eighth grade athletes who won the league meet the year before were all returning. Even though there were only nine of them, they were a power to be reckoned with. I thought we were a shoe-in for another championship at the ninth grade level.

We had our organizational meeting and began our conditioning and practice sessions on the second Monday in March. We had a large number of seventh and eighth graders out for track and the returning nine athletes for the ninth grade team. We always looked for our ninth grade team to provide leadership to the seventh and eighth grade teams, leading the younger students in stretching exercises and assisting them on their particular track event. We also called on the ninth graders to exhibit a good work ethic and model positive character traits to these younger athletes.

The first three conditioning days of practice indicated we were going to have some problems with our ninth grade team. Five of our nine ninth grade athletes failed to make those practices, and when confronted with their absences, they gave vague excuses about having appointments or having work to do at home, yet none of them brought us a note from their parents. Jerry and I accepted their excuses initially, but gave each athlete a pep talk about being leaders and setting a good example to the underclassmen. In every case, these pep talks were received with bland and unenthusiastic attitudes.

After the first three days of conditioning, the ninth grade athlete attendance to the regular practices was better. Our first track meet revealed our ninth grade team was as strong as they were the previous year—they easily won the meet with many first place finishes from the nine athletes. We also learned our seventh grade team would be very competitive as they beat the other teams at that meet.

We were having exceptional outings at a variety of league dual track meets and invitationals as we moved into the middle of April. Our ninth grade team was undefeated and seemed to be coasting to another league championship. But Jerry and I began to notice the attendance of four of the nine athletes was very spotty. We also noted that these four athletes were usually absent on the same days. They would all come to practice after being absent and give a variety of excuses such as being ill or having a doctor or dentist appointment. It got to the point that we demanded they bring us notes from their parents. After making this demand, the attendance got better; however, within two weeks, these four were absent at the beginning of the week before the next-to-last track meet of the season. When they returned to practice the next day, they gave us the same excuses as before and did not bring notes. Jerry and I chewed them out about the example they were setting for the younger athletes and threatened them with suspension from the team if their attendance pattern continued.

The high school track facility was located near the high school on the edge of the bluff overlooking downtown Lewiston. Just below the track was the YMCA, which had an outdoor pool located next to the YMCA building. You could look down on the YMCA building and the pool from the edge of the north side of the track.

The very next day, which was the day before our track meet, they were absent again. On this particular day, which was early in May, it was warm and very pleasant with the temperature in the mid-70s. Having taken attendance and noting that four of the ninth grade athletes were absent, we began practice. Since this was the last practice before the meet, our workout was going to be light. After doing their stretches and running a few laps to warm up, I took the 4×100 relay teams to the north end of the track to work on baton handoffs. While I was working with them, I could hear some hooting and howling coming from the area of the YMCA pool. Curious, I walked over to the bluff and looked down on the pool. There below were my four ninth grade track athletes frolicking in the pool with a couple of other young people. I was shocked! Here were four of my best athletes, part of a team that could possibly win another track championship, disdaining the important practice before a big track meet to go for a swim in the YMCA pool. After consulting with Jerry, we were both convinced these four had skipped practices on other days in the past in order to pursue their own pleasures. It was clear to us as coaches that the track team came second to the pursuit of their own agendas. We were now faced with the difficult question of what to do.

This situation introduced me to one of the most difficult decisions any coach has to face, which is whether or not to suspend an athlete, or in this case athletes, from a team. Removing these four would negatively impact the whole ninth grade track team. Here was a team, capable of winning a league championship, but rendered impotent by the irresponsibility of some of its team members. Our strategy was to confront the four athletes with their absences when they came to school. If they were open and honest with us about playing hooky and going for a swim, we would suspend them from the afternoon track meet. But if they lied to us about the reason for their absences, we would remove them from the team for the rest of the season, which would cost the team a possible league championship.

Before noon the next day, Jerry and I were able to contact each athlete and question him about his absence. In every case, they gave us the same excuses we had heard regarding previous absences. One said he was sick while another said he had a dentist appointment. One said he had to work at home and the other said he had a doctor's appointment. After consulting with Jerry and talking with Mr. Walker during lunch, we decided to remove all four athletes from the team.

As the head coach, it was my responsibility to break the news to the athletes. Just before the end of lunch I pulled all four athletes into my classroom and confronted them with the fact that Mr. Bafus and I had seen them at the YMCA pool during practice, and that Mr. Bafus and I were not accepting their excuses, as they contradicted what we saw with our own eyes. I also told them we believed that many of the other excuses they had made during the season were equally as fraudulent as the ones they gave for this absence. I communicated my disappointment with their conduct and lack of integrity. I also told them that the consequences of their actions would definitely have a negative impact on the other five ninth grade athletes remaining on the team. They would have to forego any possible chance at a league championship.

Their response to our decision to remove them from the team was amazing. There was no remorse and no apologies. They listened with blank, dispassionate faces and made no effort to contradict the decision. Only one of them had a response: "Well, we'll be able to go swimming every afternoon now," he said. "Is that all you want to tell us?"

I responded, "Yes, that is all I have to say." They left my room laughing and joking about the whole situation.

As a rookie coach, I was surprised by their responses. As an athlete who played basketball in college, I took great pride in being a viable part of the basketball team. I wanted to be at every practice to better my skills and enhance the skills of my team. I never thought about skipping practice and neither did any of my teammates. Here were some incredibly gifted athletes throwing away the opportunity to develop their talents and possibly hone them to the point where they could be a state track champion just to go swimming in the afternoons. One thing I noted was that these gifted athletes never made much of an impact at the high school. I don't think they ever competed in track again.

I had a hard time understanding this attitude, and yet it would rear its head throughout my teaching, coaching, and administrative career. If I focused on those attitudes and those situations, coaching and teaching would have been discouraging and I would have given it up. However, it was the responses of the five remaining ninth grade athletes on the team that inspired and encouraged Jerry and I. Surprisingly, when we told them four of their teammates had been removed from the team, there was an attitude of relief. "Well, it's about time. They've been slacking since last year," some of them said.

"They don't deserve to be on this team! We can still win some events and score well at the league meet," others said. "You did the right thing, coach!"

When we got to the league championship meet, we placed the five remaining athletes in the maximum number of events possible and they competed admirably. They worked hard at practices and performed well at the meet, going well beyond our expectations.

They were an inspiration to the lower-classmen and to Jerry and me. They also went on to make a difference at the high school level, where they all excelled. It was the attitude of these athletes and many others like them that kept Jerry and me in the teaching and coaching fields.

CHAPTER 17

Another Summer

> *The road down to Lewiston from the Palouse is a switchback road that drops about two thousand feet. A heavily loaded truck could easily gain enough speed to make navigating the switchback turns impossible, potentially causing a crash, losing the peas and possibly killing the driver. The instructor had me gear down to third gear and maintain my speed at approximately fifteen miles per hour with the help of the brakes.*

My second year as a teacher came to a close much like the first year. Student effort declined as we approached the end of the year, and I struggled to keep most of the students motivated. It was during the last month in algebra that we tackled the more difficult topics such as the quadratic formula for solving quadratic equations, defining and simplifying imaginary numbers, and dealing with irrational numbers and simplifying radical expressions. I found grades dropped dramatically as the school year wound down—but especially during this last month. Many of the students didn't seem to care and just wanted the school year to end. I have to admit I was tempted to take the same attitude, but I felt it was my duty to do my best until the final bell on the last day sounded. So I gave assignments, reviewed material, and administered tests right up to the last day.

As happened the previous year, staff members were assigned supervisory roles for closing out the year. On the last day, we were busy collecting textbooks, issuing fines, and supervising students as they cleaned out their lockers. When the bell rang to end the day, we went to our assigned areas to supervise the students as they left. Again, I was assigned the outside entrance to the school, which I wisely supervised from inside the door rather than outside. I noticed Mr. Walker had assigned the four new teachers to outside duty as well. It was fun watching them dodge water balloons and buckets of water as the students doused all who got near them. Two of the new staff members got involved in the water activities, subduing a couple of students carrying armfuls of water balloons, and—once they had taken the balloons—targeting students around them. After a few accurate attacks, the students around these staff members quickly vacated the area, which made their supervisory duties more manageable. I hadn't really thought about that approach last year, but it appeared to be working for them.

Once all the students were gone from the grounds, most of the staff again gathered in the teachers' lounge to stare at each other and come to grips with the idea that the school year was finally over. I would discover during my career as a teacher and administrator that those feelings of fatigue—and thankfulness another school year was over—were always present after the last student left the building and summer vacation was about to begin. When I got to that point, I always wondered if I could go through another year of dealing with junior high students again. It was amazing what a summer break could do, though. I always found I was full of anticipation and excitement when the summer was over and I was facing a new school year. The summer was just what I needed to re-energize myself and get ready for another year of teaching kids.

This summer was going to be different from the previous one. Marty and I were struggling to make ends meet financially, and I knew I needed to find a way to make more money during the summer months. I decided to sit out from graduate school and see if there was any summer work out there to make us more money. During the year, I found that several of the teachers at Jenifer Junior High worked for Twin City Foods driving combines, swathers, and trucks to help bring in the pea harvest during middle to late summer.

Twin City Foods had a processing plant south of the Clearwater River in Lewiston that processed sweet peas by sorting, packaging, and freezing them. A number of the farms within thirty miles of the Lewiston valley raised peas and sold them to Twin City Foods. Most of the farming was dry land farming with little irrigation provided unless a farm was located near the Snake or Clearwater Rivers. The farm ground north of Lewiston on the Palouse was especially rich, and in most cases they received just enough moisture to yield excellent crops of peas and wheat. Twin City Foods contracted with many of these farmers and provided the swathers, combines, and trucks to bring in the harvest each summer. All the farmers had to do was prepare the ground and plant the peas.

When harvest was going hot and heavy, which was usually the first of July until the middle of August, the processing plant would work two twelve-hour shifts. They would usually hire temporary workers to drive the trucks, swathers, and combines, and to man the processing lines in the plant. The pay was $7 to $8 per hour depending on experience, and there were opportunities for overtime if you had enough tenure with the company. The administrators who managed the harvesting indicated they liked to hire teachers because they were more reliable, so I decided to apply to drive a truck for the summer harvest.

When I applied for a job at Twin City Foods, the human resource employee who took my application indicated there were jobs available to drive a truck, and I should get a commercial driver's license if I was interested in the job. He also told me that as an entry-level employee, I would be assigned to the night shift and would be promoted to the day shift as I gained experience and tenure.

I obtained my commercial license by the middle of June and provided it to the human resource representative at the plant, who told me they would call me to work when the need arose. He said the night shift usually did not begin until well into the month of July.

While waiting for the pea harvest to begin, I again umpired Babe Ruth baseball games in the evening. I figured I could umpire two games a night at $10 per game until they called me to harvest. The umpiring and harvesting schedules would overlap a little in July, but I thought I could make it all work without having to give up either job. I thought I could work the night shift at Twin City Foods for a month and a half and umpire Babe Ruth games and still make more money than I did the previous summer going to graduate school and umpiring. During the month of June, my only job was umpiring in the evenings, so I had most of the day to work around the house, do a little fishing, and get some much-needed rest.

Umpiring went somewhat better this year since the parents and coaches had dealt with me the previous summer and knew what to expect. Overall, the experience was a positive one and I was able to make an extra $500, which was much needed.

There was, however, one athlete and his supportive group of parents who added a negative note to an otherwise perfect baseball season. This particular athlete was an eighth grader from Sacajawea Junior High who thought he was a gifted baseball player and, specifically, the ultimate pitcher.

I took notice of him the first time I umpired his team and he was the starting pitcher. As the game began I could see he was a sharp pitcher—he could throw a good fastball and he was one of the few who could throw a curveball. During the first few innings of the game, he threw a number of strikes using his fastball and curveball, mowing down the batters with only one batter getting a hit. Then in the top of the fourth inning, when he began to tire, he went into a wild streak, missing the strike zone badly and walking the first two players he faced.

During the first three innings, I noticed his parents and supporters yelling encouragement when he threw strikes or made a good play. I also noticed they would give me a bad time when they thought I missed a strike or a call on the bases.

He maintained his poise well and his parents were not behaving any more inappropriately than any of the other parents. That is, until the fourth inning. After he walked the first two batters in the fourth inning, the demeanor of both the parents and their son changed dramatically. When the next batter came to bat, his first pitch missed the plate badly and I called it a ball. His parents went ballistic, calling me a variety of names laced with some mild profanity. These comments were vile compared to what they were yelling the first three innings. Their comments also affected the demeanor of the pitcher. Instead of maintaining his poise and returning to the mound, he stood in front of the mound and glared at me.

"Let's play ball!" I called out, and he dramatically stalked back to the mound where he glared in for the sign from the catcher.

He delivered his next pitch, which was also off the plate, and I again called a ball. His parents went off on me once more, and he paused again to glare at me after the catcher returned the ball to him.

After getting the sign, he threw in a fastball, which was in the strike zone, so I called it a strike. A derisive cheer rose from his supporters after the call. The next two balls were wide of the plate and in the dirt, which gave a walk to the batter, loading the bases with no outs. The pitcher's team was ahead five to zero, so tensions rose with the loading of the bases.

The next batter came to the plate, and after the pitcher got the sign from the catcher, he delivered the pitch, which clipped the batter on the arm, forcing in a run for the opposing team. I was happy to note I was not being blamed for that infraction by the pitcher. The score was now five to one still with no outs. The next batter came to the plate, and the pitcher threw a curve that was just high of the strike zone, which I called a ball. With that call, the parents went wild again, yelling all kinds of profanity at me. I glanced over at the pitcher, who stood in front of the mound yelling some comments at me as well.

"TIME!" I roared.

I walked out to the mound and looked the pitcher in the eye.

"Look, I can't let you yell at me like that," I said, just loud enough so only he could hear. "If you do it again, I will toss you from this game. You just need to calm down and throw strikes. I guarantee you I'll call them strikes if they are in the strike zone. I want you to be just as successful as I want the batter at the plate to be. Take a deep breath and let's play ball."

As I spoke, he just glared into my eyes. His parents were also yelling in the background as I tried to calm things down.

After talking to the pitcher, I walked over to the parents and told them they needed to tone it down or I would have to ask them to leave. They really got upset at this, saying I had no right to kick them out since they were just spectators.

"If I have to kick you out and you refuse to leave, I will forfeit the game to your opponent," I responded. "So my advice is: don't let it get to that point. All you need to do is stop the insults and profanity. There are children here watching the game, and what you are doing is totally inappropriate for them."

This seemed to calm the situation down some. I went back behind the plate and called out, "Play ball!" The inning continued with the pitcher doing a better job of throwing strikes and keeping his poise. But the other team was able to score four more runs because of another walk and a double that cleared the bases. The score was five to five after the last out of the inning.

At the beginning of the game, heavy clouds moved into the area, and by the start of the fourth inning, it was beginning to drizzle. For this to be called a complete game we would have to finish out five innings. The pitcher of the other team had regained some of his earlier form as the home team came to bat and was able to hold them scoreless in the bottom of the fourth inning. As we moved into the top of the fifth, the drizzle changed to a steady rain. I called out, "Play ball!" as soon as the pitcher had warmed up, hoping to get five innings in before the rain got so bad I had to call the game.

The pitcher did a credible job in the top of the fifth, but his opponents scored one run on a walk and a double. At the start of the last half of the fifth inning, the score was six to five. The pitcher's team came to bat, but as we moved through the lineup, the rain fell harder. The pitcher's team was able to get men on second and third with two outs when the pitcher came to bat. The rain fell even harder as he stepped into the box, and I knew he was probably going to be the last batter before I would have to call the game because of the rain. The first pitch was on the outside corner and I called it a strike. He turned in the batter's box and glared at me as his parents and supporters returned to shouting insults and profanities. The next pitch was a ball low and away. The third pitch was right down the middle and he swung at it and missed. The count was one ball and two strikes, and the rain was really heavy now. I also noticed several of his supporters had gravitated to the backstop behind me to see if I were making the right calls. Because of the rain and situation, I chose to ignore this and focus on making the calls that would keep the game moving.

The next pitch was very close to the outside edge of the plate and I called out the third strike.

"You're out of there!" I yelled.

As I made the call, I quickly pulled the chest protector off and held it over my head, running through the gate next to the dugout to my car, which was about forty yards away, to get out of the rain that was now coming down in sheets. As I made my way to my car, the pitcher and his followers jogged after me, yelling insults and profanities and totally ignoring the rain. When I got to the car, I jumped in, both shutting and locking the door. Amazingly, the four or five supporters and this pitcher stood next to my car in a drenching rain, shaking their fists at me and cussing me out. I simply started the car, backed out of the parking space, and drove away. I looked in the rearview mirror as I drove off, and they were still standing there in the downpour yelling their insults at my fading car. I was comforted by the fact that I was somewhat wet, but not nearly as soaked as those people.

Later in the season I had a chance to talk to the coach of that pitcher's team, asking him about him and the boy's family.

"This boy is a good athlete, but his parents have turned him into a prima donna," the coach responded. "He won't take any coaching, and when I have tried to give him some discipline, the parents are all over me. I'm at a loss about what to do with him. The other athletes and parents resent their behavior, and they certainly were not supportive of their actions the night we had that big rain. It's a situation I have to live with, and I don't envy your position when he is pitching. Next year he and his parents will be gone, and that will make coaching for me and umpiring for you much easier."

I only umpired that team a couple of more times, but fortunately he was not the pitcher, although he played in the infield. The parents remembered me, though, and were on my case whenever they had the opportunity. I was quickly finding out there are a few parents out there who believe their child can do no wrong and will stick by them even when their behavior is totally inappropriate. I found this to be true with this Babe Ruth family and with the family of the girl that flipped me off during the school year. Fortunately, there are not many of those parents around, but it only takes one to make your life miserable. To maintain my sanity, I had to focus on the vast majority of kids who were well-behaved and respectful.

As the first of July came and went, I anxiously waited to receive a phone call from Twin City Foods to drive truck for the pea harvest. After the first two weeks of July passed and I had heard nothing from them, I decided to get proactive and went down to the dispatch office to inquire about when I might start working. I also wanted to communicate with them in person so they could put my name with my face.

When I got to the plant, I could see that harvest was in full swing. Trucks were coming into the yard and dumping their loads of fresh green peas and then exiting back to the pea fields. I went into the dispatch office where there were three or four men. One of the men was a teacher at the high school, and we exchanged some pleasantries. He then introduced me to the dispatcher, who greeted me cordially.

"I'm supposedly on the list as a truck driver," I said. "And I was wondering if I could get some idea of when I might start working?"

He grabbed a clipboard and looked down a list of names.

"They told me I probably would work the night shift since I'm new," I offered.

He picked up another clipboard and scanned the list of names.

"Yeah, you're here," he said. "But we will probably not start the night shift for another day or two. You are pretty low on the list, but it looks like you would be the fourth driver called. If we are working two or three fields one of those nights, you will definitely get called in. You need to be patient when it is your first year. Is there anything else I could help you with?"

"No," I replied. "Thanks for talking to me. I hope to see you in the next few days." I returned home hoping they would call before too long.

During the last week of July, after the Babe Ruth season had ended, I finally got a call to come in to work at Twin City Foods. I was to be there at 5 p.m. for some training, and the dispatcher indicated I would probably work from 6 p.m. until 6 a.m. the next morning. I reported promptly on time and was assigned to a day shift truck driver who was going out on his last run. After being introduced, the driver had me get behind the wheel to drive while he provided advice and instruction from the passenger seat.

As I drove the truck to the pea field, which was located just south of Moscow, Idaho, he briefed me on how the truck worked. It was a stick shift with eight gears, including four overdrive gears. He coached me through the shifting pattern as we made our way out of Lewiston and up the Lewiston hill. He said I wouldn't have to use the overdrive gears until I had a full load. I ground the gears a few times as we drove to the field, but had it down by the time we reached our destination. It was early evening when we arrived, but there was enough daylight to see the harvesters. He directed me down a narrow dirt road until we reached the spot where we could enter the field. After entering through the gated fence, he had me park on a hill that had been harvested already where we had a view of three combines harvesting peas.

While we sat on the hill, my instructor explained to me how the harvest worked. Each field had a mechanic, who was the foreman of the harvest crew that usually consisted of a swather, two or three pea harvesters, and at least two trucks. The foreman's job was to keep the harvesters and swathers working and keep the trucks moving to and from the plant. Time was important when it came to harvesting peas—if they weren't harvested at just the right time, they would not be firm or sweet enough for human consumption, which cost the company money. If the peas sat in a truck too long, they could sour, so it was important to get the peas from the field to the plant in an efficient and timely manner.

In the first step in the harvesting process, a swather would begin a field by cutting the pea plants and drawing them into neat, parallel rows from one end of the field to the other. The pronged wheel of the swather pulled the pea plants into the cutters, which cut the peas near ground level. The pronged wheel then funneled the cut plants into a row about four or five feet wide, which would flow from the back of the swather as it moved through the field. Then, the pea harvester would drive down each cut row picking up the pea plants with a pronged roller on the front of the machine. The roller pulled the plants onto a conveyor belt that carried the pea plants up into the guts of the machine. There, the peas were shelled and separated from the rest of the plant. The shelled peas were then conveyed to the harvest bin, which would fill up until there was enough to load onto a truck. The majority of leaves, pods, and stems of the pea plant would then be dispersed out the back of the harvester onto the ground. Usually, one swather worked quickly enough to occupy three harvesters.

He talked for about thirty minutes until another truck full of peas came by and the driver said, "You're up!" Just then, a red light on a pole above the driver of a harvester combine began to flash, and he instructed me to move out to take on a load of peas.

My instructor told me to pull the truck to the right of the combine and hang back until the driver dropped the conveyer belt arm of the harvester, which is located under the bin holding the harvested peas. The truck always takes the load on the downhill side of the harvester. The truck moves under the lowered arm as the harvester continues harvesting, matching speed with the harvester. After the peas have been dispatched to the truck, the harvester driver raises the arm and turns off his blinking red light, which indicates he is unloaded. The driver then angles away from the harvester, and moves back up on the hill to wait for another blinking light. My trainer told me if the harvest is good, a truck obtains a full load of peas in about forty-five minutes to an hour. The states of Washington and Idaho limit the tonnage the pea trucks can carry, and that was usually reached in four harvester loads.

The field foreman monitored the combines and trucks, providing maintenance and repairs if there was a breakdown. The foreman also had a radio to maintain contact with the dispatch office at the plant. When a truck filled, the driver notified the foreman and the foreman dispatched the truck back to the plant, letting the office know it was leaving the field. The process was coordinated in a way to ensure there was always a truck in the field to unload the harvesters.

After we had filled the truck, I drove over to the field foreman, who dispatched us back to the plant. This was one of the first times I'd ever driven a large, heavily loaded truck. The instructor coached me to be careful as we reached the top of the Lewiston hill.

The road down to Lewiston from the Palouse is a switchback road that drops about two thousand feet. A heavily loaded truck could easily gain enough speed to make navigating the switchback turns impossible, potentially causing a crash, losing the peas and possibly killing the driver. The instructor had me gear down to third gear and maintain my speed at approximately fifteen miles per hour with the help of the brakes. He cautioned me to refrain from braking if possible since the brakes could easily heat up.

Following his instructions, I was safely able to reach the bottom of the hill and then make my way to the plant. As we came down the hill, he pointed out escape ramps located at key spots on the hill.

"If you lose control, you want to guide the truck onto the escape ramp, which is full of deep sand or gravel," he said. "It will quickly bring you to a stop. Of course, you will have to be towed out, and the peas would spoil by the time that happens and you would be laid off for the remainder of the season. My advice is don't lose control of the truck."

When we got to the plant, he directed me to the weigh station and then to the loading dock where he showed me how to raise the bed of the truck to unload the peas. After the peas were unloaded, we returned to the weigh station attendant, who gave us a paper documenting the weight of the peas that were unloaded, which was recorded at the dispatch office.

After turning in the slip, the dispatcher asked the trainer if I was good to go.

"He'll do fine," the man replied.

So off I went back to the field once more, this time by myself. That night I made three hauls with no serious incidents and was sent home about 4:30 a.m. On the last haul, I was extremely tired and had to fight falling asleep while driving. I drove with all the windows open, which I think helped keep me awake. I was glad to get home and fall into bed.

The next afternoon, they called me again to come in and drive at 6 p.m. This time, I was dispatched to a different field, which was near Pullman, Washington. I had some trouble finding the field even though the dispatcher had given me written instructions on how to get there. I pulled into the field just as a full truck left and one of the combines was signaling it needed to dump its load. I drove right to the truck, unloaded it, and went to a spot in the field where I could see the other combines. The field foreman drove over to me and chewed me out for not getting to the field in a timely manner. I apologized and worked the rest of the night to keep things running smoothly. When I returned to the field after bringing my first load to the plant, one of the combines was down and the mechanic was busy trying to repair it. He needed a part, which I brought back from the plant after my second run. That night was pretty hectic, but I was finally sent home about 4 a.m.

I was able to work about ten hours each night for eight days straight before things began to slow down. After that stretch, I went three days without a call before being brought in again for three more short nights. Again after that stretch, I went four days without a call. I was still looking forward to getting a few more nights of work, so I called the dispatcher, who said the harvest was about over and the day shift would handle the rest of the season.

My short time harvesting peas came to an end with me having worked fourteen days and earning about $800. Since I had not worked a full thirty days, I did not have to pay union dues, so I was extremely happy in that regard; however, I was frustrated about not getting more work. I knew working the full harvest would give me just enough money to make ends meet. So I determined to work harvest during the next few summers to gain some tenure so I could work the day shift and make enough money to meet that goal. I considered this particular summer barely a success with the money I made from umpiring baseball games and working the pea harvest. But when the middle of August came, I was energized and ready for another school year teaching math and coaching track and basketball.

CHAPTER 18

General Math Foolishness

> *About halfway through the process of grading the assignment, I looked back at John to check on him and saw an amazing thing. His forehead, cheeks, and mouth were beet red and the rest of his head was bone white. I stood up in alarm and started back to his seat.*

The 1973-74 school year started just like the previous one. I was again assigned four algebra classes and two ninth grade math classes. I was also designated as the ninth grade JV basketball coach and the track coach. Like last year, we had one day to prepare for the start of the semester, which included a teachers' meeting where new staff members were introduced and policies reviewed. One of the new staff members was a gentleman by the name of Mr. K.C. Albright, who would be teaching science. He was young and enthusiastic about teaching. We gravitated towards each other as the year progressed, developing a collaborative friendship.

We spent time together during lunches and after school during this year, and during our discussions I found he had served in the military and went into teaching after his service just like I did. He and I both liked sports, especially basketball, football, and baseball; and by the end of the next summer, we were both attending classes at the University of Idaho seeking degrees in secondary education administration.

On that first day of orientation, I found he had been assigned as an assistant football coach and was interested in coaching basketball as well. During the year, he and I bounced teaching ideas off each other and voiced our concerns for programs that seemed to take away from the learning of our students. My relationship with Mr. Albright had a positive impact in forming my general philosophy of education and on my view of junior high school students.

After our preparation day, the school year began with a vengeance. I found the majority of my classes were extremely large, totaling 182 students to start the school year. Two of my algebra classes had more than 40 students enrolled. The two general math classes averaged about 24 students per class, which was just about right. These averages would change dramatically by February when students from the algebra classes opted to transfer to the general math classes because they were failing the course.

I spent the first day of class assigning seats and developing my seating chart for each class. It took me about two weeks to get all 182 names and faces down so I could call on them without having to refer to the seating chart.

Overall, the year went smoothly, but there were several incidents and circumstances that stood out in my general math classes that helped me grow and mature as a professional teacher.

One in particular involved a disruptive student in my second period general math class. I was having difficulty keeping this student focused and on task. He wanted to talk a lot and usually became defiant when confronted. During one particular lesson, I had to stop my presentation twice to ask him to stop talking. After the second time, I jumped on him pretty hard verbally.

"You need to stop talking while I'm talking," I shot at him. "If you continue disrupting the lesson, I will have to give you a detention."

I stared him down as I said this, and he defiantly returned my gaze. I often found this duel of eyes to be a student's last-ditch effort to control the situation. The loser of the confrontation was usually the one who looked away first.

In this situation I was determined to win, so I held his obstinate gaze silently until he looked away. I then turned to the chalkboard to continue my lecture. As I started to write, I heard a collective gasp from the group of students sitting around him. I quickly whirled back around to confront the student.

"Do you have something more you want to say to me?"

He just smiled at me as if nothing was wrong.

"No!" he responded.

One of the things I had learned in education classes and through experience up to this point was to have eyes in the back of my head. An effective teacher needs to notice everything and develop an entire bag of tricks to have an edge in dealing with junior high students. I knew I had to try to create the impression that students couldn't get away with anything in my classroom. They needed to worry that they still might get caught even when they thought I couldn't see what they were doing.

With this in mind, I remembered the door to my classroom had a large window set in it for security reasons. Usually, only a few of the lights in the hall were lit, leaving the hallway much darker than the classroom. If I got a peek at the window at just the right angle, I could see my class reflected in the glass—just like looking in a mirror. The students, of course, were totally unaware of this.

Having used this method of "developing eyes in the back of my head" in a previous class, I moved to the portion of the board where I could see this particular young man as a reflection in that door window. To him, it would appear that my back was to him, but from my perspective, I could clearly see him in the makeshift mirror. I turned back toward the board once more, keeping an eye on the window. What I saw was what I had suspected had occurred—he was boldly holding his right fist over his head with the middle finger extended. I was learning fast that this gesture represented the ultimate symbol of disrespect and defiance for some of the children. This was the second time in two years that gesture had been made towards me.

With my back turned to him, I paused writing on the chalkboard.

"Young man," I said, "if you flip me off again when I turn my back, I will personally come back there and physically haul you to the office!"

I turned toward the class and looked at him, "Do you understand me?"

The students around him were grinning and several laughed out loud as his face turned beet red.

"I didn't flip you off, Mr. Hammann," he insisted. "Honest! How could you possibly think I would do such a thing?"

"I know you did it, because I saw you. When I turned to the board, you lifted your right hand, made a fist, and extended your middle finger with a nasty smile on your face. Again, did you understand what I just said?"

He paused a minute.

"Yes..." he finally said with reluctance.

"Okay! Now that we have an understanding, let's get back to the lesson."

I found him to be very attentive from that point until the end of the lecture. I also made sure to make my way to his desk as I moved around the room assisting students with the assignment. I asked in a friendly manner if he needed any help on the homework, making no reference to our confrontation during the lecture. I was trying to communicate our confrontation was not personal and it would not affect my availability to him nor my respect for him. This appeared to have a positive affect on our relationship for the rest of the year. There were still times when I had to address some disruptive behavior and talking on his part, but it was less frequent and his responses were less defiant and disrespectful.

I found my effectiveness as a teacher greatly increased as I developed this hyperawareness of what went on in the classroom. I found it important to confront inappropriate behavior immediately when it was identified.

There was another incident that occurred in a general math class during the year that helped me fine-tune this hyperawareness. It took place during the second semester of the year. Three new students were assigned to my first period ninth grade math class. One of the students was a tall, gangly, likable young man named John, who appeared to have a very laid back demeanor. When he came into my class, I assigned him the seat in the back right corner of the room.

Just in front of him, I seated another new student named Bill. He was about six feet tall and weighed around 210 pounds, without an ounce of fat on him. With what seemed like muscles everywhere, it was evident he lifted weights and was physically stronger than anyone else in the room—including me. When he took his seat the first day, I could see he was intimidating to the other male students and attractive to the female students. Even I felt somewhat intimidated by his size and evident strength. But after having him in class for a week, I found he was soft spoken and not the least intimidating in his demeanor. He told me he was transferring from Sacajawea Junior High, where he had played football and wrestled.

The addition of these three students did not appear to have a negative affect on the class until about two weeks after they arrived. On this particular day, I came into class right after the bell rang. As

I moved to my desk at the front of the room, I noticed most of the students were quietly visiting as they waited for me. The peculiar thing was that every student had a toothpick in his or her mouth. I also noticed that three of the students were out of their seats, standing around John, who was seated at his desk at the back of the room. One of those three was Bill.

I walked back to see what they were up too and to ask them to be seated so we could begin the day. When I got there, I saw John was holding a small one-pint canning jar containing a number of toothpicks sitting in about an inch of fluid.

"What have you got there?" I asked him.

"These are cinnamon oil toothpicks," he said. "Do you want to try one?"

Initially, they didn't appear to be anything threatening, disruptive, or unsafe, so I took one and put it in my mouth. Sure enough it brought the taste of cinnamon to my mouth.

"Did you give one to all the students?" I asked with a look at John. "Is that what I'm seeing?"

"Yes! I thought it would make a nice change to the class. Is it okay?"

"Sure. As long as it is not disruptive."

I asked the three standing students to return to their seats and I moved back to the front of the room to take roll. By this point in the year, I could take roll by looking to see which chairs were vacant. I looked out at the class after taking roll and was alarmed to see John raising the canning jar to his lips and drinking the cinnamon oil in the jar containing the toothpicks.

"John, what in the world are you doing drinking that cinnamon oil?"

"Bill said he would give me $5 if I would drink all of it," John responded.

"And remember you can't get a drink or leave the room if you want to get paid!" Bill chimed in.

"John, that stuff is caustic," I said. "Are you okay?"

"Sure, I'm fine," he said pleasantly. Without a second thought, I instructed the students to get started with class.

"Everyone exchange papers with the person next to you so we can get them graded."

About halfway through the process of grading the assignment, I looked back at John to check on him and saw an amazing thing. His forehead, cheeks, and mouth were beet red and the rest of his head was bone white. I stood up in alarm and started back to his seat.

"John, are you all right?" I asked fervently.

He could barely croak out his answer.

"Sure. I'm okay!" The contrasting red and white parts of his face and his low, raspy voice clearly said the opposite.

"John, come out to the hall. I want to talk to you."

John got out of his chair and moved quickly to the exit. As he passed Bill, I could hear Bill mutter out of the side of his mouth, "Remember, you can't get a drink or throw up if you want the money."

I followed him out into the hall, closed the classroom door, and asked him again if he was okay.

He dropped all pretenses and bent over, grabbing his stomach with one hand and his head with the other.

"I think I'm going to die!" he groaned. "My stomach really hurts and I think I'm going to throw up!"

I touched him on the shoulder and said, "Get down to the bathroom and then meet me in the office. I'm going to call the hospital."

He immediately began shuffling toward the bathroom, bent over and gagging. After looking into the classroom and telling the students to look over the lesson in the book while I was gone, I broke into a jog heading for the stairs.

"How could I let something like this happen?" I thought as I made my way to the office. I'm going to get sued over this. He looked like death warmed over, and he is probably in the bathroom right now heaving out his guts. I might lose my job for letting a kid bring cinnamon toothpicks into the classroom! How could I not foresee this? I would eventually learn it is impossible to foresee everything. Some junior high students have fantastic imaginations and don't hesitate to act on them.

When I got to the office, I could see Mr. Walker was out so told the secretary what had happened and asked to call the hospital. She grimaced at me and pushed her phone over, pointing at the notice under her phone that had the local hospital phone number. I quickly dialed the number and was directed to a nurse after telling the hospital receptionist my dilemma. I quickly outlined the situation to the nurse.

"What ever you do don't let him throw up," she said. "Cinnamon oil is caustic and it will burn his esophagus going down and then again when it comes up. Have him drink a lot of water and then get him over to the hospital." I said okay and hung up.

My thoughts were really whirling now. How in the world do you stop someone from throwing up when they were already gagging as they ran to the bathroom? He was probably still in the bathroom emptying his stomach, I thought. I'm really in trouble now. Just then, John came into the office looking very pale, but he looked better than he had in the classroom. At least now his head and face were all white and not contrasting shades of red and white.

"Well, I threw it up," he said. "I thought I would never stop throwing up, but I'm feeling some better now. The only thing now is that my stomach and throat really burn." I instructed him to get down to the drinking fountain and drink as much water as he could.

"Then come back here. We are going to take you to the hospital."

As he moved to the drinking fountain in the hallway, Mr. Walker came into the office and I briefed him on the situation. He said he would take it from there and that I should get back to my classroom. I was certainly glad to turn this over to him so I could return to my unsupervised students.

I quickly walked back to class to find the students talking excitedly. As I entered the room, they deluged me with questions.

"What happened?"

"Is he okay?"

"Did he throw up or drink any water?" Bill asked loudly. "He knows he won't get paid if he did!"

"Everything is fine," I said, calming the murmur somewhat. "He was able to get the cinnamon oil out of his stomach and he did need to drink a lot of water to dilute the oil and minimize any harmful effects it might cause. And yes, Bill, he did throw up and did drink a lot of water. I want you to know that what you did was totally inappropriate. You are not to make wagers of that kind in this class again."

It took a few minutes to get everyone calmed down, but finally we were able to get through grading the papers and reviewing the new material. When class ended, the students left buzzing about the cinnamon incident.

At lunch, I had a chance to talk to the secretary about John and she indicated he was back in school. His mom had been called, and she met Mr. Walker and her son at the hospital, where she took custody of him and supervised his treatment. She called the office later to say the hospital had administered a liquid to him to neutralize the acidity of the oil, and it looked like he would be okay. I was relieved to hear this, and the information certainly helped the rest of my day go better.

The next day when John returned to class, I pulled him out in the hall and talked to him about the situation. I emphasized he should not make a bet to do something that might jeopardize his health or safety and to do so was just stupid. He said he understood and would make sure it didn't happen again. He apologized for his actions, which was good to hear.

Two weeks later, I heard from another student he had made a $2 bet with a fellow wood shop student to put his hand in a wood vice and allow another student to tighten it down. Needless to say, John had not learned his lesson, and I was worried he wouldn't graduate from high school alive—or without being maimed. In the teachers' lounge we talked about John and his willingness to do almost anything to get attention. Some students are like that—they will risk life and limb to be recognized by their peers, and many of their peers are very willing to encourage them to be that risky.

I learned I needed to stay on top of every situation regarding students under my supervision. And while I am not a fortuneteller, I also learned I needed to be able to try and predict all possible outcomes of every decision I made regarding student behavior. Sometimes, it may appear there is not a safety or health issue with something a student has or is doing, but it is best to err on the side of keeping students safe rather than ignoring the situation. This tempered my willingness to be too experimental or permissive.

CHAPTER 19

A Unique Basketball Season And Some Startling Surprises

> *If that wasn't humiliating enough, as soon as the horn sounded to end the game, the Pomeroy coach and his players ran into their locker room. The coach didn't come to shake my hand and he didn't provide the opportunity for his players to shake the hands of my players, which was always a tradition between the players and coaches of the teams we had played in the past.*

The fall semester of the 1973-74 school year went well in the classroom, and our football teams did well on the playing field. We were fast approaching the basketball season, and I was looking forward to another season coaching a fresh batch of JV ninth graders.

The tryouts for the ninth grade varsity basketball team began the first week of November. Mr. Crosby and I again collaborated on the drills and activities we would run during the week of tryouts. Again during the first hour of tryouts, we decided to break the athletes into small groups to work on shooting, dribbling, rebounding, and defensive drills. The last half of practice would be focused on scrimmaging so we could see their individual skills under pressure and their abilities to work as a team.

It was clearly evident from the tryouts that the talent pool was pretty small after the top eight players were removed. It looked like the varsity team would be fairly strong, but not too deep. It was clear to me the junior varsity team was really going to be lacking in talent. I would be hard pressed to have a decent ball handler, I didn't have any really good outside shooters, and we wouldn't have any height. After dividing the athletes up, the varsity had twelve players with only eight really good players. The ninth grade JV team was down to just sixteen players, who were all about the same ability. We were going to spend a lot of time working on shooting and playing defense. Our offensive patterns would have to be very disciplined and simple so we could get short jump shots or layups. I could see it was going to be a long season.

The season opened with a game against our archrival, the Sacajawea Savages. Amazingly, we won a very close game mostly because of our defense and our ability to force them to turn the ball over. They were just as weak as we were in shooting, and it was our defense that carried the day.

As the season progressed, we lost more games than we won, but the athletes loved the game and we were close as a team. We got a break in December when Coach Crosby sent down one of his players who was not getting much playing time. He was struggling with the pressure of being in a game and made a lot of mistakes. So Coach Crosby sent him down to the JV team, where he would get more playing time and maybe be able to come out of his nervousness whenever he got in a game. We were glad to get him—he had more talent than anyone else on my team. Although he still choked a lot when he got into a game, he was a positive addition. Every time we got together to practice or to play a game, I challenged them to work hard and give it their best effort, and they always responded. I watched them grow and improve and by the end of the season, our team had really shaped up.

One pair of games stood out to me from that season. Mr. Crosby scheduled all the basketball games for seventh, eighth, and ninth grades—including the JV games. Many schools did not have a JV team for the seventh, eighth, and ninth grades, so he tried to schedule games with some of the smaller districts in the area which were often 1A, 2A, or B-level schools, compared to Lewiston's 3A designation.

The little prairie town of Pomeroy, Washington, was located about thirty-five miles west of Lewiston on Highway 12. The school district was classified as a B-level school in the state of Washington, but had tried on numerous occasions to schedule varsity freshman basketball games with the big city junior high schools of Jenifer and Sacajawea. But each year, the ninth grade varsity teams of both schools filled their state-allotted number of games with commitments to the larger school districts and were unable to schedule games with Pomeroy.

With the new JV programs, Jenifer was now looking for more games for the ninth grade JV team because many of the bigger schools in Clarkston, Washington; Grangeville, Idaho; and Orofino, Idaho, did not field such teams. On this particular year, Mr. Crosby was able to schedule two games with Pomeroy, but the Pomeroy coach was adamant both games had to be played in Pomeroy. Mr. Crosby was eager to give us a full slate of games, so he agreed. The games were scheduled one week apart, with the first occurring during the second week of January.

So on a cold, sunny day in January, we loaded up our bus and made our way to Pomeroy for our first game with this small-town team. I had no idea what to expect. I didn't know much about the community or the school district. I knew it was an agricultural community that raised mostly wheat, and the main grain storage facility for the surrounding farms was located there. I had also heard the people in Pomeroy were rabid basketball fans, as were all B-level schools in eastern Washington.

After driving the thirty-five miles to the school over some snowy roads, we finally reached our destination. We eventually found the school and pulled up behind the gymnasium near the locker room entrances. I told the boys to stay in the bus until I had a chance to see where our locker room was.

As I entered the boys' locker room, a janitor who was cleaning the showers greeted me. I identified myself as the JV coach from Lewiston, and he said our team would be dressing in the girls' locker room. He showed me how to get there, and then he left me to bring my team in and get them ready for the game. When Mr. Crosby scheduled the game, he had been assured the school would provide us with towels to use on the bench and when we showered after the game, but I did not see any towels anywhere in the locker room. So I told the boys to get dressed while I looked for some towels.

There was a door at one end of the locker room that had "gym" written on it. I could hear a number of basketballs bouncing from behind the door, so I pushed through the door to see what activities were going on and to see if I could get some assistance.

As I walked into the gym, I saw about ten boys bouncing balls and shooting at the three baskets hanging from the ceiling at one end of the floor. They were all wearing basketball uniforms that said "Pomeroy Pirates" on the front. Their heads were shaved, and two of the boys were very tall. One looked to be six-feet, four-inches tall and the other appeared to be six-foot-two. Two of the shorter players were dribbling around the court, whipping the balls behind their backs and under their legs as they went. As I moved across the floor, the six-foot-four boy drove to the basket and dunked the ball with two hands. I looked on with astonishment, thinking that our team was in real trouble. We didn't have anyone over five-foot-eleven, and I didn't have anyone that could dribble under pressure, much less dribble behind his back and between his legs. I didn't even have someone who could touch the rim, much less make a two-handed dunk. And the shaved heads indicated a high level of discipline and commitment that I knew my team did not have.

Over by the chairs set up along the north side of the court for the teams was a tall, redheaded man wearing a polo shirt that had "Pomeroy Pirates" printed over the pocket. Thinking he was the coach, I moved over to him and extended my hand.

"Hi!" I said pleasantly "My name is Bob Hammann, and I am the coach of the Jenifer ninth grade team. Are you the freshman coach?"

I was hesitant to say I was the coach of the Jenifer Burros or the Jenifer Jacks, since I was still trying to come to grips with our mascot. I was already feeling intimidated by what I was seeing and didn't want to give him or his team any more motivation to beat us because of a less-than-macho mascot.

He turned, took my hand, and shook it curtly.

"Yes, I'm the freshman coach," he said gruffly. "What can I do for you?"

There was absolutely no friendliness in his voice, and he didn't even bother to introduce himself. That piqued my anger a little bit. Who did this guy think he was?

Nevertheless, I tried to maintain a friendly attitude.

"Well, we were told there would be towels available for showering and for use on the bench, and I couldn't find any in the girls' locker room. Could you help us out?"

He stared at me for a second as if trying to understand what I was saying.

"Find the custodian. He'll get you whatever you need." And with that, he turned from me abruptly, and yelled for his players to get in the locker room. He then walked away from me, following his players into the locker room.

If I was irritated before, I was fuming now! Who did this guy think he was and where did this guy think he was coming from? I'd never had another professional treat me like that in my short tenure as a coach and teacher. I left the gym floor and spent about ten minutes wandering all over the facility looking for the custodian. I finally found him cleaning one of the public restrooms near the main entrance to the gym. I told him my need and he graciously quit what he was doing and got the towels we needed. When I got back to the locker room, my athletes had dressed in their hand-me-down uniforms and were sitting on the benches waiting for the pre-game briefing and some encouraging words from me.

As I stood before them my feelings were a mixture of anger and trepidation. I was angry about the way my team and I were being treated and fearful for the outcome of this game, which appeared to be against a significantly talented and superior team.

"Guys, you will be one of the first teams from Jenifer to play the Pomeroy Pirates," I began, looking each of my players in the eye as I spoke. "I got a glimpse of them warming up in the gym when I went looking for towels and they look big, strong, disciplined, and talented. They have a couple of guys over six feet tall, who will probably give us some trouble on the boards. It also looks like they have some good ball handlers as well. We can play with them if we are disciplined on offense and work hard on defense. We will probably do some pressing to keep them on their toes. When you go out on the floor in a minute, run through our warm up drills and then spend some time shooting jump shots and set shots. You will need to get used to their baskets since you have never played in this gym before, so focus hard. We will come back in here about three minutes before the game starts to pray and go through some last-minute instructions."

I had them gather together in a circle and put their hands together and yell, "Defense!" The team then headed out in a line onto the basketball court with the captain leading the way. As they came on the floor, they crisply organized themselves into two lines for performing the layup drills.

We were past the layup portion of the drill and moving into shooting short jump shots when the Pirates came onto the floor. The big six-foot-four center led the way for the team, dribbling a basketball. They looped around the court where we were shooting, as if to make sure they had our attention, before moving to their end of the court where they started their layup drill with the six-foot-four center performing a forceful, two-handed dunk. The few fans that were in the stands roared their approval.

But for my team, it was like someone let the air out of our balloon. I was at half court and I heard a couple of players begin talking.

"Did you see that?"

"He dunked the ball with two hands!"

"Hey!" I called out to my players. "Let's stay focused on what we are doing. It's not your job to watch them warm up. Let's move on to the defensive shuffle drill."

We continued moving through our drills, but I noticed that occasionally one or two of my kids would glance over at the Pirates. I had to admit they were intimidating. Even the six-foot-two kid was doing one-handed dunks. Several players were dribbling behind their backs and making impressive passes to teammates cutting to the basket. All during the warm-up drills, the Pomeroy coach stayed down under the basket where his team was warming up. Not once did he make eye contact with me or offer any overtures in my direction. I knew deep down in my gut this was going to be an ugly game for my kids, and there wasn't much I could do about it. It was evident that this coach wanted to make some kind of statement.

As we worked through our warm-ups, the gym began to fill with fans. There was only one wall of bleachers, and both teams sat along the sideline opposite them. A small group of parents and fans from Lewiston sat on one end of the bleachers, while the other end filled up with fans from Pomeroy. Three minutes before the game was to begin, I called out to the captain to take the team to the locker room. I noticed the Pomeroy coach did the same.

I followed my team into the locker room, and as I came through the door I heard their astonished comments.

"Did you see that? He dunked the ball with two hands!"

"They have their heads shaved! What does that mean?"

"Did you see the one guy dribble behind his back?"

"Did you see their uniforms? They are brand new!"

"How are we going to beat a team like that?"

When the last comment floated up from the din, I felt anger rise in me.

"WAIT A MINUTE! HOLD ON! GIVE ME YOUR ATTENTION!" The team quickly quieted down, and I moved to a place where I could look into their faces.

"You guys are talking like you're beat before you even get on the floor! You're letting those guys intimidate you before the game even gets started, and that's exactly what they want to do. They are trying to get in your head. Your job is to go out there and play like you have been coached. Play hard, give your best effort, and keep your poise. You can play with these guys. I know you can. We are going to start the game by playing man-to-man defense, so be sure and identify who your man is when you do the jump ball. If they start out in man-to-man, we will use our spread offense when we have the ball, looking for layups and short jump shots. If they start out in a zone, run our 1-3-1-zone offense or our 2-1-2-zone offense depending on their zone defense. If they press us, use the press break pattern we've been working on in practice. Just play like we've practiced and we will stay with these guys." In my mind, I knew we were in for a long afternoon, but I wasn't going to tell them that.

After I gave my instructions, we gathered together and I prayed. It had been my practice from day one as a basketball coach to pray for both my team and the opposing team before each game. I prayed for God's protection on all the players, and I prayed He would help us compete hard and give our best. After the prayer, we put our hands together and yelled, "DEFENSE!"

With that, we jogged out onto the floor. The other team was already out there with their starting five at mid-court. My starting five shed their warm-up jackets and moved to mid-court as well. They matched up so everyone knew which player they were going to guard on defense. My center, all five-foot-eleven inches of him, lined up with their six-foot-four center at mid-court, and the game began as the official threw the ball up in the air.

The Pirate center leaped high into the air and tipped the ball to one of his players, who passed it to another player, breaking to the hash mark in their offensive end of the court. He pivoted and quickly snapped a bounce pass to the center, who had streaked toward the goal after tipping the ball. He caught the ball in full stride and jammed it through the hoop over the head of my defender with a one-handed slam that brought the crowd to its feet with a roar.

One of my guards grabbed the ball and stepped out of bounds to pass it in to the other guard. But when he turned to pass the ball in, he found himself facing the Pomeroy team already set up in a full-court zone press. The ball went to our guard, who was immediately trapped in the corner. The guard tried to pass the ball down the sideline, but the pass was picked off by one of the Pirates, who pushed toward the basket, hitting a jump shot from the free throw line. We were less than twenty seconds into the game and we were down four to zero! I immediately called a time-out and brought my team over to the bench. I reviewed the press break offense we had practiced on numerous occasions and encouraged them to use it to break the press. I encouraged them to keep their poise, step it up, and play harder. We broke the huddle with a cheer and they returned to the court.

My team inbounded the ball and, using our press break offense, we broke the press this time and went into our offense. They had fallen back into a zone, so we passed the ball and finally got off a good shot, but it was a miss. The miss was picked off the boards by the six-foot-two forward who began a fast break, passing the ball out to a guard at the hash mark. They were able to move the ball down the court for a layup before we could get back on defense. They immediately moved into the full-court press after making the shot. After two minutes had past in the first quarter, we were behind ten to zero. After breaking the press at that point, I called time-out and set up an offensive play, which was successfully executed, giving us our first score.

The game went like this for the whole half. We struggled to get the ball into our court and they continued to press. Things really got bad when I substituted some of my weaker players into the game. They were so overmatched I had to pull them out just to keep the score from being a major discouragement. By halftime, we were down fifty-four to eighteen, but I was proud of the fact we had managed eighteen points. I'd thought we could keep the game under control with our defense, but they were just an unstoppable offensive juggernaut. We tried everything, but we just couldn't keep them from scoring. When the horn sounded, my kids scurried quickly to the locker room, happy to be off the court.

When I got into the room, I could see they were discouraged. They sat on the benches with their shoulders slumped over and their heads down. One player looked up at me with tears in his eyes.

"What are we going to do?" he moaned. "We're doing the best we can, and they are just kicking our butts! What can we do, coach?"

"Alright, I have to be honest," I replied. "And I'm not going to pull any punches. We are playing a team that is well coached and highly talented. They are a whole lot better than we are and you're right. They are kicking our butts. But this experience can be used to help us get better. The thing you need to work on is execution and defense. You need to use the press break play to break the press and get the ball safely to our court. We don't have the skill to dribble through the press, so use the pass to break the press. I suspect they will take the press off eventually. When we break the press, run the appropriate play depending on the defense they play. We are going to switch to a zone defense to see if that helps us get more rebounds. Be sure to block out the two big boys if you are the one closest to them in the zone when a shot goes up. Remember to always get a hand in the shooter's face when he shoots and then block them out for the rebound. Work hard and don't worry about the score. We'll get through this together. Take a minute for now to rest, and then we will go back out and warm up for the second half."

The second half of the game was worse than the first. They kept the full-court press on and played their starters until halfway through the fourth quarter. The final score was 110 to 34—we were beaten by more than 60 points! If that wasn't humiliating enough, as soon as the horn sounded to end the game, the Pomeroy coach and his players ran into their locker room. The coach didn't come to shake my hand and he didn't provide the opportunity for his players to shake the hands of my players, which was always a tradition between the players and coaches of the teams we had played in the past. I could tell from the crowd's reaction to both the score and the behavior of the coach and players that they were somewhat embarrassed by it all.

I watched as my team picked up their stuff and made their way to the girls' locker room. When I arrived, they were all sitting on their benches exhausted and hanging their heads in humiliation. I moved to one side of the room and called for their attention, and they all turned to face me.

"Listen to me, men!" I said with as much passion as I could muster. "I'm proud of the way you played and the way you conducted yourselves today. You were faced with an overwhelmingly superior basketball team, and you played to the best of your ability and executed the defense and offense as you have been coached. You were just up against a far more talented team and sometimes that happens in life. You'll come into situations where you may find yourself in over your head. And what you should take away from what happened today is you do the best you can and learn from the experience. You are a better team for playing these guys. They may have won the game overwhelmingly, but they didn't demonstrate half the character you did!

"I can promise you this," I continued. "We will never act like that coach and his team acted today. You don't run up a score on someone like that and then run off the floor without even shaking your opponent's hand and recognizing their efforts. I will not knowingly put you through something like this again. I'm going to talk to Coach Crosby and see if he can bring the varsity back here next week to play these guys. I guarantee they won't beat our varsity 110 to 34. Now get showered up and let's get on the bus so we can get home. Despite the score, I think you played well and I'm proud of you!"

With that, they showered and got dressed and we were on the bus in twenty minutes. It's amazing how resilient kids are—in the locker room the boys were down and despondent. But by the time they got on the bus they were over it, happily talking about their planned activities for the weekend. I was proud to be associated with them. In my mind they were winners.

At school the next day, I sought Mr. Crosby and briefed him on the events of the previous night. He was more upset than I was at the conduct of the coach and the players. When I suggested he take his team to play their varsity the next week, he was in agreement, but suggested I take his starting six players with my team since my team and I were on the receiving end of this coach's insulting behavior. I protested that I didn't know his offensive plays and didn't have the rapport he had with the players, but he assured me the players would assist me with the offense and follow my leadership.

At our practice that night, Coach Crosby gathered the JV and varsity teams around him and explained what happened the previous night and told the players that six of the varsity players would go with my team the next week to provide a little payback for the drubbing the JVs had taken the night before, a plan that excited both the varsity and junior varsity players. We returned to practice scrimmaging with each other, which gave me time to review his offensive plays and work with the players who would go with me the next week.

A week later, we once again found ourselves in the unfriendly confines of the Pomeroy gymnasium, but this time I had some players that matched up fairly well with their talented team. This time when we came on the floor to warm up, I walked over to the coach when he brought his team on the floor and reintroduced myself.

"I hope you don't mind, but I brought some of the players from our ninth grade varsity to help make the game more competitive. Is that okay with you?"

He smiled knowingly.

"I was hoping you would do that," he said. "It was my intention at the last game to see if you would be motivated to bring your varsity. We have a very gifted group of freshman and we foresee them competing for a state championship when they are juniors and seniors. This will be a good match for them."

With that, he turned and walked back to watch his team practice.

I would like to say we kicked their butts during that game, but it just didn't happen. We had fewer turnovers when they pressed and were better offensively and defensively. Early in the second quarter, they took the press off, because we were getting too many easy layups. I believe we could have beat them if the six varsity players had been part of my team and I had a rapport with them, but when the game was close, they tended to do their own thing and didn't take to well to my coaching. Because of that, we ended up on the losing end of a fifty-four to forty-four score.

And once again, when the final horn ended the game, the Pomeroy coach and his team left the floor without shaking my hand or the hands of my players even though we tried to get to them. I determined to make this rude, obnoxious coach pay for his behavior if we ever played them again in the future. He was setting a bad example for his team and the community. Junior high and high school athletics are not just about winning by any means possible. There should always be mutual respect between the teams, which begins with the coaches. I was going to encourage Coach Crosby to schedule this team next year, but to be sure we played a home-and-home pair of games instead of just playing both games on his court.

Even though many of my JV players did not get to play in this game, the team left the floor with their heads up knowing we had given them a much different game than the one played the week before.

We finished out this season losing more games than we won, but I saw considerable maturation and growth in the abilities of my team from the beginning of the season to the end. And by the time this second season as a basketball coach wrapped up, I was loving the coaching experience and I was loving the boys.

After the basketball season was over, there were two surprises that caught many of us off guard. The first surprise was the announcement that because of a law called Title IX passed on June 23, 1972, we were going to have to have the same number of girls' teams as boys' teams to meet the new requirement of equal opportunity between the sexes as defined by the law. Since the passage of the Equal Opportunity Act of 1964 and the summer of 1973, a number of legislative and executive actions had been implemented to include equal opportunity for women. Initially, this only applied to employment, which I learned in my first graduate class taken the summer of 1972. But since that time, the law had been expanded to address equal opportunity beyond just the work place to equal opportunity in the classroom and sports. Thus, every school was required to have the same number of athletic opportunities for its female students as it provided for the male students. So, for the 1974-75 school year, Jenifer was going to add fall volleyball to match football. There would be varsity and junior varsity basketball teams for the seventh, eighth, and ninth grade girls to match the boys' program, and there would be softball added for ninth graders to offset the boys' baseball team. Girls would also be allowed to be a part of the seventh, eighth, and ninth grade track teams.

Because the number of teams was being doubled, the school district believed it needed to have an athletic director for each junior high to oversee the higher number of competitive events and the increased use of the facilities. Mr. Crosby was selected to be Jenifer's athletic director.

After this announcement was made, Mr. Crosby asked me if I would be willing to move up to the ninth grade varsity coach, because he would not have the time to coach basketball in addition to his duties as the athletic director. I was more than happy to accept his offer and relished the opportunity to work with the more talented basketball players. I couldn't wait for the 1974-75 year to start.

The second surprise came when Mr. Walker announced his retirement at a staff meeting in April. I was stunned! I felt comfortable working with Mr. Walker. I knew what he expected, and I could count on him to support me whether I was teaching, coaching, disciplining a student, or confronting an angry parent. The other teachers felt the same way. Now he was going to leave, and we were concerned about who was going to replace him.

We were told Mr. Roger Adams was going to move down from the district office to take Mr. Walker's position. Mr. Adams was the principal at the Lewiston McSorley Elementary School before he moved to work at the district office for a year, so he had experience as a principal. However, no one on the staff seemed to know what Mr. Adams was like, so there was some anxiety among the teachers regarding this change of leadership.

On the last day of school, we got to see a different side of Mr. Walker. Since he was an officer in the Idaho National Guard, he had arranged a special treat for the students and staff of Jenifer Junior High. He had us schedule student check-out on the last day of class to end about thirty minutes early. At that time, Harvie came on the intercom and invited staff and students to the football field to be part of a special treat provided by him to celebrate his retirement.

We excused the students and followed them out to the football field where a Sikorsky HH-53 "Super Jolly Green Giant" helicopter had landed in the middle of the field. The students swarmed over the aircraft as Mr. Walker moved around explaining various aspects of the helicopter. The students and I were very impressed. These were similar to the "Jolly Greens" I had seen operating out of Udorn Air

Force Base in Udorn, Thailand, when I was stationed there between 1969 and 1970, but this one was much more advanced. It was evident that displaying this aircraft for the students and staff had special meaning to Mr. Walker.

It was an appropriate way to end the school year—and the career of a very special leader. It was definitely a whole lot better than having to supervise another year-end water fight.

CHAPTER 20

Another Summer, a New Principal, and Some Payback

> *"The gym was rocking with fans yelling for their respective teams as we finished the time-out and returned to the floor. We took the ball out at half court just as we had planned, and they ran the play to perfection. Matt got the ball six feet from the basket and rose up high over the defender for the short jump shot. But he missed!"*

As we moved into the summer of 1974, a number of things happened that kept my family and I extremely busy. After renting for two years in the Lewiston Orchards, we decided to buy a house. So with the help of the GI Bill for veterans and redeeming a whole life insurance policy to cover the closing costs, we were able to buy a nice, older two-bedroom brick house in downtown Lewiston located at 815 11th Avenue. Since this house was about four blocks from Jenifer Junior High School and about two blocks from Webster Elementary School, I could walk to work and my children could walk to school. It was in an ideal location and—for the price of $19,000—it was a bargain. It would need some remodeling, and I would need to replace the antiquated furnace in the basement, but we could deal with that in the next two or three years.

It took us a few weekends of concentrated work to pack our things and move to our new house, but with help from people in our church and my fellow teachers, we were finally able to get all our furniture and boxes to the new site two weeks before the end of the school year. While Marty emptied the boxes and arranged things in the house, I worked to finish out the school year.

Our plan for making extra money during the summer was the same as the previous year. I would umpire baseball games in the evenings until the start of the pea harvest when I could work the night shift for Twin City Foods. When I went to make arrangements with the Babe Ruth league manager, I was surprised when he asked me if I wanted to take his place. He said he was getting a different job and would not have time to manage the league. He indicated I could make a lot more money, but it would take a lot of time and energy to schedule games, appoint coaches, address disputes, and find umpires.

I felt I wasn't quite ready for that kind of responsibility, but told him about K.C. Albright, the new teacher at Jenifer who I'd developed a strong friendship with during the previous school year. I greatly respected his teaching, coaching, organization, and leadership abilities and knew he would be a good fit for the position. As it turned out, K.C. was offered the job and took it. It turned out to be a blessing for both him and myself since we were both struggling to meet our financial needs on an $8,000 annual teacher's salary. After taking on the manager's role, K.C. gave me an umpiring schedule that would allow me to be freed up when the pea harvest began.

It was another busy summer as I helped my wife adjust to living in a new home, umpired Babe Ruth baseball games, and worked the pea harvest. Again, I had to make an appearance at the dispatcher's office at Twin City Foods to make sure I was on the list to be called when it got to be near the middle of July. This summer, I had moved up the tenure list so they gave me a few more hours, but there were still a number of workers ahead of me. Thanks to umpiring and a good pea harvest, I was able to make enough money to meet our financial needs and to provide for a small vacation at the end of August just before the new school year started.

A week before the start of school I headed to Jenifer to meet the new principal, Mr. Adams. I wanted to be proactive rather than reactive in getting to know him and to offer my assistance as he made the transition to his new position. When I got to the school, I found Mr. Adams emptying boxes and arranging his office.

Mr. Adams was totally different from Mr. Walker. Mr. Walker was a tall, burly, no-nonsense kind of man, whereas Mr. Adams was a short, thin, balding man who seemed pretty laid back. However, he had a ready smile and greeted me enthusiastically when I introduced myself and welcomed him to the school. "I don't think I need any help," he said in response to my inquiry. "The secretary and custodian are giving me all the help I need. You teach math, right?"

I responded in the affirmative.

"Yes, I've been teaching algebra and ninth grade general math up on the second floor next to Mr. Chavez's room." He took a moment to look at the class schedules, shuffling through some papers scattered on his desk. He picked up one of the sheets with an exclamation. "Oh, yeah! I've rearranged the schedule some. We have two new math teachers so I've given you four algebra classes and two eighth grade classes rather than the ninth grade math classes. I've also appointed you as head of the math department since you are the only one on staff with a math degree. All the other math teachers have only a minor in math. I hope that is okay."

As we spoke, he continued emptying boxes, not quite giving me his full attention.

Nevertheless, I was relieved to hear I would get a break from teaching ninth grade math, but I was also surprised he made me the head of the math department. "Yeah, that will work for me," I responded. "Whatever will work to meet the needs of the kids I'm willing to do."

"Great! Well, I guess I'll see you in a week, right?" he said as he worked to unpack one of his boxes.

"Yeah, I guess. I'm going to go up to my room and arrange a few things. If you need any help, let me know."

I went up to my room feeling great about my new assignment and the fact it looked like I could get along with Mr. Adams. He seemed like a nice guy—amiable and not nearly as gruff as Mr. Walker could be at times. My anxiety about the change of leadership was somewhat relieved. At least to this point, it didn't appear to be a bad thing.

The teacher in-service day was the same as it had been in the past. Mr. Adams's style of leadership was totally different from that of Mr. Walker. He was not an autocrat like Mr. Walker, who had made it clear whenever he dealt with staff members that he was in charge and expected everyone to do things the way he wanted them done. Mr. Adams's leadership style was more laissez-faire in that he expected teachers and staff to operate with little support from him. He appeared to be more diplomatic and allowed more freedom and flexibility for the staff to meet the educational needs of the students. He did have some structure, though—he laid out his expectations regarding lesson plans, student supervision, and discipline. Every Wednesday, teachers were to submit their lesson plans for the following week using blocked calendar books provided by the school. The lesson plans would include lesson objectives, the activities to meet the objectives, and a statement defining what measurement tool would be used to see how well the objectives were met. This was going to take extra time on the teacher's part. Mr. Walker had expected us to keep lesson plans, but we only had to write down the page numbers of the unit we were going to cover and detail the homework assignment. He didn't require us to state objectives or how we were going to meet them, and we didn't have to turn in our lesson plans each week; he would generally inspect them when he came to observe our class.

Mr. Adams stressed the importance of supervising students at all times. He did not want us to leave our classrooms unsupervised, and he wanted us to be out in the hallways between classes to provide supervision to students going to their lockers and making their way to class. He wanted all teachers to be in the hall five minutes before classes started at the beginning of the day and five minutes after classes ended at the end of the day to supervise students.

Finally, with regards to discipline, he wanted us to have full control of our classrooms and indicated he did not want to have any students referred to him unless we had tried everything possible to correct their behavior. This was very similar to what Mr. Walker had required, so it appeared there would be no changes in this area.

During that first teacher in-service day, I spent a lot of time with K.C. Albright and checked in occasionally with Mr. Crosby. Since this was going to be the first year for the implementation of Title IX, Mr. Crosby was busy working on scheduling practices and games for the basketball season. Mr. Albright was going to coach the ninth grade varsity girls' team and I would be coaching the ninth grade varsity boys' team, so we were interested in how he was going to work out the practice schedule. Since this was a brand new program, we thought only a few girls might turn out and there would only need to be one girls' team for each grade. We decided to wait until after our team meeting with the students who wanted to turn out before we scheduled practices. If indeed only a few girls turned out, it would ease the pressure on scheduling. The preliminary practice proposal was that some teams would have to practice before school and the others would practice after school.

The fall season was going to work out fine, as would the spring season. In the fall, the boys would be on the football field practicing and playing, which would leave the gym for the girls to practice and play their volleyball games. In the spring, the girls would practice on a softball field in the Orchards as the boys practiced and played on a Babe Ruth baseball field in the Orchards. The athletes would be bussed to the fields each day. The girls would just be assimilated into the track program, with the boys and girls practicing together.

Before the implementation of Title IX, males dominated junior high and high school sports. Female students were relegated to cheering the boys on through cheerleading and pep club. High school and junior high facilities were built with that in mind. With the implementation of Title IX, the use of these facilities, especially during the basketball season, doubled. The pressure to make the changes necessary to accommodate Title IX without any reasonable lead-time to build or remodel these facilities caused some resentment on the part of those who were given the task to make it work. The administration and the coaches were directed to provide equal availability to the new girls' programs. Addressing this problem was one of the main topics of discussion at the beginning of the school year, but no clear decisions could be made until we got close to the start of the season and knew how many girls wanted to participate.

I was going to be teaching two eighth grade math classes along with my four algebra classes this year, which was different from the previous two years. A look at my class list indicated my class sizes were going to be up, averaging almost thirty-two students per class. We were looking to adopt a new math textbook series in the next school year, so as the new department chair, I called a meeting on the first day to discuss that issue. The district would be making the selection, but they were interested in our input. So we spent some time looking over four textbook options and making a recommendation.

The first day with students started as usual. I developed seating charts by assigning seating for the eighth graders and allowing the freshman algebra students to select their own seats. I reviewed the class procedures and rules with the students and spent the day organizing the various classes. In my opinion it went very well, as it should since this was my third year as a teacher.

It wasn't until a month into the first year that I first noticed there might be a problem with the new principal. I had a confrontation with an eighth grade boy who refused to move when I directed him to a new seat because he was talking excessively during a lesson. The confrontation grew to the point where he used some insulting profanity to describe my heritage. When he did that, I wrote a short note to Mr. Adams briefly describing his behavior.

"Get your stuff together and get down to the principal's office," I told the boy. "You can talk to Mr. Adams about this." I gave him the note and sent him on his way.

Normally, I had no problem hacking a student for talking to me like that, but this student was old enough and mature enough that I didn't want to be physical with him. I felt it was better to let the principal deal with him. I had done this before when Mr. Walker was a principal, and I assumed Mr. Adams would operate the same way.

The student left my room with his books, grumbling under his breath. I went back to teaching, and about ten minutes later there was a knock at my door. When I opened it, the student I had sent to the office was standing there with a smile on his face. He reached out and handed me a note. "Mr. Adams wanted me to give this to you."

I looked at the note and it simply said, "Please let this student back into class." It didn't tell me what he did. In fact, there were no assurances Mr. Adams had punished him in any way, shape, or form. After reading the note, I looked up at the student who was still standing at the door smiling like a Cheshire cat. I was shocked to say the least. He started to enter the room, but I didn't move aside to let him back into class.

"You've got your books, right?" He nodded, still grinning.

"Sit down here in the hall. I'll bring you your assignment and you can work on it here, but you are definitely not getting back into this classroom today." That wiped the grin off his face. "But, Mr. Adams said..." he began, but I quickly interrupted.

"I really don't care what this note says or what Mr. Adams says. You aren't going to talk to me that way and then get back into my class after a ten-minute discussion with the principal. By the way, I'll be calling your parents after school today to see if they can change your attitude!"

Grumbling, he slid down to the floor and got out his math book. Propping the door open so I could keep my eye on him, I went back to my desk and wrote the assignment on a piece of paper and gave it to him. He worked on the assignment for the rest of the period in the hall while I finished the lesson and then worked with individuals in the class. I called his mother after school and talked to her about the language he used with me, and she said she would take care of it when he got home. His attitude was much better when he returned to class the next day.

Three other times that semester I sent a student down to Mr. Adams with the same result. I talked to some of the other staff members and they were having similar problems. It had to be a pretty serious misbehavior like a fight or smoking in the bathroom for him to discipline a student. By the end of the semester, most of the staff were feeling little support from our new principal. Most of us then decided to deal with disruptive students ourselves by giving them after-school detention, hacking the student, sending the student to the counselor, or calling the parents.

As November rolled around, so did the basketball season and with it, tryouts. After meeting with our prospective athletes, it was evident only a few girls were going to turn out for the seventh, eighth, and ninth grade basketball teams. There would only be enough girls to have two teams—one for ninth grade and one seventh/eighth grade team. This made the facilitating of practice easier.

In the mornings, the boys' seventh/eighth grade junior varsity team and the girls' ninth grade team would take over the courts for practice. Right after school, the girls' seventh/eighth grade team would practice alongside the boys' ninth grade junior varsity team. And between 5:30 and 7 p.m., the boys' seventh and eighth grade varsity team and the boys' ninth grade varsity team would utilize the gym. Most of the parents were supportive of the practice and game schedules, although most did not like practicing in the mornings.

This was my first year as the ninth grade varsity coach, and I found I was going to be working with the cream of the crop. I had a talented group of athletes out for the team, including a strong six-foot, four-inch center named Wade Evans who could rebound and shoot well around the basket. I also had a six-foot-two forward who was a great leaper and shooter named Matt Mosman. This was the son of the lawyer I had kicked out of the Babe Ruth baseball game my first summer in Lewiston. It turned out he was a great kid and his dad was incredibly supportive. I also had another small, quick-hustling guard/forward named Mark Parsons who could shoot the lights out when he was hot. The varsity would have two other guards who were excellent ball handlers and about four quality substitutes. This was a whole different team makeup than what I had as the junior varsity coach.

The new ninth grade JV coach was Mr. Tom Green, who taught social studies. He didn't have much experience playing basketball, but he was eager to coach and work with the athletes. He worked hard at improving his knowledge of the game and his coaching skills during the season. He and I had a great working relationship.

When the season started and the girls had their first basketball game, I remember the comments K.C. Albright made after that game. K.C. came into the teachers' lounge really grumbling. "Did you guys hear about the game last night? I can't believe it," he said to the handful of us in the lounge. "The game lasted three-and-a-half hours. There were more than eighty fouls called, and the referees called every single traveling and double-dribbling violation they saw. It was like they were going to show those girls what playing basketball was really like. They never let up. The girls were pretty discouraged by it all. They are just not very skilled, and the officials aren't helping the situation. This could be a very, very long season."

I was glad he was coaching the girls and not me. I also vowed to avoid those games as much as possible—at least until their skill levels greatly improved.

The ninth grade varsity season was going well. We were winning a few more games than we were losing. Then, we came to the games scheduled with Pomeroy. In the back of my mind, I had been looking forward to these games since the beginning of the season. I wanted to get a little payback for the treatment we had received the previous year from the Pomeroy coach.

The first game we were to play was going to be at home. This would be a single game since Pomeroy did not have a ninth grade JV team, nor did they have a ninth grade girls' team. I guess they did not have enough girls to field a team that year.

When they showed up in our gym, I was determined to treat their team differently than we had been treated the previous year. When their bus drove up, I had arranged for my team manager to be there to greet the team. He directed them to where they were to dress down and made sure they had plenty of towels.

When he and his team came on the floor and warmed up, I could see they were not as gifted height wise as they had been the year before. They had a couple of kids about six-foot-two, and they had some quick guards who could dribble well. They had butch haircuts, but they did not have shaved heads like they had the last year.

After his team began warming up, I made a point of walking over to him and greeting him, determined not to treat him like he had treated me. He was just as unfriendly with me then as he had been the previous year. I tried to carry on a conversation and develop some rapport, but he would have none of it. After a couple of attempts on my part to encourage a discourse with him, he just yelled at his kids to go into the locker room and again turned abruptly away from me to follow his team off the court.

After he and his team were off the court, I pulled my team into our locker room and we had a moment of prayer asking God to protect us, and our opponents, as we played. After the prayer, I told them the story of how the players and their coach had treated last year's ninth grade JV team.

"They beat us 110 to 34!" I said at the end of my speech. "Do you hear me? They beat us 110 to 34! They beat us by 60 points! They kept their full-court press on us until halfway through the fourth quarter. Then, after they had crushed us, they ran off the court without even shaking our hands! Do you guys think that is okay?"

"No!" they shouted.

"Are you ready to do something about it?"

"Yes!" they shouted even louder.

"Listen," I continued. "I want a little payback on these guys. You are good enough to play with any team at this level. I want you go to our full-court press right from the beginning. I want to see some great man-to-man defense. I want to see you play with poise, but I want to see you play with some fire! I want to see you running the offense like we practiced it and fast breaking at every opportunity. Keep the pressure on them and make them pay for every mistake they make. Are you with me on this?"

"Yes!" they returned in unison.

With that, we brought our hands together in a circle and shouted, "DEFENSE!" before turning to run out onto the court.

The game started with a bang. My six-four center, Wade Evans, got the tip and we broke to our offensive basket with Mark Parsons driving for a layup, which he missed—but Wade Evans was there to get the rebound and put it in for two points. We went into our press, but they were able to quickly break it and made a layup. Then they went into their full-court press, which we broke and eventually scored off a set play. We went back and forth like that for the full half. At the end of it, we were down by four points.

We had both played great defense; both our presses worked on occasion, with each team getting easy layups when they got a steal. It was pretty evident that we were evenly matched. The fans from Lewiston and the fans from Pomeroy were into it and the gym was rocking. The teams headed to their locker rooms at halftime to the cheers of both sets of fans.

When we got to the locker room, I had them drink some water and sit down to gather their strength.

"You guys are playing great! We are pretty evenly matched, so the team that wins this will be the one that works a little harder and wants it more. Do you want this victory?"

"Yes!" they responded with a shout.

"Okay, here is what we are going to do this half. We are going down to a half-court press. If they break it, we will fall back to our 1-2-2-zone defense. They haven't seen our zone yet, so maybe that will cause them some confusion and we can get some turnovers. The zone should help our rebounding as well. Keep running the man-to-man offense like you were in the first half. Be patient and try to get layups or short jump shots. If they come out in a zone defense, go to our zone offense and remember, ball movement is what will beat a zone. Matt, you and Wade and Mark need to get on the boards. You guards need to fall back when we shoot to make sure they don't get any easy layups off the break. Okay! Everyone ready to go? What you do in the next two quarters will determine the winner and the loser. You guys can beat this team. Let's go!"

We moved out on the floor and did some warm-up layups as the Pomeroy team came out and did the same thing. The horn sounded, and the ball was again tossed up at half court. This time, Pomeroy got the jump ball and moved down to their offensive end of the court where they passed the ball around for a shot against our 1-2-2-zone defense.

The second half of the game was just as hard fought as the first. We were able to come back from our four-point halftime deficit and tie the game up by the end of the third quarter. The lead went back and forth throughout the fourth quarter. At the beginning of the fourth quarter, Mark Parsons sprained his right ankle, and I had to pull him out and tape it up before he could get back in the fray. He was able to play, but he was a little gimpy.

As the game progressed, the Pomeroy coach became more and more agitated with his players. During one time-out I could hear him, over the noise of the crowd, yelling about their lack of effort and their inability to play defense. When they got back on the court, he would deride them for some miscue on offense or defense when they passed the bench. I could see it was having a negative effect on his team.

The whole game came down to the last thirty seconds. The score was tied and Pomeroy had the ball. Out of their set offensive play, one of their players took a short jump shot on the baseline and was fouled by Wade Evans. He went to the free throw line and sank two free throws, so now we were behind by two points. We had twenty seconds left as we took the ball out, so I took one of my two remaining time-outs when my guard reached half court with the ball. With fifteen seconds left in the game, I set up the offense so that Matt Mosman, our best jumping forward, could take the last shot with about six seconds to go. The gym was rocking with fans yelling for their respective teams as we finished the time-out and returned to the floor. We took the ball out at half court just as we had planned, and they ran the play to perfection. Matt got the ball six feet from the basket and rose up high over the defender for the short jump shot. But he missed! The ball bounded straight back toward Matt and his defender. They both grabbed the ball and were wrestling each other for control when the referee blew his whistle signaling a jump ball. With four seconds left, there would be a jump ball at our end of the court. I immediately called my final time-out.

When the team got to the bench, I quickly got my writing tablet and drew a picture of the free throw area on the paper and began to outline our final play to try and tie the game. The whole team was gathered around me as I knelt down in front of the five starters and said, "Look! We are going to tie this game up right now! Here is how we are going to do it. Matt, you are the jumper. I know you can control the tip. You can jump a lot higher than your defender. I want Wade to place himself right here under the basket. Now, they are going to think you are going to tip it to him, so they will sandwich him with their two tallest players. But you aren't going to tip it to him. Mark Parsons is going to be here just to the right of you, Matt. You are to tip it to Mark, and Mark, I want you to go straight up for a jump shot. I know you can get up over your defender. If he is playing you tight, give him a head fake and then go up. I know you are going to make that shot, but if not, Wade, you will turn to the basket on the tip and be in position to get the rebound and put it back in if he misses. Have you all got that?" They nodded at me, and I said, "Now, men, we are going to tie this game and force an overtime, which we are then going to win! Right?" In response they put their hands in over mine and shouted, "JACKS!" I cringed a little at that, but I was too much into the game now to care about our nickname and all the connotations that went with it. I just wanted to see my team win and Pomeroy lose.

The players returned to the floor, and my kids set up just like I showed them. The referee tossed the ball up and sure enough, Matt leaped well above his opponent and tipped the ball to Mark. It was obvious this caught them by surprise, because they just stood there flat-footed. He immediately gathered himself and jumped up, banking the ball off the backboard into the net for the tying score just as the horn sounded. The play had worked, and now we would get three minutes to win the game.

We played the overtime to perfection, winning the game by a score of eighty-four to eighty. I was grinning ear to ear as my team came off the court. I congratulated them for a great effort as I slapped their backs and backsides. I then directed them to go over and shake the hands of the players from Pomeroy, who had to go by our bench to get to the girls' locker room, so they couldn't avoid this simple courtesy.

"Good game," I said to the Pomeroy coach as I shook his hand. "Your kids played well!"

"Thanks!" he responded simply before following his team toward the locker room. As he walked away, one of his players came up alongside him.

"How was our defense, coach?"

"Defense?" the coach retorted harshly. "Do you think a score of eighty-four to eighty means we played defense? Get in the locker room!" And with that, they were gone.

In the Jenifer locker room there was shouting and laughing. I gathered the team around and congratulated them.

"You guys played a great game, and I am proud of you. You played hard and you played as a team, and that helped you beat a good team. You came back from being down at halftime and tied the game by the end of regulation time. You did a great job. Shower up, go home, get your homework done, and get some rest. We play these guys at their place next week."

A week later, we went to their place where another great game was played—except this time we lost by six points. I felt we got homered a little bit by the officials, but it's easy to use that as an excuse when you're playing away. Even though we lost, my kids played just as hard as they did when we beat Pomeroy the week before. I was proud of them and told them so.

We finished the season with a record of nine and seven, including two losses to Sacajawea, which cost us the traveling trophy. This trophy was awarded to the school that won two out of the three games played during the season. You could have a losing season, but you still felt it was a successful season if you won two out of three games from Sacajawea. I discovered this rivalry was the highlight of the basketball season, and both gyms were full to capacity whenever we played.

This was my third season coaching basketball and my first as ninth grade varsity coach. I was discovering that coaching was very rewarding, purposeful, and satisfying to me. There was no other place where I could have quite the same positive influence on young men as the athletic field or basketball court as a coach. We all spent two or more hours a day working toward a common goal. I had the opportunity to show these young ninth grade boys the values of hard work, teamwork, integrity, setting goals, and developing the discipline to reach them. I got to see them succeed and fail in the pursuit of those goals, but the most important thing was the close relationships I saw develop between the athletes and myself, as we truly became a team. By the end of each season, I came to love these young men like they were my own sons. It didn't matter if they were a regular player or bench sitter; I had the same feelings toward each one.

CHAPTER 21

The End of The School Year and a Change of Course

> *After one particular game I had umpired that summer, the paper published a story of the game on the front page of the sports section, which included a five-by-eight picture of Dwight Church and I face to face jawing about a particular call I had made during the game. I didn't think too much about it until my professor came up to me just before class started and asked me about it.*

By the time spring came around, my algebra classes were going pretty well, although I was seeing grades dropping again as we moved into solving simultaneous and quadratic equations. From what I could see, the dropping of grades was a combination of students losing their motivation because the weather was warming up and the fact the material was becoming more difficult. A higher percentage of assignments were not being completed or turned in. This particular year, I had a quarter of my algebra students receiving a "D" or an "F" for their second semester grade. I encouraged many of these struggling students to come in for extra help after school, but only a few took advantage of the offer. And once I noticed many of them were really lost, we would spend a day reviewing rather than moving on to a new topic. But it was clear to me the motivation was just not there for most of those students who were struggling.

My third season as the head track coach began with a lot of students out for the sport. The number of students out for track doubled because we now had girls on the team. They needed a lot of extra attention since most were inexperienced with many of the events, but Mr. Bafus and I found they were easier to coach because they had not developed any bad habits or techniques. We also discovered we couldn't treat them the same way as the boys. Yelling and harsh criticism did not work, whereas patiently reasoning and explaining techniques and goals were effective most of the time. The track season went well, but it wasn't nearly as satisfying as coaching basketball.

One of the issues that really drove me crazy was the complaining during track meets. This became a real issue with the girls' teams. Many of the athletes would complain about every little hurt or injury and try to use it as an excuse to withdraw from an event—especially near the end of a meet. It drove me crazy. Mr. Bafus was much more patient than I and handled it better, so I usually referred the whiners to him.

By the end of the season, I was pretty discouraged and began looking for a way to get out of the position. Unfortunately, I couldn't just drop coaching in the spring because I needed the money to meet my family's needs. Fortunately, a solution presented itself when Mr. Crosby announced at a spring coaches' meeting that the baseball coach was resigning and the position was open for the next school year. Since I had played a lot of baseball and softball since junior high and had experience umpiring at the Babe Ruth level, I notified Mr. Crosby that I was interested in being considered for the position. Mr. Crosby responded favorably to my application once he knew my experience as a player and an umpire, but he was concerned about filling my position as the head track coach. He consulted with Mr. Bafus, who indicated he was ready to move up as the head track coach. Once he knew that the track position was going to be filled, this paved the way for me being offered the ninth grade baseball coaching position for the 1975-76 school year. I was excited about coaching in the two areas where I had the most interest and experience.

I thought the school year might end differently under the leadership of Mr. Adams, but he maintained the same structure for closing out the year that had been instituted by Mr. Walker. I was prepared to watch the ensuing water fights between students from inside the school entrance, but God intervened and it rained that day, making for less chaos. Although there were still a few water balloons sailing through the air, there were not as many water fights as might have been had it not rained.

After the students were all gone and I'd spent some time in the teachers' lounge commiserating over the past year with some of the other teachers, I went to my room to evaluate the year and see where I could improve. I was concerned about the low grades in the algebra classes. The eighth grade classes had done all right with only about ten percent of the students failing. A high percentage of students had received As or Bs, and I felt what I was doing with those students was working, but I was really concerned with the algebra classes. Mr. Adams had indicated earlier in the year that he had received a few complaints from parents saying I was too hard on the students and there were too many students failing the class.

Taking that criticism into account, I decided to have the students keep a notebook containing their daily notes. I would grade the notebook at the end of each semester, giving the students 100 points for neatness and completeness. I assumed this would encourage them to take notes every day and improve their learning. I also adjusted my grading scale so students would receive an A for 90-100 percent, a B for 80 to 89, a C for 70 to 79, a D for 50 to 69, and an F for 1 to 49. I felt these two adjustments would address the criticisms and still maintain the integrity of the class. Another thing that had been heavy on my mind since the middle of the school year was the leadership style of Mr. Adams. Several of the teachers were complaining about a perceived lack of support from Mr. Adams when it came to maintaining discipline in the classroom. I was developing the growing belief that for teachers to be effective, they needed to be fully supported and encouraged by their leader. When there is a lack of either, the morale of the staff suffers and has a negative impact on learning. I was frustrated by the lack of support I felt and determined that I could have a bigger impact in educating students if I worked toward my administrator's license and took up the role as a building principal. I believed I could provide the support and encouragement to teachers that they needed to be effective.

My wife and I discussed this at length and decided I should aggressively pursue the secondary administration masters degree in the next few years. Having set that as a goal, I enrolled for a full load of classes for the summer of 1975. I took an educational administration class, a school finance class, and an educational law class. Like before, the GI Bill paid for tuition, books, and fees, and it also provided me with a small stipend. With a full class load, I did not believe I could umpire full time for the Babe Ruth League, but I could probably work in the pea harvest once the classes were over. The classes lasted until near the end of July, which made it possible to do both. This would make things a little tight financially, but we felt we could make it.

The graduate classes began the first full week after school was out. For six weeks, I would be commuting four days a week up the Lewiston hill to the University of Idaho in Moscow. Anticipating this commute and trying to save money on the cost of gasoline, I bought a used Honda 350cc motorcycle. Most of the time I used this mode of transportation to make the trek to Moscow, unless it was raining. There were a few days when I came home soaked to the bone because I didn't check the weather report the night before. Of course, I was really upset when the weatherman said the day would be clear and sunny, but it rained instead.

My classes went well. My math degree helped me along in the school finance class, and in the education law class I learned more about Title IX, the Equal Rights Act, and the events that led up to both. I was also introduced to the evolving special education laws being developed and implemented, and we reviewed the growth of collective bargaining for teachers and other public employees along with the constitutional rights of both teachers and students.

The educational administration class was also informative and helpful. One of the topics of the class included the leadership styles demonstrated by public school principals. From the information provided in the class, it was clearly evident Mr. Walker had an autocratic style of leadership and that Mr. Adams had a laissez-faire style of leadership. Neither of these styles seemed to fit my personality, and I could see that each of those styles had weaknesses, which were evident as I worked for these men.

The style that seemed to meet my personality was the democratic/servant style where the principal included the teachers, students, and parents in the decision-making process, which focused on improving teaching and student learning. I believed this would encourage ownership in the educational process by all the constituents. Of course, this must occur within the framework of the policies set by the local school board and the laws of the state.

The key to effective education, whether in public or private schools, is the teacher. If students are exposed to charismatic, innovative, motivated, and knowledgeable teachers, then learning improves exponentially. Understanding this, I believed the principal's job was to hire such teachers and/or provide a collegial environment that might encourage teachers to grow and develop into that kind of an educator. My summer classes helped me begin to develop a mental idea of what I wanted to do when the time came for me to step into the role of a secondary school principal. I was not able to umpire Babe Ruth games on a full-time basis that summer; however, about two weeks into my classes I received a call from Dwight Church asking if I would be interested in umpiring some legion baseball games. The pay for each game was about double what I got doing Babe Ruth games, and he explained I would only be needed about once each week. Some of the games would be single games and others would be double headers. I quickly jumped at the chance to umpire at that level, as long as he understood I would not be available to work near the end of July, because of the pea harvest. He was totally supportive and indicated we would be able to work that out.

During that summer, I got to see umpiring from a totally different perspective. Each of the ten games I umpired was well attended with crowds ranging from 250 to 1,000. The fans and parents were much more sophisticated in their understanding of the game and in dealing with an umpire. Close calls were respectfully booed if they didn't go their way and raucously cheered when they did.

Dealing with Dwight Church was also interesting. He rarely challenged balls and strikes, but would be in your face in a minute if a call of "out" or "safe" occurred on a close play. I also discovered during my first game, to my embarrassment, that he really knew his baseball. I called his runner out during a rundown between third base and home plate. The runner had bumped into the catcher and fallen to the ground as he ran away from the third baseman, who had the ball. The third baseman tagged him with the ball and I called the runner out, but Coach Church was right in my face telling me there had been interference and the runner should be awarded home plate.

He cited the rule in the rulebook and when I looked it up, I found he was correct and had to reverse my call. The other coach was not happy about the reversal and gave me an earful as I returned to the plate. From then on, I made sure I'd read the rulebook several times so I could deal with Coach Church's knowledge of the game.

In most cases I enjoyed umpiring and watching Dwight Church manage his team. He was very demanding of his players, and you could tell they had great respect for him. He was not afraid to harshly address their faults using the most colorful of language.

I remember one game as I was umpiring the bases when his starting pitcher was into the fifth inning and beginning to struggle. The Twins were ahead by three runs, but the bases became loaded from a couple of singles and a walk. With one out, Dwight went out to the mound and called for a new pitcher from the bullpen. As I stood between second base and the pitching mound, I watched this young man throw warm-up pitches as Dwight stood near the mound. This kid could throw heat! After about five pitches, Dwight said something encouraging to him and went back to the dugout.

The next batter came to the plate, and the pitcher blazed a fastball strike past him. The next pitch was also a blazing fastball, which the batter swung at and badly missed. It looked like he was going to get the Twins out of the inning without a mishap, but then on his third pitch he threw a lazy curveball to the plate. The batter lifted it between the left fielder and the center fielder, clearing the bases with a double. The game was now tied.

Immediately after the play was over there was an explosive "Time-out!" from Dwight Church as he stalked to the mound. Dwight marched up to the pitcher, got right in his ear, and chewed him out royally. He was red-faced and angry, but he kept his voice low enough that the crowd couldn't hear what was being said, although I was close enough to hear most it.

“I brought you in here to throw fastballs!” he said. “I did not bring you in here to throw curveballs!” He continued to make it clear that every pitch from this point forward until the end of the inning was to be nothing but heat. He interlaced this with enough profanity that I had to walk away. After making his case, Dwight stalked back to the dugout. The kid threw fastballs to the next two batters that were unbelievable. He struck them out without any of them even getting a foul ball. When the pitcher hustled over to the dugout, Dwight was there to give him a smack on his backside as he went past. They went on to win the game with no more runs from their opponent. Umpiring the legion games showed me Dwight Church was an excellent coach, although a little more colorful than I could ever be.

One of the interesting things that summer came out of umpiring American Legion baseball games and, of all things, my college finance class. The *Lewiston Tribune*, the local daily newspaper, covered the Lewis and Clark Twins intensely during the summer. Many times reporters would be at games with a camera where they took pictures that would be included with their report in the sports section of the paper. The *Lewiston Tribune*'s circulation area included most of north central Idaho, including the communities of Moscow and Pullman.

After one particular game I had umpired that summer, the paper published a story of the game on the front page of the sports section, which included a five-by-eight picture of Dwight Church and I face to face jawing about a particular call I had made during the game. I didn't think too much about it until my professor came up to me just before class started and asked me about it.

“I saw your picture on the sports page of the *Tribune* this morning. Was that you?”

“Yeah, that was me. I'm umpiring some of the legion games in the evening.”

He looked quizzically at me. "I didn't think you had it in you to be an umpire! You seem to be just too quiet and reserved to be doing that. I'm really surprised!"

His remark to me was disturbing. Did he think I didn't have the wherewithal to umpire a baseball game? If he didn't think I could umpire a baseball game, what did he think about my stepping into a role as a building administrator? I know I tend to be more of a listener than a talker, although I'll speak my mind if I feel strongly about something. But I got the feeling he thought I didn't have what it took to be a principal or a leader. I determined right there to prove him and anyone else who thought that they were dead wrong.

After summer school was over, I was again able to work about four weeks on the pea harvest until the middle of August. This change of pace during the summer again re-energized me for the new school year that started at the end of August.

CHAPTER 22

Student Problems and Coaching Baseball

> *When I first asked her, she replied with a grumpy 'No! I really don't want to.' 'Come on,' I said, trying to cajole her. 'I know you know how to do this one.' She stunned everyone with her retort. 'You don't know a damn thing about what I know! Just leave me alone!'*

The 1975-76 school year started with staff and students excited about returning to school. My schedule was going to be full. I would be teaching four algebra classes and two ninth grade general math classes. The ninth grade math classes started out pretty large with an enrollment exceeding twenty, which meant those classes would grow to be near thirty by the start of the second semester. I also had a number of students from the Northern Idaho Children's Home, which meant there would be some behavior problems in those classes. Many of the students I had in the algebra classes were students I had taught the previous year in the eighth grade math classes.

The in-service day for teachers went well, with Mr. Adams providing the same format and presentations he laid out the year before. There were a few new teachers on the staff, including a new math teacher named Mr. Neil Patterson. As the head of the math department, I visited with him some during the in-service day and found him to be quiet and reserved, but competent in the field of math. He would be teaching next to me on the second floor, so I would have Mr. Chavez on one side of my room and Mr. Patterson on the other side. He was pleasant to visit with and looked like he would be a valuable addition to the math department. As the teaching staff turned over, we were finding that a number of men were assigned to teaching on the second floor, which was fine with me. In my wing of the floor we now had myself, Mr. Crosby, Mr. Patterson, Mr. Chavez, and Mr. Thorpe teaching classes.

During in-service Mr. Adams stressed some changes in board policies. One of the new policies had to do with hacking. There had been some complaints in the community from a minority of parents that some hacks given by teachers were abusive in nature, and the board reacted by passing a policy to provide more structure to this form of discipline. The policy stated the teacher giving the hack was to ask a neighboring teacher to come out in the hall where the punishment would be applied. The teacher delivering the hack was to make sure no other students were in the hallway to view the punishment and was to state the reason for the hack before proceeding under the watchful eye of the witnessing teacher. After this new policy was outlined, I consulted with Mr. Chavez and Mr. Patterson and we agreed to be witnesses for the others if a hack was warranted.

My first day with students went well, with me again organizing the class seating charts and outlining the requirements for passing the class. I emphasized the new grading scale and assigned them the responsibility to have a math notebook for taking notes, which would be graded at the end of the quarter.

A number of things happened during this school year that stood out. One of the issues that arose had to do with the students from the Northern Idaho Children's Home. These students were sent to the home for a variety of reasons. Some were there because their parents could not control them; some were there because they were habitual runaways, while others were there because of minor skirmishes with the law. A significant number of them could be disruptive, especially in a class like general math. We had some disruptions to start the year, but I found I could get significant help from the staff at the children's home if I communicated with them.

They had a point reward system that gave the children special privileges in the home if they were well behaved at school and at the home. They could get points for maintaining passing grades and attending school regularly. They could lose points for running away and misbehaving. This seemed to work for them, especially when there was good communication between the school and the home.

I got to know many of these students during the year, and it didn't take much to get them to tell me their stories. Some had been physically and even sexually abused by a parent or a boyfriend of a mother. Some of these students had been habitually truant from school and some had run away from home several times. Some were prosecuted for habitual misdemeanor crimes. But they all had problems with submitting to authority figures and following the rules, whether they were passive aggressive in their rebellion or aggressively confrontational.

One particular boy was making significant progress at the home and at school. He was doing well in his classes and was not a problem at the home. He seemed to be on his way to rehabilitation and becoming a model student. By mid-winter he had accumulated enough points to be released from the home and sent back to his mother. One week before he was to be released, he just ran away. They found him and brought him back to the children's home within two weeks.

When he returned to my class, he came up to me with a broad grin.

"I'm back!" he said cheerfully. "They took all my points away and I have to start over."

"Why did you run away?" I asked. "You were almost ready to be sent home. Wasn't that what you wanted?" He lowered his voice and moved a little closer to me.

"If I went back home," he said quietly, "I would have to put up with my mom's boyfriend, who loves to beat on me. I like it here! At least I know I'm safe and I know what the rules are. I don't want to go home. I ran away to make sure I could stay here." With that, he moved to his seat and got ready for class. He turned out to be one of my best general math students that year. He was generally well behaved and he got good grades. It's interesting how the adolescent mind works when they are faced with difficult situations.

Another incident that stood out involved a young lady named Jennifer (not her real name), who was taking algebra. She had been in my eighth grade math class the previous year and was an outstanding student, well liked by staff and the other children. She was always well behaved and respectful in my eighth grade math class, and she worked hard enough to receive an A each semester. She always sported a ready smile and her demeanor was usually upbeat. I was delighted to see I was going to have her in my algebra class and looked forward to teaching her again. As the year started, I could see she was going to pick up where she left off in the eighth grade. She listened well in class, took good notes, and was respectful toward her fellow students and me. She received an A for the first semester.

When the second semester started, she began to change. At the start of the year, you could count on her being pleasant and smiling a lot, but as January progressed, she began to smile less and became sullen at times. There were days when she did not hand in her homework, and on the first test of the semester she got a D. There were times during our interactions in class when she made belligerent comments towards me and other students. At first, I ignored the comments, thinking she was just having a bad day, which can happen to us all. But it all came to a head on one particular day when I called on her to come up to the board and work a problem. In the past, I could always count on her to do this enthusiastically. She particularly liked working problems that stumped some of the other students.

When I first asked her, she replied with a grumpy "No! I really don't want too."

"Come on," I said pleasantly, trying to cajole her. "I know you know how to do this one."

She stunned everyone with her retort. "You don't know a damn thing about what I know! Just leave me alone!"

There was an awkward silence in the classroom. The class and I were stunned, as her comment was totally out of character. But I couldn't just let her say something like that in front of the class and get away with it.

"Young lady, you need to come out in the hall with me where we can talk. John, would you please work this problem on the board while I'm outside with Jennifer?"

Jennifer got up angrily from her desk and stomped to the door, opened it, and left, with me close behind her. As we were heading out the door, I wondered how I would confront her. This behavior was totally out of character and there had to be something unusual going on in her life to suddenly cause this kind of outburst. Instead of jumping on her verbally I gently, but firmly, said, "Look at me!" She turned, stiffened her back, and faced me. She raised her head and defiantly looked me in the eye. "Jennifer," I said gently. "What in the world is going on? This isn't like you at all! What would make you say something like that to me in front of the whole class? I thought we had a good relationship."

Immediately, her posture changed. Her shoulders slumped, and her once-defiant eyes began to fill with tears.

"Mr. Hammann, I'm so sorry," she said, starting to cry. "I can hardly stand it anymore. I'm not worth anything! I'm just a mess! My family and I have been going to counseling for the past month because my dad has been molesting me for over a year! He is in big trouble with the law and with my mom, who has kicked him out of the house. I feel like it's entirely my fault! I just want to kill myself!"

I was totally taken off guard—I couldn't believe what I was hearing! How could a parent do such a thing? This significant parent in her life wasn't even a stepfather; he was her dad! I was full of anger toward her dad, but my heart went out to her. Here was a beautiful, well-adjusted, bright young lady crushed by the actions of someone she trusted—her father. She was blaming herself for the despicable behavior of a trusted adult. "Jennifer," I said, "let's go down to the counselor and see if we can get you some help." I looked in on the teacher across the hall and asked for her to watch my class while I took a student to the office. As we walked to the office, she began to sob. I tried to comfort her.

"Jennifer, it's going to be okay," I said. "You can handle this. Whatever your dad did, it is his responsibility and you can't blame yourself. You are a great kid and I know you did nothing wrong here. You can get past this!"

When we got to the office area I found the counselor's door closed with another student sitting outside waiting to see him. I checked to see if Mr. Adams was there, but he was not available. By this time, Jennifer was a basket case. I sat her down in a spare office next to the counselor's while I tried to find someone qualified to counsel her. She sat there and sobbed as I left and was still sobbing when I came back a few minutes later. She needed help, but none was available. I got her some tissues from the teachers' lounge, which she used to wipe her eyes and dry her cheeks. As I watched her dab at the tears, I felt I just couldn't leave her there alone and suffering, so I closed the door and sat down across from her. "Jennifer, look at me," I said firmly. "Stop crying and look at me!" She began to get herself under control. The sobbing lessened until she was finally able to raise her head and look at me through puffy eyes. "Jennifer, I can't tell you I understand fully how you feel and what you are going through," I said. "But I'm a father and I have a beautiful fourth grade girl, and it upsets me that a father would molest his daughter. What he did was wrong and it is his responsibility. It is not your responsibility! He is the adult and you are the adolescent. You didn't do anything to make him do what he did. He simply broke trust and hurt you. I think it is a good thing that you are in family counseling. That means you and your family want to address what happened and make sure it never happens again. But I want to communicate this to you—you did nothing wrong. You should not feel guilty or ashamed. It's not your fault. It is his fault. I have nothing but the highest respect for you. You are one of my best and brightest students, and you have an incredible amount of potential. If anyone can deal with this and come out a stronger person, it is you. Do you hear what I'm saying?"

She looked up at me and nodded. I could see that she was getting herself under control. "I want you to go down to the faculty bathroom and clean yourself up," I said. "Then I want you to come back and wait to see the counselor. Can you do that for me?" Again, she nodded and even smiled a little. She stood and went to the bathroom.

While she was gone, I saw a student leave the counselor's office and saw Mr. Kytonen stick his head out to invite the next student into his office. I quickly motioned that I needed to talk to him, and he let me in his office. I filled him in on what Jennifer told me, and he said he would get her right in after he dealt with his next student.

I returned to the vacant office and found her sitting in her chair composed and looking much better. "Jennifer, I talked to Mr. Kytonen and he will see you in a couple of minutes. You just need to talk to him and let him know what is going on. He'll be able to help you. If you still need someone else to talk to, just let me know. I would be glad to give you a listening ear. Are you okay now?"

"I'll be okay," she responded. "Thanks for helping me." I left her there and returned to my class.

The next day when she came into my classroom, I greeted her at the door and asked if things were better. "Yes, things are much better, thank you," she said with a shy smile before walking to her desk. I could tell she was embarrassed to talk about what happened the day before, so I said little about the incident during the year other than to periodically ask her if she was okay. She always smiled and said, "Yes. I'm okay."

Based on the change of her behavior and the improvement I saw since our talk in the hall, I believe the family counseling went well and things got better for her. Her grades did come back up and her behavior in the classroom returned to what it was before this incident in her life. One of the things this taught me about teenagers is they're incredibly resilient—a bad thing happened to this girl, but she was able to bounce back and went on to graduate from high school with excellent grades. I'm sure it scarred her, but the emotional wound it caused did heal and it appeared she was able to get on with her life.

I had a great time coaching my first season of baseball. It was a much better experience than coaching the track team. Most of the athletes were on my basketball team as well, so we were familiar with each other. My biggest challenge was preparing practice activities for the athletes—I had played a lot of baseball, but I had never coached the sport.

I developed practice sessions based on what I had observed while watching some of Dwight Church's legion teams practicing during the summer months. I led off with some stretching exercises to limber up the muscles and joints followed by a couple of jogging laps around the field. The players would then divide up into pairs and throw baseballs back and forth to warm up their arms. I had an assistant coach and a manager, so we would divide the team into three groups. One of us hit fly balls to the outfielders, another hit ground balls to the infielders, and the pitchers would continue warming up and strengthening their legs by jogging laps and doing some sprints. Next, we would work on hitting with our pitchers throwing batting practice, since we did not have a batting cage or pitching machine. During the last part of practice, we would scrimmage and work on baseball situations like turning the double play and facilitating a rundown between the bases. We practiced special scenarios like when there are two outs and we are behind by one run with the bases loaded. Where should we play on the infield? Where should we play in the outfield? Where should the play go if the ball is hit to the right side? Where should the play go if it is hit to the left side? Where should we throw the ball if there is a shallow fly ball? As the year progressed and I became more experienced, I was able to fine-tune my practices to make them more efficient and meaningful.

During my first year of coaching, I gave the athletes more latitude in their play than many coaches do today. I never set up signals to relay through the catcher the pitches I wanted the pitcher to throw. Most of my pitchers were strictly fastball pitchers, and location is what helped them get a batter out. I had only a few pitchers who could throw a curveball or some other change-up pitch and was careful to make sure only a few curveballs were thrown, especially when the weather was cold. Freshmen tended to throw curves with their forearm rather than their wrist, which could cause an arm injury if it was done too much. As for our games—I absolutely loved them. When we were at bat, I always coached third base, and I had my assistant coach first. As the third base coach, I particularly liked sending instructions to the batters by giving them a signal from that position. In giving signals, you have a gesture that is a key signal. It tells the batter the batting instruction is coming next. For instance, the key signal may be touching the right side of my nose. After going through a number of gestures, I would give the key signal of touching the right side of my nose followed by the instructional signal, which might be touching my right shoulder signaling the batter to take the next pitch. If I wanted him to lay down a bunt, I would follow the key signal of touching the right side of my nose with touching my left elbow. Normally, I had a key signal and about four other signals designating instructions such as take the pitch, lay down a bunt, or swing the bat because the hit and run was on. There was also a signal to the base runners for stealing a base using the same method.

It didn't take me long to figure out I could only have a few signals as the players tended to forget them if I had too many. I found this out when my batters were calling time-out frequently to meet with me between home plate and third base to find out what I was signaling. If I kept the number of signals to about four or five, they could generally handle that.

My first year as a baseball coach went pretty well since we ended the season with a winning record, which was great. But at the end of the year, I determined to spend some time during the summer watching Dwight Church coach the Twins. I was sure I could pick up more coaching pointers by just observing him.

The school year ended much like previous years with one exception: we saw an end to the water fights. We collected books and checked kids out and then moved to our customary positions to supervise the water fights. Except this year, one of the female students was hit hard on the side of the head with a water balloon, perforating her eardrum. The mother was called to take her to the hospital where she was treated. Her mother then called the principal's office and strenuously voiced her concern regarding supervision on the last day. Mr. Adams called the staff together before we all checked out and made an executive decision that this would be the last year we would tolerate the traditional end-of-the-year water fight. He indicated we would beef up supervision and confiscate all water fight paraphernalia. He would also ask that a police officer be present to help monitor situations that day.

There was a general sigh of relief from the staff over this decision—we all felt things tended to get out of control once we released the students on the last day of school and thought this would make our supervision jobs easier knowing the principal would back any action we might take.

CHAPTER 23

Graduate School, a New School Year, and Some Union Issues

> *"I had never heard of a teacher 'warming up' before giving a hack, and I was intrigued and amused. I had to cover my mouth because I was having a hard time controlling my face. I was entertained by Mr. Patterson's serious formality and the dramatic way he was 'warming up.' In fact, I was on the verge of destroying this serious moment with a large smile or snicker, and that would not have been proper"*

After the summer of 1975, my wife and I talked extensively about increasing my efforts on obtaining a master's degree, which would allow me to qualify for an Idaho administrative certificate. I qualified for ten years of support from the GI Bill once I was discharged from the military, so I decided to try and take a class or two during the 1975-76 school year and take a full load again during the summer of 1976. Since I was not coaching a fall sport in 1975, I took a class titled Learning Theory and Teaching Strategies, which dealt with teaching techniques and methods for setting instructional goals and measuring the degree to which those goals were met. During the summer of 1976, I took two classes. One was titled Measurement and Statistics, which dealt with gathering and analyzing student learning data. The other was School Community Relations, which covered the various methods for facilitating communication between constituents in the school and the community, including students, staff, parents, and local businesses.

These classes gave me more insight into the tools I would need to be a successful principal. By the end of the summer of 1976, I had received all As in my classes except for one B in Secondary School Curriculum from my first summer in graduate school. At the end of the 1976 summer term, I met with my administrative program supervisor, and he pushed me to try and graduate by May of 1977. He said his department was under pressure from the college administration to increase graduation rates, and he was pushing all of his students to pick up their pace toward graduating. This meant I would have to take three more classes during the 1976-77 school year, but a look at my coaching responsibilities and the classes I still needed indicated I could do it. It would take a lot of time and work, but I could take one night class in the fall, do my principal internship experience during the fall semester, and take one class during the spring. This was workable since these classes only met twice a week for two hours each night and I wasn't coaching in the fall. So during the first half of the school year I took Practices in Guidance at night and did my internship with Mr. Adams during the regular school day.

My supervising professor was able to make an arrangement with Mr. Adams to allow me to work with him on administrative tasks and responsibilities. Mr. Adams was clear I would continue to teach my full load of classes and do the principal intern activities the two weeks before school started and one hour before and after school during the fall semester. The internship requirements were based on the hours spent on various projects, and a pass or fail grade was assessed based on whether those hours were fulfilled. For instance, I had to spend a specific number of hours on addressing student discipline issues, then a specific number of hours on teacher observations and evaluations. Other project topics included supervision of activities, developing class schedules, and promoting school and community communications. After fulfilling the hours for the project, I would write a report outlining and summarizing what had been done, and Mr. Adams would sign off, verifying I put in the hours and that the report was accurate. Along with taking the two summer classes, umpiring a few legion games, and working the pea harvest from mid-July to mid-August, I was now going to work two weeks before the start of the regular school year for my internship. I found myself working with Mr. Adams before the start of the year to develop teacher class assignments and student lists for each class, as well as organizing mailers for parents regarding the start of the year. I also helped enroll new students to the district and gave tours of the facilities to those students and their parents. I assisted Mr. Crosby with developing the athletic schedules for the year and also helped Mr. Adams develop the schedule for orienting teachers the first day they returned. I found myself putting in about eighty hours before I was to contractually report to school with the other teachers. Mr. Adams even allowed me to make a short presentation to the staff regarding some changes in district policy during the first day of orientation. I found the work stimulating, rewarding, and meaningful.

Orientation day for teachers went smoothly. Most staff members returned to school rested and ready to take on the challenges of another year teaching junior high students. We discovered three new teachers had been hired during the summer, with one of them qualified to teach math and science. The district administration and the school board had implemented a new philosophy for hiring teachers. This year, the primary criteria for employing new teachers straight out of college was to hire those who had the highest graduating grade point averages. The thinking was if we hired the brightest, they would turn out to be the best teachers. This turned out to be inaccurate since each one of these teachers left the district within two years. One of the new female teachers handed in her resignation before the end of the first semester after the students made her life incredibly miserable. She knew her subject matter, but she was at a loss when it came to controlling her classes.

One of the teachers, Mr. Black, would be teaching math and science just down the hall from me. Since I was the math department chairman, I spent some time the first week getting to know him. He had a degree in physics with a minor in mathematics, and I could tell he was very bright—my initial contact with him indicated he would make a great addition to our department.

When the school year started, I found myself working like a dog. Preparing and teaching my classes took much of my time, but I was putting in a significant number of hours performing internship activities. I would come in an hour before I was required to be there, and leave an hour or an hour and a half after school was out. I was handling student discipline issues and supervising home volleyball and football games. I also had to attend two school board meetings and report on my observations as part of my internship. Plus, I was attending a night class twice a week in the evenings. I was putting in more than sixty hours a week of hard work—but I was enjoying it.

Part of my internship involved dealing with discipline issues that happened near the end of the day. I dealt with a few fighting situations and quickly learned, under the supervision of Mr. Adams, to follow due process when recommending disciplinary action. Due process involved three requirements. First, written policies and rules had to be in place governing student behavior. Second, these rules and policies needed to be presented and explained to the students before they could be enforced. Third, a formal or informal hearing must be provided before any discipline could be administered. In this hearing, the student and/or his representative must be allowed to present his side of the issue. Finally, if discipline was necessary, it needed to fit the crime and be clearly stated to the student.

One fighting incident in particular occurred at the end of the awards assembly held at the end of the winter sports season. As the ninth grade varsity basketball coach, I was involved with giving letter certificates and making brief comments about my team. It was usually customary for one of the mothers of the team to bake a cake or pie for the coach as a "thank you" for his or her efforts with the student athletes. On this particular day in early spring, I was given a beautiful, large, vanilla-frosted white cake set on cardboard and covered with tin foil. It was cold as my student manager and I exited the assembly through the boys' locker room. As we walked out into the dirt parking lot, we came upon two boys in a physical altercation. One boy had pulled the other's coat over his head, forcing him to bend over. As he pulled the coat down, he began kicking the other boy in the face with his booted foot. Once I recognized what was happening, I put the cake in my left hand and shouted at them.

"That's enough! Back off! Stop kicking him!"

Incredibly, the boy stopped kicking the other and took a step back. The other boy shrugged his coat back off his head and stepped forward, throwing a vicious right hook, which landed on the side of his attacker's face. I reached out with my right hand and grabbed the student by his coat lapel and pulled him away as he pulled back his fist to deliver another blow.

There I stood, holding this beautiful, white, frosted cake in my left hand and an angry student with my right hand. Unbelievably, I was actually tempted to take that cake and smack it into the face of the student who had thrown the punch after I had said to stop. Fortunately, I restrained myself and instead handed the cake to my stunned student manager, grabbed the kid with both hands, and pushed him up against the gym wall. Initially he started to struggle, but quickly ceased once he saw who had him pressed against the wall.

"You are both going to the office with me," I said. After saying this, the student I was holding tried to pull away from me and began to protest.

"No I'm not! I'm going to kick the crap out of this guy!"

He shook himself free and moved toward the other student, who was turning to head to the office across the street. The two boys were eighth grade students weighing in the neighborhood of 120 pounds, and I was a fairly athletic man weighing 180 pounds. I quickly grabbed the defiant student and threw him over my shoulder like a sack of potatoes. He was stunned at first, shocked by the ease with which I had tossed him over my shoulder. But soon he recovered and began to struggle mightily to get free of me. I had only gone about fifteen feet when I realized there was no way I could carry him all the way to the office without one or both of us getting hurt. So I stopped and set him down still holding him by his coat.

"You can walk over to the office like a man with some dignity," I told him. "Or you can continue to resist and I will physically carry you over there. What is it going to be?"

This calmed him down significantly, and he told me he'd come along peaceably if I let him go.

"Do you give me your word on this?" I asked.

"Yes! I will not cause you anymore trouble." With that, I released him and the three of us walked across the street to the office with my student manager dutifully following along carrying my cake, which was mercifully still intact.

When we got there, Mr. Adams supervised me as I provided due process to the students. We had rules against fighting, and they both said they knew those rules. I gave them each a chance to relay their side of the situation that led to the fight. It turned out the fight started with insults and then became physical. After consulting with Mr. Adams, we decided to suspend them from school for two days. I then called their parents to have them pick up the students. When they came to the school, Mr. Adams explained the situation and his disciplinary decision to them and released the students to their care. In both incidents, the parents were supportive of our actions. This was just one of the several disciplinary issues I dealt with during my internship. I was learning as much from this internship experience as I had learned from my graduate classes combined.

One thing I learned from this experience was that reasoning with students and giving them choices can go much further than trying to be physical with them, even in emotionally charged situations. Learning this important concept went a long way toward helping me be effective as a secondary school principal later in my career.

As for my teaching assignment during this particular year, things were a little different. I was again teaching four algebra sections, but this year I also taught two eighth grade general math classes. The eighth grade classes went pretty well, but the algebra classes were a real challenge. Once we got past the first quarter, the effort from a significant number of my students plummeted. Near the end of the semester, about a third of the algebra students were receiving a D or F. Many of the students just refused to do the homework and study for the tests.

After I submitted my algebra grades to the office at the end of the first semester, Mr. Adams came to my room concerned about the number of failing grades I was giving. I pulled out my grade book and showed him the attendance patterns of some of the students, with many having more than fifteen absences. Those same students had a significant number of zeroes for their daily grades and also failed to keep a notebook, which was worth 100 points. There wasn't much he could say with the documented evidence staring him in the face, but he did make a comment as he left. "Bob, those are just too many Ds and Fs," he said. "You need to do something to reduce that number. The school board and district administration are very concerned about the number of students failing your algebra classes this year, and they wanted me to look into it. I'm just giving you a warning—you need to do something to address this."

I was stunned at his request. My grading scale was already watered down since a student had to average less than fifty percent to flunk the class. There was no way I was going to drop the grading scale any lower than that. After evaluating his comments and looking over my grading system, I decided I had enough documentation to weather any storm that might come my way this year. However, I decided to once again re-evaluate my instruction and grading requirements at the end of the year if I continued getting this kind of pressure from the administration.

Fortunately, the problem took care of itself about two weeks into the third quarter. At least half of the students receiving Ds and most of the students receiving Fs transferred to ninth grade general math. That greatly improved the grading statistics, and I did not receive any more visits that year from Mr. Adams regarding this issue.

Another issue that raised its head during the year had to do with the Lewiston Education Association (LEA), the Idaho Education Association (IEA), and the National Education Association (NEA). When I joined the Lewiston staff in January of 1972, I came in under the radar and was not approached about joining the LEA, IEA, or NEA, which were all affiliated organizations. But when the following year began, I was approached by Mr. Walker and asked if I wanted to join the LEA, IEA, and NEA. He indicated most of the teachers on the staff and in the district were members and that these were professional organizations to represent the issues of classroom teachers. Membership was optional, but if I joined the dues would amount to about $150 per year, which would be deducted from my salary on a monthly basis. I was enthusiastic about teaching and the dues did not seem to be exorbitant. I also wanted to be a supportive member of the staff and viewed as a professional, so I chose to join.

My first time attendance at an LEA meeting occurred shortly after I joined at the beginning of the 1972-73 school year. I don't recall there being many high school or junior high coaches in attendance other than Mr. Albright and myself. I think most of the other attendees were female elementary and secondary school teachers. At that meeting, we elected the officers for the LEA with most of them coming from the elementary level. The rest of the meeting was pretty much a gripe session, with some teachers complaining about pay, benefits, and working conditions, comparing their situations with those of teachers across the river in Clarkston, Washington. The discussion was pretty negative, and I decided I didn't have time to deal with this kind of thing. My main concern was teaching, coaching, and working with my junior high students. I felt strongly I had better and more important things to do than gripe about my job and the working conditions. I heard more than enough griping and grumbling in the teachers' lounge.

The issue of my continued membership with the LEA, IEA, and NEA came to a head in September 1976, when the NEA endorsed Jimmy Carter for president and supported the Democratic Party's political platform. This was the first time to my knowledge that the NEA endorsed a presidential candidate and took a stance on non-educational issues. I was initially puzzled by the stance of the NEA, since I supposed it to be a professional organization, but as I did some research and thought more about what they had done I became outraged by their stance. First, the NEA never consulted me about my opinion on these political issues, and second, I thought these teacher organizations were there to help teachers become better equipped to meet the educational needs of the students. They were using a portion of my dues to promote political issues I opposed and support a political party platform I could not endorse. And lastly, I was not in favor of electing Jimmy Carter for president.

I talked with my more conservative colleagues and found they felt the same way. What did the NEA think it was doing by taking my dues to support the election of a political candidate I did not personally support and to lobby our national legislatures about issues that had nothing to do with education? I went to the next LEA meeting and voiced my concerns, but was met with a terse, "We'll take that position under consideration, but there is little we can do at the national level."

Another issue that greatly distressed me was happening across the border in the state of Washington. Teachers in the Evergreen and Aberdeen School Districts had gone on strike in an attempt to force those districts to give them better salaries, benefits, and working conditions. I totally disagreed with this approach of trying to leverage school boards and a community to make a teacher's life easier. Those teachers in Washington were making significantly more money, getting better benefits, and their work environment was better, yet they were still demanding more. I finally came to realize the LEA, IEA, and NEA were professional organizations in name only. They were gradually morphing into unions much like the Teamsters and the United Auto Workers.

I always felt that if I was unhappy with my salary, my benefits, or my working conditions, then I could just move to another school district. I was adamantly opposed to striking and denying the community my services as a teacher just because I wanted more money or better benefits. I always felt a conscientious community would take care of its teachers to the best of its ability if the teachers could demonstrate a majority of the children in the community were learning well. I also didn't believe in tenure for a teacher—a teacher should be able to stand on his or her record based on the achievement of the students under his or her care. If a teacher couldn't perform the job adequately, then they should be removed. I didn't enter the teaching profession to get rich or have an easy life. I was in the business because I deeply cared about giving kids the skills and discipline needed to become contributing citizens of this great country we live in. I believed many other teachers felt the same way I did, but those in power at the state and national levels had developed a union mindset.

Based on the response at the LEA meeting and what I was seeing at the national level, I made my way to the district office, where I filed the paperwork to stop paying IEA and NEA dues. Since Idaho was a right-to-work state, I could do this. I did maintain my membership in the local LEA, because I knew I had a voice and they were better equipped to represent my needs to the administration and school board. But it was obvious the state and national organizations were going in the opposite direction I wished to travel, and I would have no influence there. I determined to never join such organizations again, and this particular incident further encouraged me to pursue my goal of becoming a building administrator.

The second semester came around, during which another standout and humorous incident took place. On a fateful day in the spring, I was teaching my eighth grade math class when I heard a soft knock at my door. I stopped teaching and went over and opened it. There stood Mr. Patterson with two boys behind him.

"What can I do for you, Mr. Patterson?"

"Would you mind coming out here to witness me giving these two boys a hack?" he replied, in a very soft but firm voice.

I noticed then that he was holding in his right hand a three-foot-long, one-inch-thick paddle with holes drilled through the business end of the instrument much like the one I had. "Sure!" I said. "Just give me a minute to get my students working on their assignment." By this time, my students had begun to whisper to each other as I moved to respond to the knock on the door, but they quickly went silent when they heard Mr. Patterson ask me to witness a hack. When the students knew a hack was going to be given, they would get very quiet in an attempt to hear as much as possible of the proceedings, especially the sound of the blows. I knew this because I had overheard some lengthy discussions among the students about the courage and cowardice of those who received the infamous hack. The reputations of both the students and the teachers could rise or fall based on the way a hack was received and administered.

I went to the chalkboard and wrote the math assignment on the board, stressing to the class they needed to be on task and quiet while I assisted Mr. Patterson. I knew my instructions for silence would be followed, but my instructions to work on the assignment would probably be mostly ignored, since they would be tuned in to the activities that were about to take place in the hall. I also knew this learning experience might be more valuable for them than the math.

I moved out into the hall, shutting the door behind me. I found Mr. Patterson calmly standing with the two eighth grade boys. Mr. Patterson and I looked down the hall to make sure no one was present as was required by school board policy. Just then, a student came out of Mr. Black's room just down the hall. Mr. Patterson motioned with his paddle for the student to return to class, and she quickly retreated back into the classroom. Now at least three classrooms knew a hack was about to happen in the hall.

Once the hall was clear, Mr. Patterson looked at me, cleared his throat, and said very formally, "Mr. Hammann, these young men have continued to chew gum in my class even after I warned them several times not to. The last time I caught them chewing gum, I gave them a detention, yet they came to class today again chewing gum. At the beginning of class, I had them spit out the gum they were chewing and gave them another detention, but then I noticed them again chewing gum just before I came to get you. For this defiant refusal to do as instructed, I am giving each of them a hack."

"Okay," I responded. "That sounds reasonable to me."

He turned to the two boys and spoke formally once again.

"I'm going to have you both bend over, and you're going to grab your ankles and stay in that position until I administer the hack. If you raise up before I hit your backside, you will get another one. Do you understand me?"

Both boys nodded their heads. "I want both of you to stand over here next to the wall while I warm up!" The larger of the two boys, who was about five-foot-eight, moved nervously to the far side of the hall, while the smaller boy, who was five-foot-two, moved to the wall exhibiting a small, cocky grin. I had never heard of a teacher "warming up" before giving a hack, and I was intrigued and amused. I had to cover my mouth because I was having a hard time controlling my face. I was entertained by Mr. Patterson's serious formality and the dramatic way he was "warming up." In fact, I was on the verge of destroying this serious moment with a large smile or snicker, and that would not have been proper. So I just covered my mouth as Mr. Patterson moved to the center of the hall and began "warming up." He lifted both of his arms, stretching them over his head before bending over to touch his toes a few times. He twisted his torso to the left and right as the mesmerized students looked on. Their eyes widened as Mr. Patterson slowly backed away from us, making sure he had a lot of space around him before beginning to swing his paddle slowly and then with great gusto. Amazingly, the paddle whistled loudly as he swung it forcefully like a tennis racket. I noticed the heavy-set student pale as the paddle whistled with each swing. And even the cocky grin on the other student's face receded a little bit as he swung the paddle. Of course, behind my hand my smile was growing as his was shrinking. I was really having trouble keeping my features neutral, as the humor of the situation was almost more than I could stand.

Finally, after several practice swings, he looked over to the two students.

"Who's first?" he asked firmly. The student with the cocky grin shrugged his shoulders and volunteered. He swaggered over to where Mr. Patterson stood and assumed the position, grabbing his ankles as he bent over. Mr. Patterson stood to the side of the exposed backside and took his striking position. He then leaned down toward the boy's head and reminded him of the rules.

"Remember, don't raise up or you're going to get another one!"

"Yeah, I get it!" the boy replied flippantly.

Mr. Patterson then stood up and almost faster than the eye could follow, he drew back the paddle and swiftly brought it down on the exposed backside. He swung it hard enough so it whistled just before it hit and understandably, the student flinched and started to stand up as the blow landed.

The sound of the hack resounded up and down the hall, and I knew the rest of the classes in the hall were now keenly aware of the event occurring in the hallway. I knew the hack was significant because the big kid standing next to the wall waiting his turn whimpered and crumpled to the floor.

"Please, please, I promise I will never chew gum in your class again!" he cried. "Please don't give me a hack."

Mr. Patterson ignored the pleas of the big kid crumpled on the floor and instead spoke very sorrowfully to the student he just hacked. "You raised up! I'm sorry you did that. That means you get another one. Take the position and stay down this time." The cocky grin had long disappeared from the boy's face and was now replaced by a grim frown. With tears dotting his cheeks, he again took the position. Mr. Patterson quickly struck him again, although this time he didn't do it with the same enthusiasm. The student stayed down this time, but stood up slowly after the blow was delivered, indicating he was in some pain, although I think this was more for show than for pain.

"Am I going to have any more problems with you chewing gum in my class?" Mr. Patterson asked.

The student hung his head a little and respectfully replied, "No, sir! This is the last time I'll chew gum in your class." Mr. Patterson then sent him back to his classroom. I noticed his room was exceptionally quiet as the boy opened the door and returned to his seat.

As the classroom door clicked shut, Mr. Patterson turned to the boy slumped on the floor.

"Get up here and take your medicine like a man," he told him. "You chose to defiantly disobey me, now get up here so we can get this over." The boy slowly got up on his feet and came over to Mr. Patterson. Tears were flowing down his cheeks, but he assumed the position as directed. Again, Mr. Patterson leaned down close to his ear and reminded him of the rules. With hands on his ankles and his backside in the air, the boy nodded his head in understanding. Mr. Patterson quickly swung the paddle, with less force than that applied to the first student, and fortunately the student stayed put.

After the hack was delivered, the boy stood up and Mr. Patterson made him look him in the eye.

"Am I going to have any more trouble with you chewing gum in my class in the future?" The boy shook his head and replied with a great amount of sincerity.

"No, sir, Mr. Patterson! You won't catch me chewing gum in your class ever!"

"You probably need to go down to the bathroom and clean up a little bit," Mr. Patterson said to the boy. "You look a little worse for wear. Once you get cleaned up, you need to quickly get back to my class. You got that?"

"Yes, sir!" he replied and quickly scuttled down to the bathroom at the end of the hall.

After the hall was clear, Mr. Patterson looked at me and smiled.

"I'll bet this will be the last hack I have to give this year," he said with a wink. "What do you think?"

"Neil, you just became a legend in this school," I said, breaking out into laughter. "You shouldn't have any more issues in regard to discipline the rest of this year and probably for years to come. I have to admit I have never seen anything like that in my whole teaching career."

And indeed, I never had to witness another hack given by Mr. Patterson, although he and I taught alongside each other for the next three years.

We both returned to our respective classrooms, and as I entered mine I noticed my students were quietly working like busy beavers. I marveled as they continued to work quietly and on task like this until the bell rang to end class. Later in the day, as my students trickled into the classroom, one or two of them told me they'd heard Mr. Patterson had hacked two students and it was quite the event. It's amazing how a hack can sometimes have a dramatic positive affect on the learning environment of your classroom and the behavior of practically all the students in the school. The afterglow of that hack lasted about a week before everything returned to normal.

Near the end of the week, when several teachers were in the lounge, I related my observations of what came to be known as "the hack of 1976." Mr. Patterson entered the room and listened to my story with a wide smile. Most of the teachers were impressed and looked at Mr. Patterson with a new respect. "I never had another problem with students chewing gum," Mr. Patterson told the group. "In fact, I haven't had any discipline problems to speak of since that day. I guess the hack served its purpose." Most of us agreed—and were correct—that Mr. Patterson would probably have few disciplinary problems for the rest of the year.

CHAPTER 24

Angry Students, a Master's Degree, and Searching for a Job

> *As I came around the corner, he jumped out at me—all five feet, three inches and 120 pounds of him—and tried to hit me in the face with his fisted hand. As he jumped out to cold cock me, I took a step back, which saved me from receiving the full brunt of the blow. Instead, he grazed my chin with his fist.*

From the beginning of the school year, I had the opportunity to visit with our new math teacher Mr. Black a number of times. This was his first year as a teacher, and since I was the math department chairman, he came to me on a few occasions for advice or just to vent. He seemed to have a love for teaching and for his subject matter. He also seemed to care about kids, and even volunteered to coach the seventh grade football team.

On one particular day about two weeks after the start of school, he told me he was having some disciplinary problems with his seventh and eighth grade math and science students. The noise level in his classes frustrated him, especially when he would give them time in class to work on assignments. I told him I had noticed several times as I made my way to the office that the noise level in his class was high, even when he was trying to give a lecture.

"I'm going to get this under control," he said. "I can't function in that kind of noisy atmosphere. Tell me what you do to keep students on task in your classes."

I told him I demanded quiet and their attention when we were grading papers, giving a test, or when I was making a presentation. I had to stay on them all the time, sometimes giving a detention or calling a parent when one or two students refused to comply. I told him I could stand a certain level of noise when I let the students work on assignments, because I let them work in groups of twos or threes, as I always believed student learning could be enhanced when they were helping each other work the practice problems. Certain amounts of noise could not be avoided as they were helping each other, so I just had to occasionally warn them to keep it down as they worked. I also had to tell some students to keep the discussions on the math problems and not their social lives.

After hearing me out, he told me he felt there should be absolute quiet from the students in his classroom at all times, because he believed that was the best atmosphere for learning. He indicated he was going to come up with a plan to get the absolute quiet he felt he needed. I wished him well and didn't think about this discussion until later in the school year.

As the year progressed, I noticed the noise level in his class got lower and lower each time I walked by his room on my way to the bathroom. It finally reached a point where I could walk by his class and not hear a thing coming from his room unless he was teaching. But I also noticed the attitude of the students coming to my eighth grade math classes from his science classes. Several times, some of those students came into my class saying, "I hate that science class!" Or, sometimes, "I hate Mr. Black!"

When I questioned them about their feelings, they were pretty vague.

"I just hate the class," one student said. "All we do is work and you can't say anything. If you do, you get punished. I just hate the class and the teacher!"

After I had heard several of these comments, I caught Mr. Black in his classroom after school and commented on the quiet learning environment I had observed in his classes when I went by his room.

"What did you do to get them to work so quietly?" I asked.

"I just nail them each and every time they start disrupting the class," he said with a smile. "It's reached a point where they now know better than to talk or make a lot of noise in my class. They know there are unpleasant consequences for that behavior. You'll have to stop in sometime when they are working on an assignment and see how well it is going."

I did not say anything to him about the negative comments I was getting from some of his students, but early in February I had the chance to stop by his class on my way back from a bathroom break. As I walked by his room, I noticed his door was open, so I stopped and looked in to see Mr. Black reading a book at his desk as the students were all working intensely. The room was eerily quiet, and my curiosity was such that I decided to slide into the room and talk to him about the exceptional behavior exhibited by the students. I noticed out of the corner of my eye two boys at the front of the room standing straight and tall at the chalkboard as I approached Mr. Black's desk.

"I noticed your class was exceptionally quiet today," I said to Mr. Black, "and I remembered you had invited me to come in and see what you were doing to keep the noise level down and the students on task. So I stopped in to see what was going on. What are you reading?"

Mr. Black looked up at me with a smile.

"I'm taking a graduate class in physics, and I'm doing some reading in preparation for my class tonight. As for the behavior of my students, come over here and I'll show you." He got up from his desk and directed me to follow him over to where the two boys were standing at the chalkboard. When we got to the boys, he just pointed to them.

"These two boys are here because they thought they could disrupt my class by visiting with each other while I was trying to give my lecture this morning. This is what happens when one of my students disrupts my class." I took a closer look and noticed the boys were standing ramrod straight with their hands grasped behind their backs, leaning forward with their noses in a chalked circle made on the board. There were several other small circles on the board near where these students were standing. "They get to stay in this position until the end of the period, which will be in about five minutes," Mr. Black said. "As you can see, this is pretty uncomfortable for them. I doubt they will cause me a problem in the future, right boys?"

There were grunts from the two at the chalkboard.

I turned to look at the students in their seats, but they continued to work quietly, ignoring what was transpiring at the front of the room.

"Why are these students working so industriously when it's less than five minutes until the end of the class?" I asked.

"They know that if they don't they will be standing up here like these boys for a ten-minute period tomorrow. I just don't tolerate any kind of disruption and they know it." Amazed, I told him that what he was doing seemed to be working and to keep it up. With that, I turned and left the classroom, hurrying to get back to my own class before the bell rang. As I hurried down the hall, I felt there was just something wrong with what I had seen. The student behavior in his class was what every teacher might envision as perfect, but the learning environment was off. There was good behavior, but there didn't appear to be any enthusiasm for learning from the students. They seemed to be working and complying out of fear rather than from a love for the subject matter or the teacher.

I questioned some of my better eighth grade students who came from Mr. Black's science classes during the following week about the way he ran the class. In almost every discussion, they communicated a deep negative feeling for the subject matter and the teacher. "It's as if he cares more about having a quiet room than he cares about us," one student said. "I feel pretty small and unimportant in his class. I just hate science and if I had the chance, I would never take another science class again."

Initially, I had considered instituting some of the disciplinary techniques demonstrated by Mr. Black. But after talking to some of my students, I realized that having a student stand with his or her nose in a circle at the board in front of the others was demeaning to the student being punished. It also elicited anger and negative feelings from those on the observing end. It went beyond being discipline and bordered on emotional abuse. No wonder there was a hatred for the subject matter and the teacher. I found I had to spend a lot of time in the following year helping my students overcome the anger they had from taking math from Mr. Black. In some instances, I was unable to help them overcome their feelings and appreciate the subject matter—they could not get beyond the negative experience they'd had the year before. Some of those students who moved on to high school were adamant they would never take another math class if they could help it.

I determined there had to be a balance between maintaining discipline in the classroom and loosening up enough to make math a fun subject. I did not back down from confronting inappropriate student behavior with warnings, verbal chastisements, hacks, after-school detentions, or referrals to the principal's office—but I usually implemented the discipline privately, either out in the hall or after class. I also interlaced my lesson presentations with humor whenever possible. At least two or three times a month we would play some math games to break the monotony of the everyday classroom routine. I would say the learning environment in my classroom was generally positive for most of the year. As for my classroom discipline, there was one standout incident that occurred with an angry student from the North Idaho Children's Home. He was enrolled in my eighth grade math class during the middle of the first semester, and before his first class period ended, it was clearly evident he was going to be a discipline problem. He was sullen and reluctant to follow directions from the time I assigned him a seat until the class period was over. That attitude never changed in the days that followed, but it wasn't until his fourth day in class that I had a confrontation with him. He came to class late that day without his books and slammed the door as he made his way to his desk.

"Hey!" I said sternly. "Don't slam the door like that when you come into my class. You're late and you need to be here on time."

He turned beet red and began to tell me off using a variety of vulgar words. The class was shocked, and all eyes turned to me to see what I was going to do. I kept calm and jerked my thumb toward the door.

"Let's go!" I told the student. "We are going down to see Mr. Adams. Class, the assignment is on the board. I want you to work on it while I'm gone. Let's go!"

The student jumped out of his desk and stalked belligerently through the door. I followed behind him, trying to act as calmly as possible. When I came out into the hall, he was already about fifteen feet ahead of me. I continued following him as he moved down the hall and then turned left out of sight into the hallway leading to the stairs that went down to the office.

As I came around the corner, he jumped out at me — all five feet, three inches and 120 pounds of him—and tried to hit me in the face with his fisted hand. As he jumped out to cold cock me, I took a step back, which saved me from receiving the full brunt of the blow. Instead, he grazed my chin with his fist. The wild swing and the fact that he missed my face caused him to lose his balance and stumble by me. As he stumbled, I put both hands out and pushed him forcefully away from me. I stood in front of him with my hands at my side.

"Do you really want to do this? You have attacked me, and legally I can now protect myself. Is this really what you want to do?"

He stood there for a full five seconds, glaring at me with a red face. His arms were hanging at his sides with both hands balled into fists. I was now fully alert and stood ready to defend myself and get him under control if he chose to be physical. Fortunately, he turned away and continued stalking down the stairs to the office area. I followed him, walking carefully around the three blind corners until we got to the office. By this time, he had calmed down considerably and took a seat in the main office. I stepped past him and into the office where Mr. Adams was working at his desk. I closed his door and told him about the behavior of the student in class and about him trying to hit me as I escorted him to the office. To my surprise, Mr. Adams said he would handle it and sent me back to class.

That was the last time I saw that student. I suspect the children's home removed him from school and provided his education under their direct supervision. They were known to do that with the more difficult students. During my term at Jenifer Junior High, this was the only time I had a student try to physically attack me. I was glad I was able to deal with this particular situation without having to get physical.

At the end of the fall semester, I had completed my principal internship with a "pass" grade. I had also finished the night class in the Principles and Practices in Guidance. I took my last class in the spring called Interpersonal Communication, which was probably the most valuable class in my graduate program. I learned the importance of listening and truly understanding what another was trying to communicate and how body language plays a role in listening. Asking questions and summarizing what a person said can communicate that I truly heard what he/she said. It's important not to multitask while listening, but to give the person my full attention when he/she is talking. We were taught a variety of interpersonal communication methods and given the opportunity to practice them in class. It proved to be a very valuable class when it came to disciplining students, dealing with parents and business leaders, and dealing with educational peers.

After I finished this class in the spring of the year, I had one more task to complete to meet the requirements for the master's degree in secondary school administration, and that was to take a comprehensive exam. A person completing a master's program at the University of Idaho had to submit an in-depth written dissertation or take a comprehensive essay exam over all the course material taken in the program. Because of my coaching duties during the spring of the year, I chose to take the exam.

On April 18, I sat down with several other graduate students in a classroom on the campus of the University of Idaho and took the exam. I had kept copious notes from each course taken in my graduate program and had used them to prepare. At the beginning of the testing period, the exam proctor passed out some notebook paper and a blue book containing several pages of blank lined paper and gave each of us the essay questions associated with our programs. He indicated we could use blank lined notepaper to make a draft, but our final answers were to be written in ink in the blue book. He said the notebook paper, for security reasons, had to be submitted with the blue book at the end of the exam period.

I was a math teacher and at that time, writing was not my forte. My handwriting looked like chicken scratch and I struggled with putting together grammatically correct sentences and developing paragraphs that made sense. I spent the first hour and a half writing my draft and then the last half hour copying the answers in ink to the blue book. I turned the exam in with great trepidation. I knew the answers to the questions, but I was concerned about communicating that knowledge in writing.

My program advisor told me I had to have a "pass" grade to qualify for the degree. A failing grade would mean I had to retake the exam, which wouldn't occur until the end of the next semester. I was relieved when two weeks later I received notification that I had passed the test and would be graduating in the middle of May.

Anticipating the possibility I would be obtaining a degree in May and getting an Idaho principal's certificate, I had begun the process of applying for principal jobs in Idaho, Oregon, and Washington. I had set up a placement file with Boise State University when I attended there in the fall of 1970, so I just updated the file with a new resume and a copy of my transcripts. I also included letters of recommendation from Mr. Adams, one college professor, and three of the teachers who worked with me. I then sent out about ten applications tied to principal jobs open in the area and had Boise State send out copies of my placement file to those districts.

I did not receive a single interview. All I received were "Dear John" rejection letters that basically said, "We appreciate your interest in our position, but we have chosen to go with someone else." I decided the rejections might be because I did not have a principal's certificate in hand, plus I was lacking administrative experience.

More than half the rejection letters contained comments that my experience did not meet their requirements. It was evident I was not quite ready to enter the field of administration and would need to gain some kind of administrative experience.

Fortunately, Mr. Crosby, our athletic director, came to me at the beginning of April and said he was resigning from his position as athletic director to be more involved with his sons as they played football, basketball, and participated in track.

"I've watched you working with the basketball and baseball teams, and you were a significant help when we did the scheduling and supervision during your principal internship last fall," he told me. "I think you could do this job. You are going to get your master's degree, and I know you would do a great job in this position. If it is okay with you, I'm going to recommend you to Mr. Adams for the position. What do you say?"

I was stunned—what a great opportunity! I could coach basketball and baseball and be the athletic director. The additional pay would also ease our financial situation at home as I would now be able to make about $12,000 in the year to come. I also would gain some administrative experience that might help me get a principal's job in the future. I was quick to respond. "Phil, I'd be really interested in doing that next year!"

"I'll talk to Roger tomorrow, and he should make a decision soon. I don't know of anyone else interested in the position, so you should get it. You will need to go to the league meeting with me in May to set up the athletic schedules for the fall and winter sports. I'll help you get organized so you can make the transition."

Within a week, Mr. Adams came to me and offered me the position, which I quickly accepted.

I entered May with a full plate of activities. With Mr. Crosby's help, I met with the athletic directors from our league and set the schedules for fall and winter sports. I called some schools outside our league to set up non-league games to fill out the schedules for volleyball, football, basketball, and wrestling. I contacted the director of officials and gave him the schedules so he could assign officials for the ninth grade sports. We usually paid our own coaches and staff to officiate games below the ninth grade level, since there were no state rules regarding that level. I had officiated a number of seventh and eighth grade football and basketball games myself since joining the staff.

As the end of the school year came, I made preparations to attend the University of Idaho graduation ceremonies scheduled on a Sunday afternoon in the middle of May. I would have skipped the ceremonies, but my wife and my parents insisted I go through it so they could be there to commemorate the achievement.

I remember gathering with the rest of the master's candidates to get our robes and sashes before our program supervisor gave us directions regarding marching into the University of Idaho Kibbie Dome for the ceremonies. The administration and faculty would march in first followed by the doctoral candidates. The master's candidates would follow grouped by their disciplines. The last to enter would be the undergraduate candidates. After the instructions were given and we had put on our robes, the supervisor moved around our group offering congratulations to each of us.

There were about eight of us receiving master of secondary school administration degrees. In that group, we had one female. Because of Title IX, the university had gone to great lengths to recruit more women to enroll in this program, since most high school principals and many junior high principals were men. I had observed this lone female candidate working her way through the program. The professors seemed to spend more time encouraging and assisting her than they did many of her male peers. As we prepared ourselves for the ceremonies, the program supervisor and a number of professors hugged her and congratulated her for her accomplishment. It seemed like they just gushed over her accomplishments, while I, along with several of the other male graduates, received only a curt handshake and brief comment of congratulations.

I was to learn that in many cases, getting an administrator job was greatly affected by the "good old boy" system, or in this case "the good old boy and girl" system. I learned to disdain that process of upward mobility in the administrative ranks—I always believed a person should be selected to lead a school or district because they were the most qualified person for the position. They should not be selected because they knew someone in a position of power. Many times when that process was used, poor leaders were selected for positions that would have a negative impact on the safety, welfare, and learning of the students under their care.

The graduation ceremonies went well, and my wife and parents were able to proudly watch me receive my advanced degree and help me celebrate this accomplishment in my life. I now faced the summer and the next school year with a major accomplishment behind me.

During the summer, my total focus was on making as much money as possible. I umpired Babe Ruth baseball games until the pea harvest started and then worked the pea harvest until the end of the season. By now, I had enough tenure to work the day shift, and my wife was fortunate enough to be hired to work the night shift sorting peas. One of us was always home with our kids when the other was working. Our kids were old enough to fend for themselves while my wife slept during the day, and I could sleep at night when they slept. By the middle of August when the harvest ended, we were both pretty exhausted. We had a little more than a week to get ready for another year of school. By the time the 1977-78 school year started, I was ready to take on some new challenges.

CHAPTER 25

Athletic Director, Coach, and a Wildly Strange School Year

> *"What's the ruling on this situation?' the head official asked. 'Can a ball dropped by a punt receiver be advanced by the kicking team?' I had reviewed the football rulebook sitting in my locker in the gymnasium, but I still wasn't certain of the ruling either. I was the ranking 'expert' on the subject, since I was the athletic director, and they were looking at me to make a quick decision, so I decided to be assertive. 'Sure! You can advance a fumble!' Mr. Albright looked at me questioningly!"*

Near the end of July 1977, I stopped by the school district office to sign my contract for the school year and was told Mr. Adams had retired from public education and Mr. Vaughn Jasper, the principal of Sacajawea Junior High School, had been reassigned to our school. This would be my third principal in six years, and I was finding changes in leadership at the principal level had a significant impact on my anxiety level. I determined to be proactive as I had been when Mr. Adams took over for Mr. Walker. So a week before school was to start, I went to the principal's office to introduce myself and greet our new administrator. I had seen him at a few of the basketball games when we played Sacajawea, but I had never had a chance to visit with him.

My initial impression was that he was very different from both Mr. Adams and Mr. Walker. He was an athletic-looking man standing about six feet, three inches tall. He had a reputation as an excellent golfer, and I learned he played a number of sports while in high school. He greeted me amiably as I walked into his office to introduce myself.

"Well, Mr. Hammann, I guess you are the new athletic director, right?" he asked after I'd shaken his hand.

"Yes," I said. "Mr. Adams assigned me that position before he left, which I hope is okay with you. I just came in to see if I could be of any assistance as you make your transition to Jenifer."

"I can assure you I certainly don't plan on changing any teaching or administrative assignments," he said. "Your reputation as a teacher and coach is well known to me, and I am glad you are in the position of athletic director. You also coach the ninth grade basketball and baseball teams, right?"

I responded in the affirmative and he continued, "I'm really not going to need any help making the transition to the principal position here. I'll be doing the same thing I did when I was up at Sacajawea. However, you could give me a review of the situation for the fall and winter sports seasons. Have you got the schedules done for the fall? Where are you with getting the winter schedules set up for basketball and wrestling?"

I told him I would give him the written schedule of the fall events so he could take a look at them and made an appointment with him for later in the week to review those schedules and my progress on filling the winter sports schedules.

After visiting with him about a few inconsequential non-educational issues, I made my way to my small athletic director's office down the hall, where I retrieved the fall sports schedules and left them with his secretary before I returned to my office to make phone calls to finish the winter sports schedules. I quickly discovered it was difficult this time of year to make connections with non-league schools to make arrangements for winter basketball games and wrestling matches. Most coaches, principals, and athletic directors were unavailable, and it took several calls to finally make a connection. I finally completed the schedules near the end of the third week of the school year, and it took many hours on the phone to finally get the job done. I also spent a couple of hours that afternoon readying my room for the new school year. After reviewing memos from the principal along with the new teacher handbooks, I saw my teaching schedule for the new school year had again changed. I was assigned three sections of algebra classes and two sections of ninth grade general math classes. I was also relieved to find I was given a full class period at the end of each day to take care of my responsibilities as athletic director, rather than having to deal with them before or after school. A few days later, I met with Mr. Jasper, and he seemed very pleased with the fall schedules and my progress on the winter schedules. I found him to be very supportive and encouraging and was looking forward to working with him in the coming school year.

The teacher in-service day came and went like all the others had—Mr. Jasper was well organized and had the staff ready to go when the students came through the door on Monday. Before the first week was out, I discovered I had a great group of students in my math classes. It also didn't take me long to see the big adjustment for the year would be learning to integrate my athletic director responsibilities with my teaching and coaching responsibilities. The duties of the athletic director turned out to be extensive: my job entailed scheduling seven football games, seventeen to eighteen boys' and girls' basketball games, volleyball games, and six wrestling matches for the seventh, eighth, and ninth grade teams in each sport. During the winter months, I put together the spring sports schedules for baseball, softball, and track. And of course, during the spring months I developed the schedules for the next year's fall sports. During my first year as the athletic director, I found my duties to be formidable, involving many hours on the phone and attending several late-afternoon and evening meetings.

Not only did I have to schedule events for all three sports seasons, but also I had to make sure I had officials assigned for each event where they were needed. There were a few occasions when I was unable to find a football or basketball official and found myself filling that role. It was also expected that I attend all home events as the athletic director to provide supervision and to assist the coaches if an issue arose. By the middle of the winter sports season, I found myself averaging twelve hours a day during a five-day workweek. There were many nights when I went home totally exhausted. I remember returning home one Thursday night extremely tired after practicing with my basketball team at 7 a.m. in the morning, teaching five periods of math, and then supervising three home basketball games that evening. I remember coming into my house around 9 p.m., shuffling directly to my bedroom, flopping into bed still in my street clothes, and instantly falling asleep until the alarm went off at 6 a.m. the next morning. I rolled over and shut off the alarm, still tired, but extremely glad it was Friday since there were usually no junior high athletic events on Fridays.

One of my first "executive decisions" as the Jenifer Junior High School athletic director involved an eighth grade football game where our team was playing Sacajawea. The game was on a late Thursday afternoon under the lights at the high school football field behind our gymnasium. I was there to supervise the game and had assigned three of our coaches from other teams to officiate. Mr. Albright was the eighth grade football coach, and his team was pretty good, jumping off on this particular night to a thirteen-point lead. But in the second quarter, the Sacajawea team was punting when our athlete receiving the punt muffed the catch at the twenty-yard line. One of their players picked the ball up off the ground and raced into the end zone where the officials signaled it as a touchdown.

Mr. Albright immediately ran onto the field and contested the call to the head official, saying he was pretty sure the kicking team could not advance a muffed catch. The head official and those working with him were not sure of the rule, so he and Mr. Albright ran over to where I was standing at the back of the end zone to get my opinion.

"What's the ruling on this situation?" the head official asked. "Can a ball dropped by a punt receiver be advanced by the kicking team?"

I had reviewed the football rulebook sitting in my locker in the gymnasium, but I still wasn't certain of the ruling either. I was the ranking "expert" on the subject, since I was the athletic director, and they were looking at me to make a quick decision, so I decided to be assertive.

"Sure! You can advance a fumble!"

Mr. Albright looked at me questioningly.

"I think you are wrong on that," he said. "But you're the boss. Let's play ball!"

They returned to play with Sacajawea making the extra point and kicking off to our team. As the game continued, I made a quick side trip to the gymnasium and took a look at the rulebook stored in my locker. Sure enough, the rule stated the opposing team could not advance a muffed punt or kickoff. I had made a spur-of-the-moment decision to help expedite the game and had cost my team seven points.

I wandered back to the football field, and when halftime came, I caught up with the head official and Mr. Albright.

"I was wrong about the muffed kick ruling," I said. "I looked it up in the rulebook and the rule clearly states a muffed ball cannot be advanced by the kicking team. I'm sorry about that, but I will make sure we have a rulebook available in the future to provide some help when we have questions like this."

Mr. Albright looked at me with a widening smile.

"I tried to tell you," he said good-naturedly. "You owe me one on this, you know. But I'm not too upset about it since we are still up by fourteen points even after giving them that touchdown."

My "executive" football decision was the talk of the teachers' lounge for the next week. Every time I came into the lounge, one of the teachers would make some smart remark about my ability to make quick, authoritative, and quality decisions. I took the jabs with a smile, but I determined from that point on to make sure I had all the facts before I made a decision. If I didn't know the facts, I would say I didn't know and seek what was needed to make the right decision.

As fall continued, my work increased dramatically as I balanced teaching with my athletic director duties. The pressure increased even more when the basketball season started. On the first Monday in November, Mr. Green and I had our tryout week for the ninth grade basketball teams. This was going to be my fifth year as the ninth grade varsity basketball coach, and I knew I was going to have a great group of athletes. I watched these guys play in the eighth grade, and I could see they were very good.

After our team meeting the week before tryouts, it looked like we were going to have thirty-four boys out for the two teams, and Mr. Jasper had made it clear that we could not cut anyone from the program. It was almost impossible for me to mold a team into a cohesive, competitive unit if I had more than twelve boys. So the plan was for me to pick the best eight or nine players and then negotiate with Mr. Green for the next three or four players to fill out my twelve-man roster. We wanted to make sure he had two or three good players on his junior varsity team so they were competitive. This would mean I would have twelve on my team, and he would carry about twenty-two on his team.

Mr. Green and I discussed ways we might reduce the numbers trying out for the teams to make the numbers more manageable and still stay within the parameters of Mr. Jasper's directive that no one could be cut. To do this, we made our tryouts very strenuous. Our tryouts started at 5 p.m. and lasted about two hours. Practice began with the athletes running two laps around the gym and then sprinting two suicides at full speed. We did two suicides at five different times during the practice, with athletes running in groups of fifteen while Mr. Green and I shouted encouragement for them to run as fast as possible. We increased the total number of suicides each practice from ten on the first day of practice to twenty-five by the last day. Needless to say, we had a few athletes throwing up by the last set of suicides that first and second day of tryouts.

Most of the basketball drills during practice involved a lot of movement and running. We did full-court defensive drills, fast break drills, and full-court dribbling and passing drills. We ended practice every day with forty-five minutes of full-court scrimmaging on the two courts in the gym. We ran the students very hard! They needed to be in shape, and we wanted to see who would work hard and who wouldn't, and by the end of the five-day tryouts, we were down to twenty-eight athletes.

On day three of tryouts, we had a new student who had enrolled earlier in the week turn out for the team. The school secretary told me his father said he was a great basketball player, claiming his boy averaged over twenty points a game at the school he attended before moving to Lewiston. He showed up Wednesday and he looked pretty fit; he was stocky and could jump well. When we started practice with four suicides, he did pretty well. He was fast, worked hard, and looked fair in the scrimmages. I was pretty excited about him. I didn't think he would make my varsity team, but he would make a great addition to Mr. Green's junior varsity team. However, all our projections about him came to an abrupt end during the last set of suicides we ran at the end of practice. We were into the third suicide when this athlete sprinted to the end line, then ran past it, only giving me a glance as he hit the safety bar on the door that led to the parking lot. He sprinted through the door never to be seen at practice again. I caught him later in the week to see what was wrong, and he told me it looked like playing for me would just be too much work.

On the other hand, there was another student out for the team who was overweight and definitely out of shape. He made every practice, worked hard, and ran every suicide to the best of his ability. Most of the time he was the last one across the line in his group. He threw up at least once in the first three days of practice, but his attitude was positive the whole time. At the end of the last day of practice, he approached me.

"Coach Hammann, I'm not much of a basketball player," he said. "And I probably won't play much even if I'm on the junior varsity team, but I want to be a part of the team. Would you take me on as a student manager? I'd be willing to do whatever I could to help the team." Of course, I accepted his offer, and he turned out to be the best student manager I ever had. He was conscientious about everything from collecting uniforms and towels to taking statistics during ball games. It was a joy to have him as part of the team.

Mr. Green and I finished practice Friday and retreated to the coach's office to make our selections. The team I selected was one of the best teams of my coaching career at Jenifer Junior High. The team included Dan Stellmon, the son of the school board member I had tossed from a baseball game my first summer umpiring Babe Ruth. Other members of the team included Brid Alford, Brad Martin, Joe Venkus, Dan Anderson, Bruce Gage, Curt Peterson, Doug Jones, Steve Day, Steve Gates, Mike Grow, and Todd Trigsted, the son of the high school football coach. Bob Winterbottom, Mitch Espy, and Mike Tews were my managers. Mitch Espy was the young man who made it through tryouts and asked to become the student manager.

This team finished the season with a ten and seven record. We beat Sacajawea two out of three times and even beat the Lewiston High School sophomore team with a combined Sacajawea/Jenifer team late in the season. But there is one game in particular that stands out to me from that season.

We were playing the Moscow Junior High team on our home court, and one of my best players, Todd Trigsted, came to me during the pre-game warm-ups saying he was having difficulty catching his breath during the layup drill. I talked to him about what he had eaten and if there were any other problems. He indicated he was just having problems breathing, so I told him to finish the warm-ups and see if it got any better.

Just before the start of the game, I checked on him and he said he was still having problems. He was one of my starters, so I told him to sit on the bench and see if resting would help him get better. I informed the game officials I was changing the starting lineup by starting one of my other players in place of Todd.

The game began, and it turned out to be a barnburner. The lead went back and forth throughout the first half, and we entered halftime down by three points. I checked with Todd as we headed into the locker room, and he said he was doing some better, but he was still having trouble getting his breath. His dad stopped me just before I went into the locker room and asked me why Todd had not started. I briefly explained the situation and said I was concerned about his health. He asked that I send Todd out to him while I met with the team during the half-time break, which I did. In the locker room, I told the team they were playing well, but we needed to pick up our intensity on defense. After making some further adjustments in our defense and offense, we returned to the floor to warm up for the second half. Todd flagged me down as I came on the floor.

"Coach," he said, "I'm still struggling some, but I think I could play."

"Todd, we could certainly use you, but I don't want to send you in unless you are sure you are okay," I replied. "Can you assure me that right now you are okay?"

He looked at me and shook his head.

"Well, just sit on the bench and let's see if that works," I said. He reluctantly went back to the bench as the rest of the team warmed up.

The second half was just as much a battle as the first. Both teams played great defensive basketball, with the game ending in a tie as the Moscow team barely missed a long jump shot at the buzzer. When the team returned to the bench, all of them were grinning. "Men, this is what basketball and competing is all about," I said. "Moscow is playing hard to win, but we need to go out there now and play harder than they do. You have to want this win enough to give it your all. Can you do that?"

"Yeah, we can do it!" they said.

I told them to go to our half-court press and fall back into a 2-1-2 zone if the opposing team broke the press. I instructed them to use our passing game offense if they played man to man, or use the zone offense if they were in a zone.

Just before I sent them onto the floor, Todd came to me and said he was feeling much better and was ready to play. I looked him in the eye warily.

"Are you sure you are okay?"

He responded with a grin. "Yeah coach, I'm ready to play!"

I gave him a nod and he moved to the officials' desk and checked in.

He and the rest of the team played an outstanding game in the three-minute overtime, winning the game by five points. The fans and the team were ecstatic about the win, but I noticed Todd was not as enthusiastic, and he was looking pretty pale as we made our way to the door of the locker room. I asked him how he was doing, noting his colorless face. He shook his head.

"I'm still having trouble catching my breath," he said. "I just can't seem to get enough air!"

I motioned for him to follow me, and we made our way to where his dad was standing in the stands.

"Mr. Trigsted," I said, "it probably isn't anything serious, but I recommend you get Todd to the emergency room. He's still having trouble getting his breath and he is looking pretty pale. It's your call, but I think he should see a doctor."

Mr. Trigsted nodded his head and told Todd to shower and meet him outside the locker room door to head to the emergency room. I figured whatever was wrong was probably not a big deal, but I was glad they were going to get him checked out.

I didn't think much about Todd's situation until I received a call late that evening from Mrs. Trigsted, who said Todd was admitted to the Lewiston Hospital with a collapsed lung. I told her I would be right over. When I got the hospital room, I found Mr. and Mrs. Trigsted sitting by his bed. As I came up on the other side of the bed, I noticed a small tube protruding from his chest, and he looked even paler than he had at the game. He must have seen how shocked I was at his condition.

"Coach, it's okay," Todd reassured me. "I just have a collapsed lung. They have this tube here to help it re-inflate. The doctor said

I would be out by tomorrow and that I can play basketball again in a couple of days."

"Did he say what caused it or how this happened?" I inquired.

"The doctor said that almost anything can cause it," Todd's dad replied. "Stress, an injury, or even strenuous exercise can cause it. He said it was not that uncommon among athletes. The doctor assured us that he would be all right. It's okay—you did the right thing to have him sit out most of the game. Things might have been worse had you not done that."

I stayed and visited with him and his folks for a while and then left to go home, relieved that Todd was alright. Winning a game was not as important as the health and safety of my players. I loved them as if they were my own sons, and I knew I would be greatly grieved if anything bad happened to them.

There was one other incident that year that was absolutely bizarre. It was during this year that "streaking" became a fad, especially among the high school and college crowds. Streaking, of course, was when a person—in almost every case a male person—removed all his clothes except for shoes and a mask to cover his face, and ran naked through a public place. Streaking was happening all around the country at football games, in malls, down the main street of small towns, and around public facilities. Even locally, there was an increase of streaking incidents on the college campuses of Lewis-Clark State College, the University of Idaho, and Washington State University.

And it looked like streaking had also caught the eye of our local high school students. There was a report floating around the school during the spring semester that a streaker had appeared at the McDonald's restaurant in Lewiston. Allegedly, a truck had pulled up to the drive-through and a young male adult, probably a high school student, had exited the idling truck naked except for a ski mask covering his face. He proceeded to run as fast as he could around the McDonald's restaurant, much to the consternation of many older adults and the amusement of the younger crowd who observed the scene. When he got back to his truck, he pulled on the door handle to open it and make a clean getaway, but found he had locked the door with his keys still in the ignition. He yanked frantically on the door three or four times, but it was not to be. It took those observing his frantic behavior only a moment to figure out what had happened before they began to laugh uproariously.

Once he realized his situation and he saw the laughter of the people in the cars behind him, the streaker made a quick decision and fled the area, leaving his locked, idling truck parked at the drive-through window. He was last seen stopping traffic as he crossed the busy thoroughfare naked and fleeing into the neighborhood located across from McDonald's.

He must have lived close by or had a friend living close by who allowed him to make a phone call, because the story went that an older man, probably his father, showed up about a half hour later to sheepishly unlock the door and take possession of the truck. Of course, this caused a major disruption to business because the drive-through was inaccessible until the truck could be moved. It was my understanding the police were not involved, which was a good thing for him and his parents.

This leads me to the legendary incident that occurred at Jenifer Junior High shortly after this story circulated through the school. I came to school early on a May morning to finish up some of my athletic director duties. The spring sporting events were about over and we were preparing to end the school year. After making a few phone calls to schedule games for the fall football season, I wandered into the teachers' lounge where three teachers were having a cup of coffee in preparation for another school day. "Did you hear what's going to happen this afternoon after school?" Mr. Green asked me excitedly.

I had been too busy during the last two weeks coaching and teaching to make it into the teachers' lounge to catch up on the gossip.

"No!" I said. "What's going to happen?" I took a seat next to him, and he leaned over conspiratorially and spoke in a low whisper.

"Two of our male athletes are going to come out of the gym entrance buck naked, streak down the street on the north side of the main building, and jump into a truck that will be waiting for them at the end of the block."

"Really! Who are the athletes?" I was both surprised and concerned one of them might be one of my baseball players.

"We don't know for sure," he said. "But I've heard that one of the athletes will be Phil Crosby's kid." Mr. Crosby's youngest son was a freshman, who played football and ran track. He was considered one of the "good" kids who never got into trouble.

"Really?" I said incredulously. "I have a hard time believing he would do something like that. How reliable is your source?"

"He's pretty reliable."

"Has anyone said anything to Mr. Jasper or to Mr. Crosby?"

"No!" Mr. Green said quickly. "No one has said anything to them. All the staff members I talked to want to just wait and see if it will really take place. It will take some guts for these kids to do something like that—they will probably chicken out."

We talked about a few other things, and then I went to my room to get ready for class. When the bell rang to start the day, freshmen poured into my classroom with an air of excitement. The second student through the door came over to my desk where I was sitting.

"Mr. Hammann, have you heard?" he asked excitedly. "A couple of students are going to streak down the street just outside your window at the end of the day. Did you know that? Boy, if they do that it will make the whole school year!"

"Come on now, I can't believe a couple of our students are going to sprint naked down the street," I said. "They wouldn't have the guts to do that. Besides, they could get in real trouble."

"I'll bet you five dollars it will happen," he said with a smile.

"No, I'm not going to bet on it, but I doubt it is going to happen. By the way, who are these two students?"

He grinned again.

"Can't say! Someone might try to stop them, and I wouldn't want to see that."

All through the day, I had students coming into my class talking about the coming streaker event. The excitement among the student body steadily mounted as the day progressed. Even a couple of teachers at lunch commented the students seemed pretty excited about something. Mr. Green, who had said something to me in the lounge just before school started, looked over at me after one comment and winked.

The last period of the day came, and I found myself sitting in my room alone working on the fall sports schedules, since this was my athletic director period. Just about five minutes before the bell to end the day rang, I heard a knock at my door and when I opened it, I found the English teacher standing there with all of her class behind her. She gave me a beaming smile.

"Mr. Hammann, would it be okay if my class and I came in here to see if there really is going to be some streaking at the end of the day? The kids are telling me that two of our boys are going to streak out of the main gym entrance and run down the full length of the street outside your room. Could we come in and watch to see if it really is going to happen?"

"Yes!" I said as I smiled back at her. "You and your class can surely come in to see that event. I wouldn't want anyone to miss such a thing, but don't be disappointed if it doesn't happen."

I stood back to let her and her class in, and all the students immediately flew to the windows and opened each and every one of them, poking their heads out so they could have a clear view of the gym entrance.

Curious about this whole phenomenon, I too poked my head out one of the windows looking toward the gym entrance. I was stunned by what I saw as I looked toward the gymnasium entrance. Every window on my side of the two-story building was open and had student heads poking out, looking toward the gym entrance. I even saw a couple of teachers with their heads out the window waiting to see if there would be any streakers bold enough to sprint the full block past our hopeful eyes. No one was outside on the street or the grounds. I didn't see Mr. Jasper or any other adult outside our building or in front of the gym. For the next three minutes, there was a hushed silence from all those staring at the gymnasium entrance.

Suddenly, a red pickup truck heading south on the main street on the east side of the building skidded to a screeching halt. The driver backed around the corner so the back of his truck was facing the gym entrance just over a block away. The tailgate of his pickup was down as if ready to have it loaded, and he sat there with the motor running. As the truck backed around the corner, a cheer went up from all the students standing with their heads out the open windows.

The truck was about thirty yards from my position, and I could see the driver was none other than Dan Stellmon, the school board chairman's son. We made eye contact and he grinned like a Cheshire cat. I just grinned back and shook my head.

After the brief cheer from those at the windows, everyone got silent again waiting for the anticipated streak. All we could hear was the idling engine of the truck. After about a minute, the bell rang to end the day, and like the starting gun at a track meet, it caused a flurry of activity. The doors to the gymnasium burst open and two naked boys wearing only tennis shoes and ski masks began sprinting for all they were worth down the street toward the waiting truck. A great volume of cheers arose from the students and staff at the windows. Most were shouting, "GO! GO! GO!" which seemed to spur the streakers on toward their goal of the truck and safety. I could see one of the streakers was indeed none other than Mr. Crosby's son. I wondered what his dad was thinking, as I knew he was surely looking out the window and shouting along with everyone else. I suspect he was getting a big kick out of this—he had that kind of sense of humor.

As they approached the halfway point of their sprint, I and several students in the room began to yell at Dan Stellmon to leave them behind.

"Leave them! GO! GO! GO! Leave them!"

That would have made this legendary event even more memorable. But Dan just yelled back.

"If I leave, they promised they would kill me! I gave my word and there is no way I'm going to leave!"

Finally, amongst the cheers of the students and staff at the windows, the two streakers jumped into the back of the pickup, pulled up the tailgate, and shouted for Dan to take off. With the squeal of tires, the truck lurched around the corner and continued to peel rubber as it made its way up the main street. The crowd continued to cheer until the sound of squealing tires faded into the distance. For a minute, there was quiet and then every head ducked back into the building and the students began to leave for the day, excitedly chatting about the streaking event.

No disciplinary action was ever taken to my knowledge, but for the next two weeks, the topic of informal discussions amongst students and staff usually turned to that eventful day. The students held Dan Stellmon and the two streakers in high esteem, while the staff just shook their heads and smiled whenever they saw the students.

This was pretty much the event that brought closure to the 1977-78 school year.

CHAPTER 26

Teaching the Handicapped and a Positive Coaching Experience

> *When the Grangeville player tried to pass the ball down the sideline to his teammate, Brad Behrens was there to intercept and move toward our basket. He saw Jeff Lang cutting to the basket and made a great pass, allowing Jeff to score an easy layup. The home crowd went wild as the ball fell through the net.*

During the summer of 1978, I did not apply for any administrative positions believing I should have at least two years of experience at my current position as the Jenifer Junior High athletic director. So for most of the summer, I umpired Babe Ruth and legion games and then worked the pea harvest when it began in July. My wife also worked the pea harvest on the assembly line sorting peas. The summer culminated with a two-week vacation to southern California, where we enjoyed the experience of Disneyland.

When I returned, I was well rested and ready to start my seventh full year as a math teacher at Jenifer Junior High. But I also returned determined to find an administrative position somewhere in the northwest.

Just before the beginning of the school year, I was surprised when the special education teacher came to my room and told me I would be getting one of her special education students in my algebra class. At first I was confused because I couldn't see a student classified as having special needs being able to take an algebra class. But my confusion was short-lived when she told me the student was blind. She said the female student was more than able to deal with the learning material, she just couldn't see. This would mean I had to take more care when I lectured and worked problems. The student would be recording my lessons to review later, and I would also have to give her the tests and quizzes orally before or after school.

On the first day of class, the special education teacher brought the student to my door just after class started. The girl came in with her red-tipped cane and introduced herself. The special education teacher asked for her to be assigned a desk at the front of the classroom near the door. This would make it easier for her to find her seat independently. She would usually come to class on the arm of a classmate, who would help her find the room. The teacher also demonstrated to me how to assist the young girl if she needed to move about the room by letting her grasp one of my upper arms and leading her to where she needed to go.

After this quick briefing given in front of the class, we scrambled to rearrange the seating in the room to accommodate the student. Once she was in her seat and had her recorder on, we began the day by orienting the students to the rules of the classroom and my expectations for work and assignments.

I was immediately sensitive to the words and actions I used to communicate with the class. I found myself referring to items I had written on the board and my classroom rules by pointing to them rather than stating them for the benefit of the blind student.

The student impressed me right from the beginning by raising her hand and asking me to read things aloud.

"Mr. Hammann, would you mind stating the rules and expectations so I can get that on my recorder?"

"Sorry about that," I said, somewhat embarrassed. "Sure, I will be glad to state them. Be sure and interrupt me if you need more clarification."

The class went well and I was impressed with the other students in the class, who were respectful of her and patient with my forgetfulness when she asked for clarifications. When the class ended, a student came up to her and said she was her escort. The blind student grabbed her arm, and they made their way out of the classroom and on to the next class.

I found her presence in the class to be one of the joys of teaching that year. She struggled some when it came to taking tests and quizzes. She was a perfectionist and during the first semester she got an "A" on every quiz and test. When the second semester started, the material got tougher and she got a "B" or a "C" on some of the tests and quizzes. When this happened she got very upset, and we even had some tears. But she adjusted and ended the course with an "A" grade.

One of the things that impressed me was the fact that she heard me say many things that went right over the heads of the rest of the class. I remember one time in the middle of a lecture on reducing algebra fractions when I cracked a joke.

"You take this y cubed in the denominator of the fraction and write it out as y, y, y. Just like some of you are thinking y, y, y did I take this class!"

The blind student burst out into laughter as the rest of the class just looked dumbly at her. I had to explain the humor and the fact that she caught it and the rest of the class had not. Once they understood, they chuckled as well. All during the year things like this happened—she heard things the rest of the class did not.

What impressed me most was she never used her handicap as an excuse for failure. She was determined to learn and succeed in spite of it. I was inspired by her example, and it made me proud to have her in my class. I believe she did well at whatever endeavor she chose to pursue.

When the school year started, I found my class load was similar to the previous year with three algebra classes, two general math classes, and one prep period for my athletic director duties. One of the new things I was determined to try this year was to make a positive personal contact with the parents of every student I had in class. I believed this would help me understand my students better and communicate to the parents that their students were doing good work in my class. Most of the time when the school called a parent, it was because there was a problem. I wanted to try and change that perspective. This turned out to be a formidable task.

During the first semester, I kept a notebook at my desk, and at the end of each class period, I would jot down positive things I observed by individual students during that period. At the end of the first two weeks, I began the process of trying to contact each parent. Sometimes I would see a student with his or her parents at an athletic event and I could make some positive comments at that time. That worked well because I could do this in front of the student. However, most of the time I had to try and reach them at home with a phone call. I found that most parents were not home right after school, so I tried making calls around dinnertime in the evening. This proved to be more effective, and by the end of the semester, I could finally say I made at least one positive contact with each of the parents. Each parent I spoke to was appreciative of my effort and was glad to hear some positive news from the school regarding their student. Some parents said it was the first time anyone from the school had made an effort to communicate anything positive. You would think this would have a good effect on classroom discipline and the effort put forth from my students, but that was not always the case. I came to accept the fact that it would take more than just being positive to make my students behave and care about working hard in my math classes. I do believe it improved public relations between the school and the parents, but it had little effect in my classroom. It was one of those situations where I tried something to improve the education of the students, and it proved to be less than what I expected. I decided not to continue this into the second semester of the year—it was just too much effort considering my workload as a teacher, coach, and athletic director.

As basketball season started up again, Mr. Green and I worked the tryout week the same way we did the year before. I ended up with twelve boys on my team and he with eighteen. Whenever his team played, we tried to play a fifth quarter to make sure all his players got some playing time. There were some teams we played that had only eight players, and the Idaho High School Athletic Association would only allow a student to play four quarters in a day, so we were unable to play a fifth quarter in those situations.

The team I selected to compete at the varsity level was composed of Paul Schaufele, Doug Huddleston, Glenn Pfautsch, Brad Behrens, Joby Watson, Rob Dammarell, Bob Thorson, Jeff Lang, Tod Burr, Jim Russel, Jeff Moser, and Geoff Johnson. I had two great managers in Scott Carlton and Joe Moscrip. The team had some good athletes, but we won only four games out of seventeen. Brad Behrens and Jeff Lang were my best players, but if they were off their game, we struggled to win, and there were several games where we were beaten badly. But there was one game that stood out from all the rest—in fact, this may have been the best basketball game I ever had the opportunity to coach.

We were playing the Grangeville Bulldogs for the second time. The first time, we had played them at Grangeville in December, where we won by twelve points. They had one really good player and some pretty good supporting players. It was late January when they came to our gymnasium for a rematch. I prepped my team to play them the same way we had played them when we were at Grangeville, planning to play man-to-man defense and go to a 2-1-2 zone if needed. We would also run our zone full-court press when we played zone.

But from the tipoff until half-time, we played lethargically. We were unable to get any turnovers off our press, and they shot well over our zone, so I took them out of it early and went to a man-to-man defense. On offense, we turned the ball over several times—non-forced turnovers, even—as we tried to bring the ball down the floor and when we attacked their defense. They were shooting hot and we were not. I called two time-outs to try and get us moving, but to no avail. By the end of the half, we were down by sixteen points.

As we made our way into the locker room, I was struggling to come up with the words I needed to say to try and get them motivated. A team they had beaten badly back in December was hammering them. I prided myself on how I was usually able to upgrade the team's play after halftime. Normally I could find something to say to inspire them to play harder. Sometimes I would raise my voice and give them a blistering, critical speech to try and shame them into working harder. Sometimes I could take a positive approach and just encourage them and suggest some offensive or defensive adjustment—but this situation was different. We were losing because we were not making an honest effort, and this was the first time

I had faced this. All my teams to this point had worked hard and were highly motivated, but for some reason this team had failed to give their best during that first half of the game. What could I say to get them going?

After everyone had settled on the benches and looked at me expectantly, I pulled up a box in front of them all and just stared them down. I didn't say anything, just moved my eyes to each athlete, pausing to stare into his eyes. I did this for about two or three minutes until I could see they were very uncomfortable. Then I spoke.

"You're getting your butts kicked by a team you should be beating," I said intensely, keeping my voice low as I swept my eyes from one end of the bench to the other. "We beat them once this season, but I think you came into this game thinking it would be a cakewalk. You thought if you just showed up they would roll over and let you run away with the game. Listen to me now. They came to play! Remember what I've been saying all season long? You always respect your opponent no matter how good or how bad they play. You never take your opponent for granted. But that is what you've done today, and now it is half-time and we are down sixteen points. What are you going to do about it?

"Well, here is what I'm going to do—I'm putting our starters out there, and we are going to play our full-court zone press for the entire half until we regain the lead," I said. "And **we will regain the lead!** I want you to play harder and execute the zone press like you've never done before. If the players I have in there can't execute, then I will play someone else who can. Do you guys understand me?" They all nodded their heads vigorously.

"I want you to go out there and go through your layup drill until the horn sounds to start the half, and then our comeback will begin. Remember, we go into the press after every basket we make. Now bring you hands in here and we will break with 'defense!' "

We gathered in a compact circle and put our hands on top of each other in the center.

"One, two, three ..."

"... **DEFENSE**!"

They broke out of the locker room with a new intensity and purpose, crisply performing their layup drill until the horn sounded to start the second half. We took the ball out at half court, moved quickly into our offense, and got off a jump shot that missed. Our opponents nabbed the rebound and moved slowly and deliberately down the court into their offense. Their good player hit a nice jump shot from the baseline, putting us down eighteen points. I didn't think this was a good start, but all we needed was one turnover to get things going. As my team came back down the court on offense, I shouted encouragement to them.

"It's okay!" I bellowed out. "Play hard and it will turn our way!"

We went into our passing game offense since they were in a man-to-man defense, and we got a jump shot off at the foul line that missed. One of my players was in position to get the rebound, but it went off his hand and bounced out of bounds. As Grangeville moved to take the ball out at the end line I began shouting, "Press, press, press!" My players responded quickly and moved into our 1-2-1-1 full-court press. In this press, you let the offense pass the ball in, and then you try to trap the player with the ball along the sidelines. The two players who are not trapping then try to anticipate where the ball will be passed, attempt to intercept, and look for a fast break basket going the other way. On this particular inbound pass, the trap worked perfectly, pinning the player with the ball against the sideline. When the Grangeville player tried to pass the ball down the sideline to his teammate, Brad Behrens was there to intercept and move toward our basket. He saw Jeff Lang cutting to the basket and made a great pass, allowing Jeff to score an easy layup. The home crowd went wild as the ball fell through the net.

After the basket, we went right back into the zone press. Grangeville passed the ball in, and the player with the ball once again found himself in a trap, but he was able to dribble free and move quickly down the court. As the player and his teammate attacked the basket, the player could either make the layup or pass off to his teammate cutting to the basket. The player was challenged by our last man on defense and decided to pass to his teammate cutting to the basket.

Now I had always coached our team to never give up on the press even if the front three players got beat. Those three players should always hustle in retreat to fill the passing lanes and possibly pick off a pass even underneath our own basket. Their hustle paid off in this case, because one of our players picked off the pass, and we moved down the floor and scored a jump shot out of our offensive set. We were now down by only fourteen points.

After that basket, the Grangeville coach called time-out to calm his players down and go through their procedures for breaking a press. As the players grouped around me, I looked over at the Grangeville huddle and I heard the coach say, "Listen, we practiced all week on how to break their press! You did it well in the first half. Just go back to what you did then."

I smiled to myself at hearing that and knelt down before my team for a pep talk. "Men, we are going to beat these guys! I finally saw you come to life. You just need to keep the press on them and not let up. They are probably going to have the person taking the ball out cut down the middle of the court, and they'll have their trapped man passing to him rather than the man down the sideline. Look to pick that pass off. They are rattled and you need to keep the heat on, even if they break the press and score. Remember to always look to pick off a pass if they break the front three of the zone press. Just keep playing hard!"

We put our hands together for another chant. "One, two, three, **defense**!"

The team broke out of our huddle with even more vigor and enthusiasm. Grangeville brought the ball in from the end line and broke our press, although with some difficulty. They set up their offense and failed to score, but we got the rebound and scored with a fast break layup. We were now down twelve points.

The game continued back and forth until the end of the third quarter, when we were down eight points. As the quarter came to an end, the crowd was really starting to get into it. They were cheering at every turnover and every made basket. They seemed to sense they might get to see a great comeback from our ninth grade varsity team.

After making some adjustments to our offense and encouraging them to keep the pressure on with the press, I sent them back out to the floor. Because we were pressing all the time, I had to make a lot of substitutes. I was playing ten players, and each substitute who went in did his part. They hustled and worked with the starters in the game. It was magical watching what was happening on the floor. We kept narrowing the lead throughout the fourth quarter, and by the time we reached the two-minute mark, Brad Behrens made another steal and layup to tie the game. When that happened, the crowd of about 400 went wild. This just inspired my players to work harder, and by the time we got to the one-minute mark, we had taken the lead. We finished the game winning by five points.

After we shook hands with the Grangeville team, we jogged off to our locker room where the players slumped on the benches, exhausted but grinning like clowns at each other. "Men, what an incredible comeback. You were down eighteen points in the second half and came back to win the game by five! You showed grit and great hustle. You never gave up and every member of this team played their role to make this happen. I'm incredibly proud of you! This is what sports are all about! You got off on the wrong foot, but you were able to change your mindset, pick up your hustle, make some adjustments, and turn things around. This is just a game and you played a very good game today, but what you experienced here needs to be taken with you into life. In life you should always work hard, never give up, and trust in your teammate to help you win. I am so proud of you. Let's get cleaned up so you guys can go home and do a little celebrating. We'll be back at practice tomorrow afternoon."

I think every one of those boys went home that evening feeling satisfied. As I watched them leave the locker room, they each seemed to stand a little taller, and I knew they were anxious to retell the game to their parents and friends. I know because my family got to hear me retell the game at least twice that week alone.

The year continued well, and since this was my second year as the athletic director, things were much easier with some experience already under my belt. I was still frustrated with my general math classes, but the learning going on in my algebra classes offset that. Six years of teaching algebra helped me develop a variety of methods for teaching the more complex aspects of the material. Students who applied themselves in the class were learning the concepts, and feedback from the high school math teachers indicated most of my students were ready for the algebra two course offered to the sophomores at the high school.

I was feeling good about my progress as a math teacher at the junior high level and was interested in pursuing some new challenges—especially using my master's degree in secondary school administration. And by the end of the basketball season, I felt I was ready to seriously pursue a principal's job for the 1979-80 school year.

CHAPTER 27

Pursuing a Secondary Principal's Position

> *"Did you know that I just took an unpaid day from my teaching job in Lewiston to come to an interview that was scheduled by your office?' I said as calmly as possible given the situation. 'I left after school Thursday and spent the night in Boise in a motel. I got up early this morning to get here, and now you are telling me I don't have an interview?'"*

After the basketball season ended in 1979, I consulted with my wife and we both agreed I should make a serious effort to obtain a principal's position in the northwest. So in March, I updated my placement file at Boise State College—now Boise State University—by including recommendations from Mr. Jasper, Mr. Adams, and Mr. Crosby focusing on my administrative experience as the athletic director at Jenifer Junior High School. When April came I began to comb through job postings in the states of Idaho, Washington, Oregon, and Alaska. I relied heavily on the Boise State University job-posting flyer that was sent out weekly, since it appeared to contain most of the administrative openings for the western part of the United States. I began to send out application letters, resumes, and placement files to both large and small school districts in hopes of snagging a position. My professors at the University of

Idaho had indicated many of the quality jobs in the northwest were generally posted in April and May. As those jobs were filled, there was a domino affect that occurred. Candidates with administrative experience would usually obtain the early jobs because they were seeking to move up in the profession. Their vacated positions would then be opened and posted in May and June. The dominoes would continue to fall until the end of the summer where someone like myself, with a limited amount of experience, might have a chance of entering the administration field as a rookie. I sent out at least ten applications during the first two weeks of April. As had occurred two years earlier, I received the typical "Dear John" letters thanking me for my interest in their district, but indicating I was not considered qualified enough on paper to be offered an interview. As the month of April came and went and then the month of May began, I was discouraged with the fact I was not getting any interviews.

During the first week of May, I sent out another group of applications including one to the Genesee School District located between Moscow and Lewiston and one to the Blaine County School District, which served the communities of Hailey, Ketchum, Bellevue, and Carey, Idaho, in the ski resort area of Sun Valley. The Genesee School District was looking for a high school principal and the Blaine County School District was looking for a junior high principal.

With those two applications I hit pay dirt! One evening during the second week of May, I received a phone call from the secretary for the superintendent of the Blaine County School District asking me to come for an interview on the fourth Friday in May. This would be my first opportunity to interview for a principal's job, and I was not going to let it pass, so I enthusiastically jumped at the chance. I told her I was very interested in coming for the interview, which she said was scheduled for 1 p.m. a week from Friday. The superintendent and the search team looked forward to visiting with me, she said, and they would be eagerly awaiting my arrival on the assigned date and time.

I hung up the phone and excitedly told Marty I would have my first principal interview in a little over a week, and it would be important for her to go along with me so we could get a lay of the land and see if it would be a viable place to live and work. My family had never been to the Sun Valley area, so we were anxious to find it on the map and do some research about the towns and surrounding area. We discovered Sun Valley is located in south central Idaho at the base of Bald Mountain and Dollar Mountain, which are known as popular skiing sites during the winter months. A small group of locals live there year-round, but the population of the area expands greatly during the winter months of the skiing season. It was known as a popular resort for the rich and famous. Celebrities such as Clint Eastwood, Tom Hanks, Jamie Lee Curtis, Richard Dreyfuss, and Arnold Schwarzenegger frequented the slopes during the winter months. It looked like a good place to begin an administrative career, and we were excited about the interview.

When I talked to Mr. Jasper about getting a day off for the interview, he said I would have to take the day without pay. School would be out the first week of June, but I felt I could fit the interview in and still take care of closing out the school year as a teacher and the athletic director. Our family budget was pretty tight, but we thought the investment would pay off, so I made arrangements for Marty and I to head down to Sun Valley while some friends picked up the kids after school on Thursday and watched them until we returned late Friday evening. We were going to leave right after school on Thursday and make the five-hour trip to Boise, Idaho, where we would spend the night. We would then get up early Friday morning and make the three-hour trip to Sun Valley. This would give us enough time to drive around the area and get a feel for the country and the community. After the interview, we would still have some time to check out the community if we needed to before we headed back to Lewiston.

Excitedly, we left Lewiston Thursday night before the interview. Since it was late spring, we had a pleasant trip traveling the two-lane, winding roads that took us through the beautiful Idaho mountains and valleys to Boise. We arrived around 9 p.m., and we were able to get a room in a Motel 6. We got up early the next morning, had breakfast and made the three-hour trek to Hailey, Idaho, arriving about 10 a.m. in the morning.

As we drove through the community of Hailey and a little way into the mountains toward the ski resorts, we found the country to be beautiful beyond description. The town was relatively small compared to Lewiston, but as we made our way up into the mountains we saw a number of magnificent chateaus and A-frame houses set into the mountainsides. It was spring and flowers were in bloom, everything was green, and we were enthralled with the beauty of the place. We talked excitedly about the possibility of working there and being a part of the community. We had done a little skiing while we were in Lewiston and were excited about focusing more on the sport if I got a job there.

It was obvious most of the winter crowds were gone since we observed very little traffic as we drove around Hailey. We stopped at a convenience store to get gas for the car on our way back into town. Since it was at least an hour before my interview and there was no one else in the store, I took the opportunity to ply the middle-aged clerk at the cash register with questions about the community and schools. As I paid the bill, I introduced myself, told him I was interviewing for the junior high principal position, and asked if I could ask him some questions about the area. "Sure," he replied guardedly. "I'll try and tell you what I know. Shoot!"

"Can you tell me what the community is like?"

"Sure!" he said with a smile. "This is a resort community. Things are pretty quiet now, but things really pick up when the ski season starts. We get a lot of rich people and celebrities in here. If you like to ski, this is a great place to live. If you like to hunt and fish, this is a great place to live as well. I like it here. Most of the locals are friendly and easy to get along with."

I then asked him, "What do you know about the school system?"

"Well, my kids have been out of school for a couple of years now. Their experience was okay, but the population of the school fluctuates, which can cause some problems. The population goes up in the winter when the skiing starts and drops in the spring, summer, and fall when skiing is not available. Considering all that, my kids got a pretty good education. I have one in college right now and she's doing okay."

I asked him what he knew about the school administration and he frowned slightly. "I don't know too much. My kids never got into much trouble, so I never had to deal with a principal. One thing I do know is there seems to be a frequent turnover of administrators in this district. In fact, I think they are looking for a new superintendent and high school principal right now as well." Just then someone came in and he excused himself to help the new customer. I thanked him for his help and we moved out to the car to make our way to the district office. As I drove to the district office, we discussed what the clerk had said. Marty was concerned about the frequent turnover in administrators, but was still excited, as was I, about the possibility of working there.

We arrived at the district office about five minutes before my scheduled interview. Marty waited in the car as I made my way to the entrance of the building.

As I walked into the district office, I found the entryway in disarray. There were boxes—some closed and taped, some only partially filled—sitting outside the door marked "superintendent." At a desk outside of the superintendent's office, I saw a disheveled middle-aged woman filling a box with books. The door to the office was open, and I could see a man inside pulling books off a bookshelf.

I smiled at the woman good-naturedly and introduced myself. "Good afternoon! My name is Robert Hammann, and I am here to interview for the junior high principal position." She frowned, moved over to her desk, looked at a desk calendar, and then looked back up to me.

"Robert Hammann?" she said, obviously confused. "You say you have an appointment for an interview for the junior high principal's position?"

"Yes, ma'am! I talked to the superintendent's secretary two weeks ago, who told me I had an appointment for an interview at 1 p.m. this afternoon."

She looked blankly at me. "The superintendent's secretary just left on vacation and I'm filling in for her," she said. "I see nothing on her calendar regarding an interview today. I'm in the process of helping our superintendent move out as he is taking a job in Nevada. Maybe he can help you." As she spoke, a sinking feeling was filling my stomach. I couldn't believe they didn't have me down for an interview. Were they saying my wife and I took unpaid leaves from our jobs, paid the expenses and took the trouble to have someone take care of our children, traveled 400 miles, and they didn't even know I had an interview? I was just about to express this thought when the man in the superintendent's office came out looking a little frantic.

"Who did you say you were?" he asked.

"I'm Robert Hammann," I said, hopeful he would make sense of this. "I applied for the administrative job at the junior high. A secretary in this office told me two weeks ago I had been selected for an interview with the superintendent and search committee at 1 p.m. today."

He got a desperate look on his face.

"Look, things are really hectic right now," he said. "I was the superintendent here two weeks ago, and I remember selecting you for an interview, but now I've taken a job in Nevada. In the last two weeks, most of the other administrators in the district have been released or have taken new jobs elsewhere. The only administrator left is the junior high principal, who has been appointed as the high school principal next year. I don't know why my secretary scheduled you for an interview now, but I'm not going to be able give you one. I couldn't possibly conduct interviews and make a recommendation to the board since I'm leaving. I'm sorry about all this!"

This revelation raised my ire, but I contained my anger to some degree.

"Did you know that I just took an unpaid day from my teaching job in Lewiston to come to an interview that was scheduled by your office?" I said as calmly as possible given the situation. "I left after school Thursday and spent the night in Boise in a motel. I got up early this morning to get here, and now you are telling me I don't have an interview?"

He grimaced and looked away.

"Look, I'm sorry but that seems to be the case," he said, embarrassed. "The best I can do is send you over to the junior high where the new high school principal is packing up to go to his new office. I'll have him give you a tour of the junior high building and give you an abbreviated interview. Would that be okay?"

My mind was racing, full of confusion, disappointment, and anger. I was trying to make sense of it all. Who was at fault for this situation? Who was going to be held accountable for this miscommunication and my loss of time and money? I didn't know what to say or what to do to reconcile the situation and my feelings. I was dumbfounded his solution for me was to have the new high school principal give me a tour of the junior high building and provide me with an interview that would have no meaning. I didn't know what else to say, so I agreed.

"Yeah, I guess that will have to do. Since I came all this way, I'd like to at least see the building and talk to the previous principal."

"I'm really sorry about this, but that's the best I can do," the superintendent said.

"Where is the junior high located and could you call and let him know I'm coming?" He agreed and moved to the secretary's phone, where he called the junior high, found the principal, and let him know I was coming. He asked the principal to give me a tour and an impromptu interview as he escorted me around the building. When he was finished he hung up the phone and gave me directions to the Wood River Junior High.

"I can pretty much assume I'm not going to be considered seriously for this job," I said. "Since it will probably be a new superintendent who will make the selection, but thanks for your help anyway."

With that comment, I left the office and went to my car. As we made our way to the junior high, I filled Marty in on the situation. She was furious, demanding that I take her back to the district office where she would have a few choice words for the outgoing superintendent and anyone else within earshot! I was upset as well, but I knew an angry reaction on our part would not correct the situation or make my position any better. I told her we just needed to make the best of a bad situation. I said the tour and informal interview might help me with any future interviews I might get.

I drove up to a parking spot in front of the junior high, left my still-steaming wife in the car, and made my way through the open entrance to the building where a young man, who introduced himself as the new high school principal, greeted me.

"I've only got about a half hour," he said. "Would it be okay if I give you a tour and we talk about the situation as we make our way around the building?" I agreed and he began to give me a tour of the facility.

As we walked through the building, I could see that they had a great facility. Everything was brand new, and it was evident the building had been built recently.

"I'm really sorry about all this," he said to me as we walked. "The district is in real turmoil and has been for the last three years. One elementary principal and I are the only administrators left in the district. The superintendent is leaving, the high school principal and the other elementary principal resigned, and I'm moving to the high school. The board has some interviews set to hire a new superintendent, but he won't be on board until mid-June. As you can see, the facilities and the equipment are top notch. There is plenty of money available in this community to support the schools. Money from the state income and sales taxes, plus the property taxes, is more than sufficient."

"You said that you and one other person were the only ones left from the original administrative team," I said, interrupting him. "I also heard from one of the clerks at a convenience store downtown that there has been a lot of turnover in the administrative ranks over the years. What's that all about?"

His response made the whole situation clear. "The Blaine County School District is a rich school district by Idaho standards. There are a lot of wealthy people living in the district and many of them are very picky about how their children are treated," he said. "An influential group in the community pretty much drove the superintendent out, because he stood for high learning and behavioral standards for the staff and students. The high school principal left because he was frustrated by the constant pressure to compromise learning and behavior standards to meet the demands of a few of these wealthy families in the district. Another issue was the constant fluctuation in student enrollment. Enrollment would go up when the ski season started and then it would drop when the season ended. All the principals were having a hard time with student attendance. If a great day of skiing came along, some parents would let their children go skiing and write them notes demanding they be excused from class. There was also a general lack of support from the school board when parents complained about disciplinary action taken by principals at board meetings. These are pretty much the main reasons for the administrative turnover in the district."

Once I realized the situation, I knew this might not be a good place to begin an administrative career.

As we continued our tour of the building, he asked questions about my education and my teaching and administrative experience. I told him about my seven years of teaching math in Lewiston, coaching various sports, and the two years of experience I had as the junior high athletic director. After hearing my story he helpfully indicated I was probably a little short when it came to experience if I wanted to get an administrative job early in the summer. He told me to be patient and to keep applying, because a person with my limited administrative experience might get a job late in the summer when the number of available candidates declined. He told me that some small districts might take on a younger inexperienced candidate because they couldn't find a quality candidate with experience. He said that was how he got his first job as an assistant principal.

The interview/tour took about thirty minutes, but it was a very valuable thirty minutes for me. From one perspective, I felt the trip was a waste of time and money because I wasn't going to be considered as a viable candidate for the position and I would not have the experience of a formal interview. But on the other hand, I learned a lot about the importance of evaluating a community and school district and making that a part of any consideration for taking an administrative position. Marty and I drove home disappointed, but after much discussion we both felt I was more knowledgeable about how to be better prepared for the next interview.

I was just getting over the disappointment of the Sun Valley experience when, two weeks later after the end of the school year, I received a call from the secretary to the superintendent in the Genesee School District asking me to come to an interview for the Genesee High School principal position. She said there would be three candidates interviewing for the position, and I was being invited to be the first one interviewed. She said the interview would last about forty-five minutes and would be in the boardroom located in the administrative office at the high school. I could also get a tour of the facilities from one of the high school students if I came a half hour early. I asked the secretary several times if she was sure I was on the list for an interview and had her repeat back to me the time and place of the interview. I'm sure she thought I was a little strange, but I certainly didn't want to have another experience like the one with the Blaine County School District. Finally, once I was assured that I was a viable candidate for the position, I told her I would be honored to be there to meet with the superintendent and the board at the appointed time and date.

After hanging up the phone, I excitedly told Marty and the rest of the family about the upcoming interview, and we spent the next hour talking about the possibility of getting a job in Genesee, which was only about twenty miles away.

Before the date of the interview, we made a short trip to Genesee to look at the community and the schools. Genesee was very small compared to the community of Lewiston, and the high school was classified as a 1A school, which is the smallest classification in the state of Idaho. The district served less than 300 students grades K-12. It was considered a rural community, but was located halfway between Lewiston and Moscow, making it also a bedroom community for those two cities. Taking an administrative job in this town would be a real change for me, but I was determined to get an administrative position even if I had to start in a small community like Genesee.

The day of the interview came, and I did my best to look the part of a responsible candidate for the position of high school principal. I put on my best suit and tie and arrived forty-five minutes early. As promised, they had a student there to give me a tour of the high school, which was in a separate part of a three-story building that also housed the junior high and grade schools. The building was older and must have been built in the 1930s or '40s, but had gone through some renovations including the addition of several classrooms. I noticed the desks in some of the rooms were the older one-piece desks with a storage area under the seat. Some of these desks were defaced with names gouged on the top surface. The gymnasium was older but well maintained—more than sufficient for a high school enrollment of fewer than 150 students.

One thing of particular interest to me was a small classroom that had been transformed into a student lounge. There were some old, dirty couches and easy chairs circled in a corner of the room against walls desperately in need of paint. I could also see a number of dark spots on the wooden floor that contained small, dried globs of chewing tobacco. But the thing that really jumped out at me was a couple of holes in the wall about six inches above the floor. "What happened here?" I asked the young man giving me a tour.

"I think a couple of the seniors got mad and kicked the holes in the wall," he said. "Sometimes things get a little rowdy in here."

"Really! What happened to the guys that kicked the holes in the wall?"

"I'm not really sure," he said blankly. "I don't think they ever found out who did that. It happened about three weeks before school was out, and we were all anxious for the school year to come to an end." I also asked him about the chewing tobacco spots on the floor and he just shrugged.

"This is the student lounge and the teachers and the principal leave the students pretty much alone during the lunch hour and before and after school," he said. "Occasionally I've seen some of the boys chewing in here."

"Don't you have rules against chewing tobacco?"

"Yeah, we have rules against chewing, but not much is done if you get caught."

He turned toward the door suddenly and changed the subject.

"It's about time to get you back to the interview, so let's go." He seemed anxious to get out of the lounge and away from this line of questioning.

As we made our way back to the waiting area for the interview, I weighed what I had seen during the tour and what the student had told me. It was evident there were some discipline issues in the district—the defacing of the desks and the vandalism in the student lounge indicated I would have to take some steps to address those issues if I was to be the principal. The holes in the student lounge should have been repaired as soon as possible after the damage was noticed, and the worn-out furniture should have been replaced along with a new coat of paint on the walls to help the students take pride in their lounge. The defaced desktops should also be sanded and re-varnished, and I would need to be diligent in enforcing the rules against chewing tobacco on the school grounds. I thought the information I gathered from the tour would certainly be helpful for my upcoming interview.

After returning to the administrative offices, I was greeted by the superintendent, who introduced himself and led me up some narrow stairs into an unfinished loft on the third floor. The small room contained a large rectangular table with five men seated near the far end. A vacant chair was set at the end of the table near the door, which I assumed was for me once we began the formal aspect of the interview. As I entered the room, they all stood and the superintendent introduced me and identified each board member by name. He said I was the first candidate of three to be interviewed. I moved about the room shaking each man's hand firmly as I looked him in the eye and said, "It's a pleasure to meet you."

Once I had greeted everyone, the superintendent directed me to the empty chair at the end of the table. There was a pause as the superintendent opened a file in front of him and passed out a few sheets of paper to each board member. While he did that, I looked around the table to evaluate the men. It was obvious most of them were farmers as some were still in their work clothes. I noticed one man was dressed casually, possibly a local businessperson. Most of them seemed to be interested in me as I watched them look me over as the superintendent passed out the paperwork.

The superintendent began the interview by asking me to tell the committee a little about my general background, my education, and my teaching experience. I did so, highlighting my upbringing in a military family, my educational degrees, my own military experience during the Vietnam conflict, and my teaching, coaching, and athletic director experience in the Lewiston School District. Each board member and the superintendent then plied me with questions about my educational philosophy, my style of administration, my view of high school students, how I would manage and evaluate the teaching staff, and my thoughts about working in a small school district like Genesee. As I had done with my introductory comments, I kept my answers as succinct as possible. My students and those who know me would say I'm not a person who likes to talk just to talk.

As the interview progressed, I was feeling good about my responses to their questions and the body language they were exhibiting. All of them were leaning forward at the table, giving me their full attention as I responded to their questions. As we approached the end of the interview, I was thinking I might have a real chance at getting the job. But then, one of the board members at the end of the table asked me to define my role when it came to maintaining discipline in the school.

"I believe it is the principal's job to see that rules regarding student behavior are fairly and uniformly enforced while making sure a student's right to due process is observed," I responded.

I talked then about some of my observations when I made the tour of the building and expressed my concern about the student lounge, including the chewing tobacco stains on the floor.

When I mentioned the tobacco stains, the board member at the end of the table leaned forward.

"What would you do if you caught one of the high school boys chewing tobacco in the lounge?" he asked as he put a Styrofoam cup up to his mouth, which I'd seen him do a few times over the course of the interview, assuming it was coffee.

"My understanding is that the high school has a rule against students chewing tobacco on the school grounds," I said. "I would bring the student in, confirm he was chewing, and check to see if he had tobacco on his person or in his locker. If I found tobacco, I would then call his parents and possibly suspend him for a day if it was a repeat offense."

The board member looked at me, lifted up his cup to his mouth again, and dramatically spit a wad of chew into his cup.

"Really?"

"Yes, sir," I said. "That is what I would do!"

From then on, the body language of this board member and two others changed completely. It was clear my response to that question had pretty much eliminated me from serious consideration for the job. The board asked a question or two more, but it was obvious the committee had lost interest in my responses. After a few more perfunctory questions, the superintendent indicated the interview was over and led me down the steps to the administrative office area. Just as I got to the bottom of the stairs, I heard a loud roar of laughter from the men upstairs, and I then knew for sure that I had blown any chance of consideration for this job. I was disappointed, but felt it was for the best. I learned from this interview that I needed to be more guarded about answering questions specifically directed at a school's problems—I would have been better served if I had premised my answer regarding the problem of chewing in school with an acknowledgement that the activity was inappropriate and should be dealt with assertively. I was on solid ground in regard to calling the parents, but should have made sure I knew board policies and administrative directives before I talked about suspending a student from school. My answer to the board member's question reflected my lack of experience and was scorned because of it. It would have been far more effective, had I known, to only talk about how I had dealt with such problems before and detail how I had previously addressed the issue.

Two weeks after my interview, I received a "Dear John" letter from the Genesee District indicating I was an unsuccessful candidate, and they were offering the position to someone with more experience.

My summer progressed with my usual schedule of umpiring baseball games and driving pea trucks for Twin City Foods. Even though I was working, I continued sending out applications and placement files to districts of interest hoping the possibility of a job offer might come late in the summer. I took consolation in the fact I was now at least getting a few interviews, which was a big encouragement.

CHAPTER 28

The Big Break Comes

I was just raising a fork full of the hot beef sandwich to my mouth when he said the last sentence...'you and I...' The bread and beef froze halfway to my mouth with gravy dripping back onto my plate as I processed what he was saying. He was talking like I was already on board as the principal. Was this an indirect way of offering me this job?

By the time the end of July came, I was fully into driving truck for the pea harvest. I was working ten to twelve-hour days, and even though I spent a lot of time sitting in a truck in a pea field and hauling four or five loads of peas to Lewiston during that time, the work was exhausting. Working six days straight and maneuvering down the Lewiston hill was tense work. If a truck carrying a load of peas was lost coming down that hill with an eight percent grade, you could lose your life and, if you survived, would definitely lose your job. So every evening when I got home, all I wanted to do was eat, spend a little quality time with my wife and kids, and sleep.

During the first part of July, I sent out another batch of job applications to districts in Idaho, Washington, and Oregon, but I had yet to receive an interview. However, in the middle of July, I received a call from the superintendent of a small district in Nevada asking me to apply for a junior high principal job that was open there. Surprisingly, the caller identified himself as the former superintendent of the Blaine County School District. He said he wanted to make it up to me for the lack of a job interview in May. I listened to his invitation and then respectfully declined. I still had a bad taste in my mouth from that whole experience and was not interested in working in Nevada.

The last day of July came, and it looked like I was going to get to the end of summer without any more interviews or even a glimmer of a job offer. The pea harvest was going well, but it looked like we would have about another week of solid work. I had worked two ten-hour days and was in the middle of my third when I got a phone call that shook things up.

I had just dumped my second load of peas at the plant when the truck dispatcher caught me and told me I had a call from my wife. He said she had stressed that it was really important I get back to her before I went back to the field. I called her and when she answered the phone and heard my voice, she got excited.

"Bob, you got a call from a Bruce Anderson, who is the superintendent of the Adrian School District in Adrian, Oregon," she said. "He said it was very important you get back to him as soon as possible. I tried to ask him what it was all about, but he got pretty nasty with me saying he wanted to talk to you only. I explained you were driving truck and wouldn't be available until after 6 p.m. this evening. He just said it was really important for you call him as soon as you get home, and he gave me his home phone number."

"Did he give you any idea what he wanted?" I asked. "Did he say anything about an interview?" I remembered I had submitted an application and placement file to a district in eastern Oregon looking for a high school principal and athletic director, but I couldn't remember the name of the district.

"No, he didn't say," Marty said. "Every time I tried to get more information he got pretty short with me."

"Okay," I sighed. "I'll call him when I get home. Thanks!"

I returned to the pea fields and spent the rest of the day excitedly speculating on the reason for the call. Was he going to give me an interview over the phone like Mr. Walker did? Was he going to invite me to come down for an interview? I thought there was a real possibility of a face-to-face interview if the phone call went well. By the time I got home at 6:30 in the evening, I was anxious to call Mr. Anderson.

After a quick meal with my wife and family, Marty gave me Mr. Anderson's phone number.

"He said that no matter the time, you were to call him as soon as you could," Marty said. "He was pretty adamant you call tonight."

"Well, here goes!" I said as I took the number from her. "Maybe this will lead to another interview and maybe even a job offer!"

I picked up the phone and dialed the number. After the third ring, a woman came on the line and said, "This is the Andersons'. How can I help you?"

"I'm Robert Hammann, an applicant for a principal's job there in Adrian," I told her. "And Mr. Anderson said I should contact him at home as soon as possible when I got home from work. Is he there?"

She asked me to hold while she went to get him. A few seconds passed before I heard a male voice.

"Are you Mr. Robert Hammann, a math teacher and athletic director in the Lewiston School District?" he asked without even a "hello."

"Yes, I'm Robert Hammann," I replied.

"I'm Bruce Anderson, the new superintendent of schools at Adrian," he said. "Are you still interested in the grade seven through twelve principal position here in Adrian, or have you taken another job?"

"No, I haven't taken another job and yes, I'm still interested in the position at Adrian."

"Okay," he said. "I'm sorry about the delay in contacting you, but I was just hired as the superintendent, and it's taken me awhile to get organized enough to fill the secondary principal's position. This is a small district that serves about 350 students, and there are two administrative positions in the district. I'm the superintendent and the elementary principal, and we are looking to fill the secondary principal position, which serves grades seven through twelve. This position also includes the duties of the athletic director. I've looked through all the applicants and you appear to be the best on paper. The other candidates are so below standard that it is either going to be you or nobody. In fact, if you are not the guy, I will probably try to operate on my own until I can do a proper search next spring. Are you interested in coming down for an interview?"

"Sure," I said, trying to suppress my excitement and sound professional. "I would be glad to come down for an interview."

"Alright. I need you to be here tomorrow morning to interview with the chairman of the school board and myself. What time do you think you can get here?"

I was stunned.

"You want me to be there in the morning? That's at least a five-hour trip by car, and I just got off a twelve-hour shift hauling peas! I can't use my only car, because my wife needs it to go to work in the morning. How in the world am I supposed to do that?"

His voice became gruff and curt.

"You want to be a principal, right?"

"Yes!"

"Then figure it out," he said. "Make your travel arrangements and then call me back so I'll know what time you will be here. By the way, who is in charge at your house? Is it you or your wife?"

The last question threw me off guard, so I replied simply, "Sir, I run things in my home. What do you mean by that question?"

"Well, it seemed like your wife ran things when I called earlier in the day," he said. "I just want to make sure you are the man in charge at home since you might be asked to be the man in charge of my high school."

"Let me assure you I'm the head of this house. I will call you back in the next half hour with my travel arrangements."

After I hung up, Marty and I began to frantically make plans for me to be in Adrian, Oregon, by the next morning. Possible travel arrangements included flying, which would be very expensive, or taking a bus, which would be significantly cheaper. I took out the phone book, found the number for the bus station, and gave them a call. The representative said one of their busses was stopping at the downtown Safeway store around 10 p.m. that evening to pick up passengers and would be heading to Ontario, Oregon, arriving at about 7:30 a.m. the next morning. The round-trip fare was about $40, and they said there would be room for me on the bus. I then thanked him for his help and hung up.

I called Mr. Anderson back and told him when I'd be arriving in Ontario.

"Can someone be there to pick me up when I get off the bus?" I asked.

"Yes," he replied. "I will be there to pick you up, and we will drive directly to the school, which is about twenty-five miles away. The board chairman will be there, and we will begin the interview as soon as possible after we get there. Will that be alright?"

"That's fine," I said. "I look forward to meeting you. How will I identify you?"

"I'll be the guy with the red hair. See you soon." With that, he hung up.

All our conversations on the phone were short, curt, and to the point. I suspected he had a military background, because he came across as in charge and somewhat demanding—exactly how my commanding officers were in the Air Force.

I spent the next hour showering and cleaning up from my day of harvesting and then packed for the trip. I wore jeans and a light shirt thinking I needed to wear clothing comfortable enough for riding in a bus for nine hours. For my interview, I carefully folded up my best suit into a duffle bag along with a change of underwear and my shaving kit. Marty had an aunt and uncle who lived in Nyssa, Oregon, which turned out to be about eighteen miles from Adrian. She also had three brothers living in the area, and we had visited them on a couple of occasions when we lived in Mountain Home, Idaho, so we were familiar with the region. Marty made a call to her aunt and uncle Kenneth and Cleta Saunders to see if I could spend the next night with them—they were excited to hear I was being considered for a job in Adrian and were glad to put me up for the night.

By the time we packed and made all these arrangements, it was time for me to go and meet the bus. Marty drove me down to Safeway, where I bought a round-trip ticket. I asked the clerk why the bus took nearly nine hours to go from Lewiston to Ontario, and she said it made numerous stops along the way. After purchasing my ticket, Marty and I waited in the car for the bus to arrive and talked about the job, my conversation with Mr. Anderson, and that region of Oregon.

The bus finally arrived about fifteen minutes late. My wife wished me luck and after a goodbye kiss, I gave my duffle bag to the driver, who loaded it into the storage compartment of the bus. I then took my seat to begin my journey toward a possible major career change.

In the past, I had taken a few long bus trips from college to home. On those trips I learned that I hated riding the bus. The seats would recline, but never into a position where a person could sleep comfortably. People were allowed to smoke in the back of the bus, but the smoke always made its way to everyone in the bus. I had a hard time coping with the smell of cigarettes. On this particular trip, there were only a few travelers, so there was more room to sprawl out and I was able to sit in a row all to myself, but that did little to make the trip enjoyable. I had worked all day and was stiff from lack of exercise. I was dead tired, but I was also emotionally high regarding the prospect of getting a principal's job. I tried to sleep, but the combination of fatigue, emotional excitement, and the inability to find a comfortable position made it difficult. Every time I dozed off, the bus would stop and some passengers would disembark while others would board and make their way to a seat, usually brushing me as they passed. I tried sleeping with the seat set as far back as it would go. I tried sleeping in a fetal position on the row of seats I had selected. It really didn't matter what position I tried, I just couldn't get comfortable enough. So for nine hours I tossed and turned and dozed, getting very little sleep or rest. By the time the bus pulled into the Ontario bus station at about 8 a.m., I was exhausted, worried, and totally dazed. What worried me most was that I would be too tired to professionally present myself and make a positive impression during the interview.

As soon as I got off the bus, I grabbed my duffle bag and went to the men's restroom to prepare myself to meet Mr. Anderson. I shaved and put on my suit and tie. When I looked in the mirror, I looked pretty good, except my suit was somewhat wrinkled from being stuffed in a duffle bag for ten hours. I took one final look in the mirror, straightened my tie, and headed into the bus lobby to wait for Mr. Anderson.

Amazingly, a short, stocky, auburn-haired man wearing slacks and a casual pullover shirt came through the lobby entrance just as I walked out of the men's room. He walked right up to me.

"Are you Mr. Hammann?"

I reached out my hand, which he grasped firmly.

"Yes sir, and you must be Mr. Anderson."

"That's me," he said. "I have a car out here in the parking lot. Why don't we load up your luggage and we will get started toward Adrian? The board chairman will be waiting for us in my office."

I grabbed my bag and followed him to his car. I tossed the bag in the back seat and got in on the passenger side of the vehicle. Mr. Anderson got in, started up the engine, and abruptly started speaking as we pulled away.

"We might as well make good use of our time as we make our way to Adrian," he said. "We'll treat this as a preliminary interview for the job. First, my name is Bruce Anderson. You can call be Bruce, but never call me 'Brucie.' That name is offensive to me and I won't put up with it. I want to start by making sure you understand that."

He looked over at me to make sure I knew he was serious.

"All right, Bruce," I said. "I usually go by Bob even though my legal first name is Robert."

"Okay Bob, let me give you a little background about myself and the recent history of the district and the position you are applying for. I spent four years in the army as an officer during the Vietnam conflict. When I got out of the military, I took my education degree in industrial arts and used it to teach for a while. I then got my master's degree in school administration, which allowed me to eventually head up a large public education industrial arts program in California. This is my first job as a superintendent and first time working in the state of Oregon. I want you to know it will be a successful endeavor for me."

He said this last bit firmly and with passion. My face-to-face meeting with him had confirmed what I'd gathered previously from our phone conversations—he was military and pretty much all business. He was not shy about speaking bluntly and at times profanely, but I found out later he had a sharp sense of humor. "The Adrian District is coming out of some major turmoil," he continued. "The superintendent had to be removed from his position, and this past semester the district has been under the leadership of a retired superintendent put in place by the new school board. At the beginning of the last school year, two administrators were hired to manage the district. One of them had a master's degree and was hired to be the high school principal and superintendent. The other administrator had a doctorate degree and was hired to be the K through eight principal. Evidently, there was a lot of conflict between the two. I think it had to do with the one having a doctorate and the other having a master's degree. Anyway, the superintendent was doing some totally inappropriate things. He bought some batteries for his snowmobiles using district funds. He was also filling his car and snowmobile machines with gas from the district pumps, which are used to fuel district vehicles and the busses. The grade school principal found out about it and instead of going to the school board, who appeared to be very supportive of the superintendent, he went out into the community and gathered support to confront the superintendent and school board. I guess the board meeting where this all came to a head was pretty exciting. I heard there were about sixty people at that meeting, which is a lot for a community the size of Adrian. This battle between the administrators was so intense that many of the patrons in the district chose sides. Those folks ended up the real losers, because many of those same people were offended when the administrators were removed. The feelings of those people are so deeply damaged they won't even speak to each other now. It has been really bad!"

I sat in a daze as Bruce spoke, slowly becoming more amazed at his story. I had felt unbalanced and out of control ever since I got off the bus, and this new revelation about the district was not helping me regain any semblance of balance. I had put in ten hours of work the previous day and only been able to get about two hours of fitful napping during the bus ride. I had been awake for more than twenty-four hours, and it was taking all my energy to focus on what he was saying and try to make sense of it. The longer he talked, the more it sounded like this district was really in a mess. What had I gotten myself into?

"Right after the big board meeting," Bruce continued, "a representative from COSA, the Confederation of Oregon School Administrators, was called in to assist the district. To make a long story short, there was a recall vote in the middle of the school year with all but one of the five board members ousted from their positions. A new board was elected, and the new board fired the superintendent and accepted an experienced interim superintendent recommended by COSA, who had retired a few years ago from the Ontario School District. This man was a highly respected administrator in the region since he was the superintendent in Ontario for nearly twenty years.

"Since the elementary principal was a major part of the problem, the interim superintendent assigned him to work strictly from his desk until the end of the school year. When his contract ran out at the end of June, he was non-renewed. Once the administrators were removed, the new board began the process of seeking a new superintendent and hired me. Because of my commitment to my other job, I was not able to take control of the district until about three weeks ago, which is why I'm so late in my efforts to hire a new high school principal. That kind of gives you an overview of the situation leading up to this interview," he said. "But I've been talking a lot ever since we got into the car, so why don't you tell me a little about your background including your military experience, your education, and your teaching experience."

I gave a brief outline of my family life before attending Bethany Nazarene College. I stated my undergraduate and graduate degrees and highlighted my background in the military. I then spent a little more time talking about my experience as a math teacher, coach, and athletic director. He drove silently, taking in what I had to say and asking only a few questions to clarify. I mentioned my coaching experience and how much I enjoyed it, and he responded quickly and firmly.

"If you get this job as a principal, you won't be doing any coaching," he said. "You just won't have the time, plus I don't believe that should be part of an administrator's role in a school." I was somewhat disappointed at this, but I knew he was speaking the truth. I suspected I would be spending an inordinate amount of time pursuing my administrative duties, especially if I was to act as the athletic director for the high school and the junior high. I loved coaching, but was willing to drop that activity if it was necessary.

After giving Bruce a brief history of my experience, he told me a bit more about what I'd be doing in the position. "The main reason the superintendent got away with buying batteries and using district gas for his private vehicles is because the district had poorly written and outdated policies and administrative rules," he said. "So the new principal and I will be spending a lot of time working on rewriting board policies and administrative rules. We will also be upgrading the evaluation procedures for the certified and classified staff members in the district. Tell me a little more about your responsibilities as the athletic director at Jenifer Junior High."

I outlined my duties regarding scheduling games and officials and supervising coaches and the various athletic events. Bruce then gave me some background about the communities of Ontario, Nyssa, and Adrian, and described the farming activities that supported those towns. He said Ontario was one of the larger towns in eastern

Oregon and had a major processing plant for potatoes and storage facilities for other crops. The community of Nyssa had a sugar beet plant, and most of the sugar beets in the region were brought there for processing. As we drove, we passed a number of small twenty- to forty-acre plots of beets, potatoes, corn, onions, wheat, and mint. Since it was August, the wheat fields were mostly harvested, but the other fields were green, showing exceptional growth compared to the Lewiston region. We passed numerous farm vehicles, and I commented on one onion field where several Hispanic people were working. He pointed out there was a large contingent of migrant workers that lived in and around Nyssa and Ontario, who were there to assist the farmers with their onion and beet fields. An extensive amount of weeding by hand was needed for the onion fields, and that was what they were doing in that field. He said the farmers could make or lose a lot of money in onions, so they usually kept those fields to twenty acres or smaller.

About twelve miles beyond Nyssa, we finally came to the "bustling" town of Adrian. All during our ride from Nyssa to Adrian we had been traveling on a highway that ran parallel to the Snake River, which meandered slowly through the valley. As we came to Adrian, I noticed the land around the town was flat with various fields crisscrossed with irrigation ditches and dirt roads. There were nice farmhouses, a few small older houses, and some camps of temporary housing for the migrant workers and their families. Many of the fields were still green, but there was a lot of dust in the August air since there had been no rain for several weeks. As we came to the edge of the town of Adrian, Mr. Anderson pointed out the school to the left, located on a small hill adjacent to the highway. There were a few small, white houses scattered around the campus, which Mr. Anderson referred to as "teacherages." He said the houses were available for school employees to rent if a teacher wanted to live close to the school. The rent was low in order to encourage teachers and administrators to live and work in the district. Mr. Anderson said it was hard to find appropriate housing in Adrian. He also indicated one of the two-bedroom units was available to the new principal should he need housing—the school board required all the administrators to live in the district.

Bruce pointed out that just south of the teacherages were the main school facilities. The building closest to the highway was the elementary building, separated from the highway by a chain-link fence. Between the chain-link fence and the building was a playground with a merry-go-round, a couple of basketball goals, a couple of swings, and some tetherball poles. The equipment looked old but functional. Most of the grass around the equipment and in front of the building was brown, with only a few areas of green evident. Bruce said the upkeep of the grounds had been neglected since last spring because of the turmoil in the district, and he had just recently hired a new maintenance and bus supervisor to begin the work of greening up the grounds, caring for the busses, and maintaining the facilities.

As we turned left off the highway into the drive that led up to the elementary facility, he indicated that behind the elementary facility—separated by a dirt driveway—was the high school facility and the athletic fields. The district lunchroom and activity center were attached to the east side of the elementary building, and the gymnasium was attached to the northeast side of the high school. Both the gym and lunchroom were shared between the two schools. We drove up into the parking lot between the teacherages and the elementary facility, and my first impression was not positive. The grounds and facilities looked run down and ill kept. It was clear that the facilities were in need of some serious work. From my conversation with Bruce, it was evident there was a distrust of the administration and serious divisions among the patrons of the district. But Bruce said he believed a new administrative team could address these issues, so I put these thoughts in the back of my mind and made a mental note to address this during the interview.

Bruce parked in a slot near the entrance to the elementary school and escorted me into the office area of the school building. He introduced me to his secretary, who had a desk just outside of his office, and led me directly into his office where a tall middle-aged man sat at a conference table in the middle of the fairly large room.

After introductions, Bruce had us all sit at one end of the table where he moved quickly into the interview process without small talk or pleasantries. He asked me to share my education and teaching experience background for the benefit of the board chairman, and then the two of them plied me with questions about my leadership style and my methods and procedures for maintaining school discipline. They asked me how I would supervise and evaluate teachers and how I would establish and maintain high academic standards for the students and the staff. They asked me how I would facilitate positive communications with the parents and community.

I answered the questions as clearly and succinctly as possible. In my answers I indicated that I believed in a modified democratic style of leadership, where I wanted input from staff regarding decisions or policies that affected them. I expected students to be respectful and orderly and would support and implement policies that encouraged such behavior. I told them I wanted to spend a lot of time in the classroom observing, supervising, and evaluating teachers, but also wanted to be visible to the students during the school day and at extracurricular events, which was an important component for me in maintaining discipline. They asked several follow-up questions, asking me to give examples from my own experiences to support my answers, which I was able to provide in most instances.

Near the end of the interview, they gave me the opportunity to ask some questions. I asked about the makeup of the community, the number of teachers, and number of students in the district. I was also curious how the district planned to address the community's perception of their school district after the incident with the past two administrators, and they said they were working to write policies to correct the situation. The board chairman said they hired Mr. Anderson to help them develop and implement those policies. The board was also looking to hire a high school principal who would assist them with this process. Their answers to my questions were encouraging to me. The salary and benefit package would definitely be better than what I was going to get in Lewiston, although I would be working more days as a principal. I would still get about five or six weeks off during the summer, plus I would get some time off during Christmas and spring breaks. Oregon was definitely a better paying state than Idaho, and that was attractive to me.

As we came to the end of the interview, I could not get a read on how well I was doing. I thought the interview definitely went better than the ones in Sun Valley or Genesee, but I was tired and still in a daze from lack of sleep. It was about 10:30 in the morning when we finished, and I had not had a decent amount of sleep for more than twenty-eight hours. As the interview wrapped up, Mr. Anderson asked me to step out of the room for a few minutes so he and the board chairman could talk.

I left his office, closed the door, and stepped into the reception area. The secretary, who was doing some typing, invited me to sit in a chair near her desk while I waited. I sat musing over the interview while the secretary returned to her work. I knew I had not done my best. I felt ill prepared and was certainly unrested and less than alert. I couldn't tell if Mr. Anderson and the chairman were interested in hiring me or not. Because of my fatigue, I felt pretty negative about the whole experience and thought this would just be another exercise in futility. But like my previous interviews, I would try and learn something that would help me down the road.

After a few minutes, I shook off my feelings and asked the secretary about the school and the community. She pretty much gave me the same information Mr. Anderson had briefed me with as we drove in from the bus station. The demeanor of the secretary was very pleasant and supportive as she talked with me, which made me feel welcome as a potential employee of the district.

Twenty minutes after I had stepped out, the board chairman came out of Bruce's office. "Thank you for making the effort to interview for this position," he said. "I appreciated the opportunity to get to know you, and I hope you have a safe trip home. Mr. Anderson said he would take you to lunch. I would like to go, but I have a lot of work to do at the farm. Thanks again for coming." He shook my hand and left the building, having given me no indication whether we might see each other again. I thought for sure I must have come up short as the successful candidate.

I was just sitting back down when Bruce opened the door of his office and waved me in with a smile.

"Let's go up and take a look at the high school, and then I'll take you to lunch at the one and only restaurant in Adrian," he said. "How does that sound?"

"Sure! I'd like to get a look at the high school facility."

We headed out of the administrative office area, turned left down a short hallway and into the lunchroom facility, where Bruce pointed out the kitchen and eating areas. He said all the students ate there, and the food provided by the kitchen staff was said to be top notch. We then headed out of the building, crossed the dirt road, and climbed up a flight of stairs to a sidewalk that led us to the main entrance of the high school. I noticed the grass around the building was brown, but there had been some work done in the flower garden beds near the entrance to the building. In front of the high school was a gravel parking lot large enough for about forty cars. Mr. Anderson pointed out that students shared the lot with the staff, who had been allotted spots closest to the building.

As we entered, he pointed to the small glassed-in office complex on the left where there was a reception area with a secretary's desk and some chairs along the wall. There were also two offices, one for the principal and the other for the part-time counselor. I looked into the principal's office and saw a desk, a nice adjustable business chair on rollers, two straight-back chairs, and a number of bookshelves. It wasn't large or spacious, but it was functional. Bruce took me down another hallway, pointing out the gymnasium and classrooms as we passed.

He took me to the left and showed me the only bathrooms available to the staff and students. The boys' bathroom had two urinals and three wooden toilet stalls with no doors on them.

"They've had some problems with students coming in here to smoke," Bruce said after I asked about the stalls. "So they took the doors off."

"What about the girls' bathroom? Do they have the doors off the stalls as well?"

"No," he said. "They didn't have a smoking problem in there, so the doors were left on. Plus, there would be more of a ruckus from the female students if they didn't have doors on the stalls."

"Where is the staff's bathroom?" I asked.

"Right here! These are the only bathrooms outside of the gymnasium area, so these are used by staff and students."

That is definitely a problem, I thought. If I became principal, I was going to take another look at having bathroom stalls with no doors, especially when staff also used those bathrooms.

Bruce quickly ushered me down the classroom hallway and into the teachers' lounge next to the bathrooms. The small, narrow room contained a rectangular table in the middle surrounded by about eight chairs. Along two of the walls were a refrigerator, a coffee pot, and a number of cabinets. We continued our tour and I saw six classrooms. One was a business classroom with about twenty typewriters, and there were several regular classrooms with updated desks, used to teach social studies, math, Spanish, and English. One classroom was even set up to teach home economics with ranges, countertops, and a refrigerator.

Bruce then walked me back down the hallway and into the gymnasium, a box-like facility with rolled-up bleachers on one side and a stage on the end. The basketball court was not regulation size, but the floor was in good shape. On the southeast corner of the gym was a well-equipped science classroom, and in the northeast corner was a music classroom. On the one side of the stage was a stairway that led down to two small boys' and girls' locker rooms, which were located under the stage and gym floor.

Set apart from the main building was a well-equipped shop classroom for agriculture classes and another building containing an art classroom and a small weight and exercise room. There were also football and baseball fields beyond the agriculture building.

As we toured, I could see that the facilities were less than what I was accustomed to in Lewiston. The buildings were much older, and there was little to accommodate the needs of staff. The faculty lounge was basically a renovated storage closet, but it was appropriately equipped. The grounds really needed attention, but the football field looked to be in good shape. The small set of football bleachers and the press box at the top were old and in desperate need of paint. The city of Adrian was smaller than any city I had ever lived in—major shopping areas were at least eighteen miles away. I was also to discover that the closest gas station was that far as well.

But I also saw some potentially good things. The school board and superintendent were taking steps to write and implement a whole new set of policies to govern the district. The new administrators would be on the ground floor of writing and implementing those policies. The salary and benefits package was significantly better than anything Idaho could offer. The board chairman and the superintendent's secretary were friendly and seemed easy to get along with. Bruce was abrupt at times, but I could tell he was a man who could get things done. If I came to this district, my family and I could live in one of the teacherages and save some money. There were both positive and negative things to be considered if I was offered this position. After the tour, Bruce took me to his car and we set off for a quick tour of the town before heading to the local restaurant.

After turning left on the main highway from the elementary school parking lot, we immediately entered the city of Adrian. There were businesses on either side of the main highway for about two city blocks. On the right was an automobile repair shop, which also housed the volunteer fire department. And on the left were a small café, a bar, and a small grocery and hardware store. We reached the end of the "business district" and turned left into a loosely organized group of houses. Most of them were older, with many sitting on one or two acres of land. We exited the neighborhood onto a dirt road that ran along the Snake River. The river was down, because it was August, but it was a beautiful setting. There were a few nice houses set along the river. The road only went about a mile outside of Adrian and Bruce pointed out a nice-looking modular home and said the band teacher, Bucky Gould, lived there.

When we got to the driveway leading down to Bucky's house near the river, Bruce turned around and drove back to the café.

"That's about all there is to Adrian," he said. "It's incredibly small, but it's a great place to start a career in administration. You have no where to go but up!"

We pulled up in front of the café, and Bruce warned it was a bit of a "greasy spoon."

"But they have some great hamburgers," he said. "This is where all the farmers meet to chew the fat, especially early in the morning. I make it a habit to drop down here when the farmers are here so I can keep a finger on the pulse of the community. It's a great place to get the local news and promote the interests of the school district. Come on in. The district is going to pick up our lunch tab, and we can talk a little more about the principal's position while we eat." The café was large enough to seat about thirty people. As we entered, I noticed a counter with several stools—most of which were empty—manned by a cook and a waitress. The rest of the room had a number of older tables and chairs occupied by several people. In the back was another room separated from the main café room by a wide doorway, where Bruce said the Adrian Lions Club met on a weekly basis. Bruce suggested we sit at one end of the counter, away from two people seated at the other end.

We ordered some sandwiches and while we waited for our orders, Bruce and I talked about sports, athletics, and a few other mundane issues. Bruce became more businesslike after our meals came and we began to eat.

"Now Bob, I want to assure you that the district is on a sound financial footing," he said. "These people have passed their local tax levies every year, and there seems to be a commitment from the board to upgrade the facilities. I'm sure you could see they needed some work when I gave you the tour. There is enough money in the budget to pay the bills, buy the equipment we need to run our programs, and pay the staff. There are still some hard feelings in the district about the firing of the last two administrators, but I think you and I could take care of that issue and draw the community together."

I was just raising a fork full of the hot beef sandwich to my mouth when he said the last sentence..."**you and I**..." The bread and beef froze halfway to my mouth with gravy dripping back onto my plate as I processed what he was saying. He was talking like I was already on board as the principal. Was this an indirect way of offering me this job? If I was loopy before because of lack of sleep and the speed by which this whole process was moving, I was now totally dumbfounded. I felt like I was in a dream.

I put my fork back down.

"Wait a minute," I said. "You just said **you and I** could address this issue of a divided community. What are you really saying here?"

"Let me get right to the heart of the matter," Bruce said with a smile. "The board chairman and I agreed we want to offer you the contract for the high school principal's job pending, of course, a visit to the Lewiston District by two of the board members. Since they had such a bad experience with the last two administrators, they want to visit the district where you work to verify your background and evaluate your effectiveness in the job you currently hold. They visited my district before they offered me a contract, and they want to do the same for the new principal's position. What do you say? I've made up my mind that we either hire you, or we will go through the next year without a high school principal. I'd rather hire you than try to manage the district by myself, but I'm prepared to do that if you turn the position down. I need you to make a decision today. Would you be willing to come back to my office to sign a contract when we are done eating here? My secretary is typing it up as we speak."

Now my mind was really reeling. He was really offering me this position, and he wanted me to make a decision right now!

"Mr. Anderson, I'm stunned!" I said. "You're offering me the principal's job, and you want me to make a decision right now?"

"Yep, I need you to give me your decision right now. I need to have the high school principal on board in two weeks, and I'm offering it to you. What do you say?"

I tried to think everything through in the few minutes he was giving me to make a decision. I weighed the pros and cons of the position—the attractiveness of the district was equally balanced with the negative things I had seen and heard in the two-and-a-half hours I was with Bruce. What was I to do?

"I need a little time to think this through," I said. "Can you give me until tomorrow?"

"No!" Bruce said firmly with a frown. "I need you to make a decision now, and if you choose to take the position, you need to sign a contract today before you return to Lewiston! What do you say?"

I was unable to just come out and say yes or no.

"Listen, I'm willing to make a decision today," I said. "But I want to at least call my wife and talk to her about the offer. After we eat, we can go back to your office and I can give her a call. I need to run this by my wife."

Bruce really frowned hard when I said that.

"Bob, I thought you told me on the phone yesterday that you run your house," he said. "Do you make the decisions in your home or does she?" This time, his comment and question angered me.

"Look, Bruce!" I said. "My wife and I are a team. I make the decisions in my house regarding where I work and for whom I work, but I always consult my wife and get her input. We've operated that way from the first day of our marriage until now. I'm not going to change that. If you want a decision today, then I will need to consult with my wife, and once I do that I will give you a decision. That's the way it has to be for me! Can you live with that?"

"I can understand that," Bruce said, backing off. "In fact, I respect it, but I wanted to make sure you are the one making the decisions, because you are going to be asked to make a lot of big decisions if you accept this administrative position. Let's finish our lunch and then we will go back to my office so you can make your call."

We went back to eating, and the conversation changed to general topics of education, some humorous stories associated with our past teaching experiences, and athletics. After eating, we made our way back to his office, and he left me to call my wife while he stepped out to see if his secretary had the new contract typed up. I took a deep breath to calm myself and dialed my home phone. It was about 1 p.m., and I was pretty sure Marty would be home. She answered on the third ring.

"Good afternoon. This is the Hammann residence."

"Marty, this is your husband."

"Bob, it is so good to hear your voice," she said. "How did the interview go?"

"Marty, you aren't going to believe this," I said frantically. "They offered me the job! Right after the interview, Mr. Anderson took me to lunch and offered me the job! I'm so tired and weary I'm having a hard time processing all this. He wants me to make a decision right now. He wasn't willing to give me a day or two to think it over. I have to make the decision now or the offer will be withdrawn."

"Well, tell me a little about the job," she said.

"I would have to start in two weeks," I said. "But what I would make here is much better than what I make in Lewiston. They pay for our health insurance, so I wouldn't have to pay for you and the kids like I do in Lewiston. I have an expense account for travel, and they pay for a $50,000 life insurance policy. I have to work more days as a principal, but I still get about five weeks off in the summer along with some days off during spring break and at Christmas. The situation here is pretty rough, though. The previous two administrators were fired; one for misusing district funds and the other for dividing the community over the issue. All but one of the school board members were recalled, and the new board wants to hire a younger and more energetic pair of administrators. Bruce is a little aggressive, but I think I can work for him. The facilities need some work, but Bruce and the board seem committed to seeing that this happens. They have a two-bedroom teacherage available to live in if I choose to take the job. They are really pressing me to make a decision right now. What do you think?"

Marty was silent for a minute. "What does your gut say?" she asked. "You are the one who is there. What do you think?"

"I think, if I want to really get into administration, this is a good place to start," I said. "I'd definitely be starting at the bottom, but like Bruce said, there is nowhere to go but up. I believe that's true. I'm leaning toward taking the job. We've already sold our house, and we have some earnest money on another house there in Lewiston. You've been packing to make the move to the new house, so we are well on the way to make a move. I think we could back out of buying the new house and get our earnest money back. I think everything is just right to jump into this career change."

"Well, go for it!" she said. "I'm with you! Let's do it!"

"Okay, I'm going to tell them yes and sign the contract. Bruce said I could get a temporary Oregon Administrative Certificate for the next two years and take some classes to meet the state's requirements during that two-year period. He wants me to start in two weeks. Thanks, Marty! I needed to get your input on this. I'll call you back when I get to Kenneth and Cleta's house."

After hanging up the phone, I went out to the secretary's desk, where I found Mr. Anderson and his secretary discussing a particular item in the contract she was typing. He looked up as me. "Well?" he asked.

"I'll take the position!" I said, looking him in the eye.

"Good!" he said with a smile. "Sit here a minute while my secretary finishes typing the contract and then you can bring it into my office and we will get it signed." When she had completed the contract, the secretary gave it to me, and I went back into Mr. Anderson's office. He was on the phone and motioned for me to sit at the conference table while he finished the call. It was obvious from his conversation on the phone that he was talking to the chairman of the board and communicating my decision to take the job. After a few minutes, he ended the conversation and hung up. He then came over to sit next to me with a big grin.

"Let's get this signed and we will go over a few things."

I handed him the typed contract, and he took a few minutes to review what had been written.

"This looks okay," he said. "What you need to do now is sign and date it right here on the line that says principal's signature. The board will act on the contract, and I will sign it over here where it says superintendent's signature. The board will act on the contract at their next meeting, which should be after the two board members visit your district."

I took the contract and looked it over. It covered the 180 days of school plus another 40 days for administrative planning and work. It indicated my family and I would have full Blue Cross/Blue Shield medical and dental coverage. I would be given a salary of $20,000, which was a whole lot better than the $6,500 I made during my first year of teaching. It included a $50,000 life insurance policy and indicated I would be enrolled in the Oregon Retirement System, which would require donations from my salary and from the district six months into the job. The one stipulation was that I had to qualify for the job with a temporary administrative certificate from the state of Oregon.

After looking the contract over and taking a deep breath, I signed and put the proper date on the appropriate lines. Mr. Anderson took the contract and said I would get a copy when I reported to work in two weeks.

"All right Bob, let's cover a few things before I take you back to Nyssa. You need to report for work on August 15, which is two weeks before the start of school. If you want to rent that two-bedroom teacherage, you need to let me know, otherwise I will be offering it to another staff member. As far as I know, we will not need to hire any new staff members, so that will make things easier. On August 15, the two of us will be traveling to Salem for a New Administrator Workshop sponsored by COSA. We will do some preliminary planning for the school year on that trip. The district will pick up the tab for the motel accommodations, food, and travel expenses.

"You will need to apply for a temporary Oregon Principal's Certificate as soon as possible. I have a copy of the application, and I will give it to you before you leave. If I were you, I would give them a call to let them know you are submitting an application. You will need to submit the application, all official copies of your college transcripts, and a form signed by the superintendent of the Lewiston District outlining the number of years you taught in their district. I would get that application off in the next two or three days. The certificate may not come until after August 15, but that will be okay if I can call and verify they will be sending one out. Get this all done and you will be ready to go."

"I can tell you now that we will take the teacherage rental at least for the coming year," I said. "I will be here August 15 to get started, and I will do my best to get things done for the Oregon certificate. Is there anything else?"

"Yes, there is one more thing," he said. "Two board members will be coming to your community next week to check you out. They will call you to let you know they are there, and they will probably want to meet with you when they get done consulting with your colleagues. I'm sure this investigation will work out fine. I've talked to your principal and district superintendent, and they all gave you high praise. I'm excited about having you on the team—I feel like we are going to do some great things in this district."

After giving me the application for a temporary Oregon administrator's license, we shook hands and then went out to his car, where he took me to Ken and Cleta Saunders' house. Not much was said during the twenty-minute drive back. I sat in the passenger's seat with my head spinning. What in the world had I done? One minute I was a teacher in Lewiston, Idaho, and now I was going to become a principal in Adrian, Oregon. I was tired and weary and felt my life was totally out of control, but I knew I had done the right thing. I mentally began to make plans to resign from the pea harvest, withdraw from the purchase of our new home, resign from my teaching position, and apply for the temporary Oregon Principal's Certificate. Marty and I would continue the process of packing our things and making arrangements to transport the furniture and boxes to our new home in Adrian. We would need to say goodbye to our neighbors, friends, and church family. I would also have to notify my parents, my sister, and my brother of the new job. I would contact Mic Wimer, K.C. Albright, and Mr. Jasper to let them know I got a principal's job and would not be back next year. I was going to be very busy in the next two weeks, and just the thought of it all made me depressed, but I knew that after I got some rest I would be up to the challenge.

I was finishing seven-and-a-half years of teaching at Jenifer Junior High and was getting ready to begin a new career in the area of school administration. I enjoyed those years in Lewiston and all the experiences that went with them. Those years helped me grow and mature as an educator. But now I felt ready for the new challenge. After all, how much more difficult might that challenge be?

Well, that is the topic for another time. My experiences as a principal were just as diverse and unique as those I had as a teacher. My two years in Adrian proved to be vastly different from my time in Lewiston. My *Teacher's Tale* is over, but my *Principal's Tale* is just beginning.

Postlude

I hope you enjoyed this book of my experiences as a junior high public school teacher during the 1970s in the state of Idaho. I was only able to provide a highlight of the events and experiences, as well as my thoughts as I grew and matured as a teacher. My perspective about teaching, the students I served, my colleagues, and the public education system as a whole changed greatly as I taught those seven years. Through the experience, I developed a deep love for my students and a genuine respect for the dedicated teachers I had the privilege to work with.

I would like to have expanded the book to include the impact teaching had on my family and my belief system, but time and space would not allow it. When I write my next book on my experiences as a principal, I hope to have that opportunity.

Education today has changed greatly with the addition of computers and the Internet, and I'm sorry to say that in many cases it may not have been for the best. I hope to address that issue in a following book as well.

I would like to close by saying that during my tenure as an educator, I came to believe the public education system is one of the American institutions that made this country great. The effectiveness of the institution was not due to the curriculum, the teaching theories espoused by college professors who sit in their ivory towers, or the laws established by politicians. Its effectiveness was due to the support of parents who demanded a quality education for their children and supported the teachers who provided that quality. It also was due to the dedicated work of exceptional teachers who knew instinctively how to teach and had a deep love for their students. Many times they were able to make a difference in the learning of their students in spite of difficult circumstances and sometimes in spite of the educational system itself.

www.ingramcontent.com/pod-product-compliance
Lightning Source LLC
Chambersburg PA
CBHW051412090426
42737CB00014B/2627

* 9 7 8 0 9 9 7 4 6 5 9 1 4 *